DATE DUE

NOV 0 3 1989	
NOV 21 1995	
DEC 1 8 1995	

Modern Developments in Public Finance:
Essays in Honor of Arnold Harberger

Modern Developments in Public Finance:
Essays in Honor of Arnold Harberger

Edited by

MICHAEL J. BOSKIN

Basil Blackwell

Copyright © Basil Blackwell Ltd, 1987

First published 1987

Basil Blackwell Ltd
108 Cowley Road, Oxford OX4 1JF, UK

Basil Blackwell Inc.
432 Park Avenue South, Suite 1505
New York, NY 10016, USA

British Library Cataloguing in Publication Data

Modern developments in public finance:
  essays in honor of Arnold Harberger.
  1. Finance, Public
  I. Harberger, Arnold II. Boskin, Michael J.
  336   HJ141

  ISBN 0–631–15595–3

Library of Congress Cataloging-in-Publication Data

Modern developments in public finance.

  Edited by *Michael Boskin*.
  Includes index.
  1. Finance, Public. 2. Harberger, Arnold C.
I. Harberger, Arnold C. II. Boskin, Michael J.
HJ141.M59 1987   336   87–6568
ISBN 0–631–15595–3

Typeset in 10½ on 12 pt Times
by Photo·graphics, Honiton, Devon
Printed in Great Britain by T J Press, Padstow, Cornwall

Contents

Contributors		vi
Introduction		vii
1	**The Welfare Cost of Social Security's Impact on Private Saving** Martin Feldstein	1
2	**The Federal Budget and Federal Insurance Programs** Michael J. Boskin, Brad Barham, Kenneth Cone and Sule Ozler	14
3	**Weighted-Average Discount Rates in Public Expenditure Analysis: a Generalization** Alan J. Auerbach	40
4	**Taxation and the Size and Composition of the Capital Stock: an Asset Price Approach** Lawrence H. Summers	61
5	**The Welfare Cost of Resource Taxation** Marc S. Robinson	95
6	**The Value-Added Tax: the Efficiency Cost of Achieving Progressivity by using Exemptions** Charles L. Ballard and John B. Shoven	109
7	**The Wage–Productivity Hypothesis: its Economic Consequences and Policy Implications** Joseph E. Stiglitz	130
8	**Commercial Policy for Panama in the 1980s** Larry A. Sjaastad	166
9	**Costs and Consequences of the New Protectionism. The Case of Canada's Clothing Sector** Glenn P. Jenkins	217
Index		254

Contributors

ALAN J. AUERBACH, University of Pennsylvania and NBER

CHARLES L. BALLARD, Michigan State University

BRAD BARHAM, Stanford University

MICHAEL J. BOSKIN, Stanford University and NBER

KENNETH CONE, Manufacturers Hanover Trust Co., Chicago

MARTIN FELDSTEIN, Harvard University and NBER

GLENN P. JENKINS, Harvard University

SULE OZLER, University of California, Los Angeles

MARC S. ROBINSON, General Motors Research Laboratories, Warren, Michigan

JOHN B. SHOVEN, Stanford University and NBER

LARRY A. SJAASTAD, University of Chicago

JOSEPH E. STIGLITZ, Princeton University

LAWRENCE H. SUMMERS, Harvard University and NBER

Introduction

Almost a decade ago, Joseph Stiglitz and I entitled a paper 'Some Lessons from the New Public Finance.' The new public finance became standard public finance very rapidly. It has an interesting and important genealogy; tracing its roots to Edgeworth, Dupuit, Pigou, and Ramsey, with several important early post-World War II contributions by Samuelson and others. The theory of optimal tax and transfer policy, the positive theory of tax incidence, and attempts to measure the social welfare lost from tax-induced price distortions, dominate the thinking of academic economists and, occasionally, policy makers today.

Arnold Harberger stands as an important bridge between the earlier developments in public finance and the new public finance. Modern public finance owes much to Harberger. His pioneering work on the measurement of waste, corporate tax incidence, and the social opportunity cost of public funds has greatly influenced an entire subsequent generation of public finance economists. Harberger himself has devoted much of his career, from the training of students to consulting for international organizations, to the professionalization of the analysis of economic policy. That imprint and its impact spreads through hundreds of economists in dozens of countries. While it does not lead to better cost–benefit analyses on all occasions in every country, sometimes it does do so. That is indeed an impressive achievement.

The essays in this volume contain contributions from some of the world's leading public finance economists. While the range of topics is broad, the papers uniformly reflect several important themes. Each represents an important application of modern public finance analysis to an interesting and important public economic issue.

These range from the choice of discount rates in public expenditure analysis through various analyses of taxation to an evaluation of such major components of public spending as insurance programs and social security.

Martin Feldstein presents an analysis of the welfare cost of social security's impact on private saving. In all advanced economies, social security, retirement, disability, and hospital benefit programs are a large and growing fraction of government budgets. Large fractions of the population receive the benefits and virtually the entire working population pays substantial taxes to finance them. A major debate has arisen concerning the extent to which the anticipation of future social security benefits affects private saving decisions. While it is not my place here to evaluate that econometric literature, the general consensus is that social security has indeed affected private saving, although the effect may well be only a third or a half dollar of decreased private saving per dollar of expected present value of future social security benefits. If this is the case, Feldstein demonstrates that, except in a special case, the welfare loss is large both absolutely and in relation to the size of the social security program. The excess of the productivity of real capital over the implicit rate of return earned on taxes paid to an unfunded social security causes a loss to each generation of workers participating in the program.[1] An initial generation, of course, receives benefits without paying any taxes. The net welfare effect balances the gains of the first generation against the loss to all future generations. Feldstein extends the classic Samuelson overlapping-generations model and analyses the welfare cost of social security. In some illustrative calculations, Feldstein estimates that the net loss can be several times the present value of taxes. Feldstein's analysis should be an important input to thinking about the appropriateness of changes in existing social insurance programs in the world's major economies.

The paper by Michael Boskin, Brad Barham, Ken Cone and Sule Ozler begins with the observation that governments, like many individuals, simply cannot take Polonius' advice: Neither a borrower nor a lender be. The substantial borrowing by governments in most economies is common knowledge. Less obvious, but also of great importance, is the lending, loan guarantees, and subsidies to lending provided by virtually all governments. Systematic thinking about government lending policies has been almost non-existent in the United States. In fact, when the government borrows, it probably crowds out precisely those potential investors it attempts to help in special lending programs, since these are likely to be the residual claimants for the funds: small businesses, farmers, students, etc. Boskin et al. highlight the misleading treatment of lending programs in the United States federal budget, suggest alternative ways of thinking about lending programs, guarantees, and subsidies which highlight the expected value of future expenditures (to compare with the potential benefits of the programs). The accounting anomalies with which the US federal budget treats lending programs is a special case of a more general phenomenon. The US budget does not separate capital and current operating accounts, excludes many items, fails to adjust par to market values, and has a myriad of other important accounting, conceptual, and measurement problems that decrease its usefulness for implementing sensible cost–benefit analyses of government programs.

The paper by Alan J. Auerbach extends the analysis of discounting for public expenditure in the standard two-period model. Auerbach shows that the weighted-average approach, pioneered by Harberger and others, remains valid with multiple commodities, given certain conditions regarding the availability of government instruments such as excise taxes or full control of public production. Thus, Auerbach's paper neatly highlights a variety of important features of weighted-average discount rates formulae, and the need to assign shadow values for the opportunity cost of public funds.

The paper by Lawrence H. Summers is a pioneering attempt to deal with short- and intermediate-run responses to changes in tax policy. The path-breaking development of general equilibrium tax incidence models by Harberger, elaborated in the work of Shoven and others, has generally examined long-run comparative static effects of tax policy changes, assuming no cost of adjustment impeding the accumulation or reallocation of capital. Thus, the marginal products of capital are always equated everywhere. Summers demonstrates that this implies that there is no scope for variation in the asset price of existing capital goods. He argues that the extreme volatility of asset prices in the real world suggests that capitalization effects can be important, and also demonstrates that a distinction between new and old capital, as well as types of capital, may be more meaningfully analysed in a simple asset price approach to the analysis of investment incentives. He concludes that these capitalization and adjustment effects are important and also presents hypothetical experiments. For example, the transition path of the economy following full indexation of the tax system is analysed and he shows that the windfall conferred on existing shareholders from indexation is about ten per cent, whereas capital losses of about five per cent would be suffered by the owners of land. These types of effects are ignored in traditional general equilibrium tax incidence models. Summers' research adds significantly to our ability to understand the full nature of the incidence of taxation. It also highlights many of the issues involved in the attempt to reform taxation in the political process.

The paper by Marc Robinson analyses the welfare cost of resource taxation. The appropriate tax treatment of extractive resources is a subject of intense debate in virtually all economies, and virtually all economies use resource taxation. Resource taxes, however, often have numerous special features. Robinson builds on the analysis of the optimal extraction rate for an exhaustible resource, noting that inter-temporal choice is an essential part of the production decision, and that various tax policies can affect the time path of production. Robinson uses the usual second-best applied welfare economics of modern public finance theory to analyse exhaustible-resource taxation. He notes that despite the complexity of the producer's optimization problem, the welfare cost of a distortionary tax can be expressed in simple form. He analyses both single- and multi-period taxes, as well as the existence of capital taxes. His analysis suggests that taxes on exhaustible resources have relatively low welfare costs, even if they do distort the time path of production, so long as they are permanent. He compares these welfare costs relative to those of other types of taxes.

A tax in common use in Europe is the value-added tax. Both Japan and the United States have been considering the option of a value-added tax, despite severe opposition. The paper by Charles Ballard and John Shoven analyzes the efficiency costs of achieving progressivity in a value-added tax by using exemptions. Most European value-added taxes exempt certain commodities (e.g. food) on the grounds that this will aid particularly needy persons. However, if the commodity is exempted, it is exempted for rich and poor alike, and this may be a very inefficient means for compensating low-income persons for their value-added taxes. Ballard and Shoven compute the efficiency–equity trade-off implicit in a value-added tax, using an applied general equilibrium model of the US economy. They conclude that the attempt to generate greater progressivity via exemption loses a large part of the potential efficiency advantages of a consumption-type VAT. Noting that with the exception of the Scandinavian countries, most of Europe has failed to maintain a relatively flat-rate VAT, Ballard and Shoven conclude that much of the efficiency gains will be lost with substantial differentiation among products. It is not surprising, therefore, that many VAT proponents argue that the way to relieve the potential regressivity of this tax is to provide a refundable credit.

The paper by Joseph Stiglitz focuses on a particularly important issue in cost–benefit analysis in less developed countries: the determination of the shadow wage rate when a worker's productivity depends upon his or her wage. Stiglitz explores both the causes of this wage productivity nexus and its consequence for a variety of policy issues, in addition to the determination of shadow wages. The analysis builds on earlier work by Harberger, which noted that the number of unemployed individuals may be endogenous and hence when the government hires an additional worker, for example, it may displace more than one worker from the rural sector, thus generating a social opportunity cost of hiring one worker in the urban sector that exceeds the real wage. Stiglitz notes three important regularities in less developed countries: the persistence of large urban unemployment; the persistence of a wage differential between the urban and rural sector, and the wage differentials across industries within the urban sector; and the persistence of the differences in employment rates among different groups within the population. By examining the wage–productivity hypothesis, Stiglitz strengthens Harberger's original insight: the opportunity cost of labor will in general exceed the real wage.

The paper by Larry Sjaastad applies the principles of applied welfare economics to determine an optimal foreign trade policy for Panama. After discussing important distinguishing features of the Panamanian economy, and developing the formal analytical model, Sjaastad defines alternative means by which Panama could best exploit her geographic position and follows this with a statistical investigation of the issue. Sjaastad concludes that a more rational commercial policy in Panama would be enhancement of import tariff revenues.

A related paper by Glenn Jenkins analyses the costs and consequences of the new protectionism in Canada by making particular reference to the Canadian clothing sector. The Canadian government has been highly protectionist with respect to textiles, knitting, clothing and footwear. The justification has been that there are substantial costs of adjustment to lost employment in this sector of the economy. Jenkins points out that this analysis ignores the cost of protection rather than adjustment. Jenkins argues that estimates of both the private and social cost of labor adjustment are modest (although severe for a small segment of the affected labor market). He therefore compares these costs with the economic and private costs of the protectionist policies that have stifled industrial adjustment. He analyses the impact of Canadian tariff and bilateral quantitative restrictions for clothing on the welfare of consumers and producers, on the resource cost of the policy for Canada as a whole, and on the future development of the clothing sector. He concludes that this relatively important Canadian industry has been protected to the detriment of the Canadian economy as a whole and generated a perverse restructuring of the industry.

The papers in this volume cover a wide range of issues in public economics, with applications to particular economic environments, from less developed countries (LDCs) to advanced economies, but they all carry the same message. It is the message that Harberger himself has been conveying throughout his eminent career: the conviction that economists can make a contribution to the analysis of policy issues by insuring that scarce resources are wisely allocated, and that costs and benefits of various policies are carefully and professionally evaluated. These evaluations can then be used as an important input into the political decision-making governing public economic policy.

The other authors of essays in this volume join with me in celebrating Arnold Harberger's distinguished career and numerous contributions to public economics and to the analysis of public policy. These *Modern Developments in Public Finance* are presented in his honor.

Michael J. Boskin
Stanford, California

Notes

[1] Assuming the economy is not operating with an inefficiently large capital stock.

1 The Welfare Cost of Social Security's Impact on Private Saving

MARTIN FELDSTEIN

Among Al Harberger's major contributions, there may be none with greater long-term significance than his emphasis on quantifying the excess burden of distortionary taxation. Harberger's famous triangle formulae have become part of the standard toolbox of all public finance economists. As a result, the excess burden of taxation has evolved from an abstract concept to a concrete measure of the magnitude of the potential benefit of changing tax rules. The present paper uses a Harbergerian approach to excess burden to evaluate the distortionary effects of the social security program of retirement benefits.

In recent years a substantial number of econometric studies have examined the effect of social security retirement pensions on the level of price saving.[1] Implicit in these studies is the presumption that reduced saving implies a welfare cost. It is surprising therefore that there have been no explicit attempts to evaluate the size of this welfare cost in a manner analogous to the measurement of the welfare cost of distortionary fees (see, e.g., Harberger (1964) and the studies cited in Atkinson and Stiglitz (1980)). The purpose of the present study is to provide such an evaluation.

The analysis here shows that in an important special case a social security program can reduce private saving without imposing any

Martin Feldstein, Harvard University and the National Bureau of Economic Research. This paper is part of the NBER Study of Public and Private Pensions. The views expressed here are the author's and should not be attributed to any organization.

welfare loss. In more realistic cases, however, the welfare loss is large both absolutely and in relation to the size of the social security program.

The primary rationale for universal social security pensions is, of course, to provide retirement income to those who lack the foresight to provide for themselves. An evaluation of the net effect of social security therefore requires balancing the welfare gain from this type of transfer payment against the welfare loss caused by the savings distortion. A more complete analysis would also include the distortion in retirement behavior and in pre-retirement labor supply caused by social security taxes and benefits. An evaluation of the welfare loss of the induced reduction in savings is however a useful starting place and a natural sequel to the econometric studies of the effect of social security on saving.

The present paper therefore makes the extreme assumption that labor supply and retirement behavior are exogenously fixed and that each dollar of 'social security wealth' (that is, the present value of social security benefits) reduces private saving by one dollar. The latter assumption implies that social security does not raise consumption during retirement. I want to emphasize that this extreme assumption[2] is not meant to represent reality but to focus the analysis on the welfare cost of reduced capital accumulation.

The reduction in private saving could, of course, be offset or more than offset by accumulating a large trust fund with which to pay future social security benefits (Samuelson, 1975; Feldstein, 1977a). In practice, however, the social security program in the United States and in most other industrial countries is unfunded. I shall therefore assume that there is no funding and no change in other public capital accumulation to offset the reduction in private capital accumulation.

The first section of this paper develops the analytic framework for evaluating the net loss of reduced private saving. The second section presents some illustrative numerical calculations. Then in the third section I examine the effect of a finite horizon on the value of the welfare loss. There is a brief concluding section that indicates the direction for future research on this subject.

The Analytic Framework

In a very important paper, Paul Samuelson (1958) extended the life cycle theory by developing an explicit overlapping-generations model and used this framework to analyse the effect of social security. Since Samuelson assumed an economy without a productive capital stock or other durable store of value, social security could play the welfare-increasing role of permitting individuals to finance retirement consumption.

The absence of a capital stock is of course critical to Samuelson's conclusion that an unfunded social security program increases the welfare of all generations. In a model with a productive capital stock, the substitution of unfunded social security for private saving raises the welfare of all generations only if the economy is initially producing with an inefficiently large capital stock.[3] When this is not true, the excess of the productivity of real capital over the implicit rate of return earned on the taxes paid to an unfunded social security program causes a loss to each generation of workers who participate in the program. Since members of the initial generation of retirees receive benefits without paying any taxes, their welfare is unambiguously increased. The net welfare effect depends on balancing the gain to the first generation of retirees against the loss to all future generations.

The framework for the present analysis will be an extended version of Samuelson's overlapping-generations model. Each individual lives for two periods, working in the first period and retiring in the second period. All individuals are alike and earn a wage w_t if they work in period t. The labor force grows at rate n per period and the real wage rate grows at rate g per period. The basic difference from the Samuelson model is that savings may be invested in real capital. To avoid the complexities of an endogenous and time-varying rate of return, I shall assume that the marginal product of capital remains constant at rate ρ per period.

The number of aged retirees in each period (A_t) is equal to the number of workers in the previous period (L_{t-1}). Since the population grows at rate n per period, $L_t = (1+n)L_{t-1}$ and $L_t = (1+n)A_t$.

Consider a social security program that imposes a tax at rate θ on wage income in each period. The workers in period t pay a tax of $T_t = \theta w_t L_t$ and, because of the unfunded pay-as-you-go nature of the program, receive benefits when they retire equal to the taxes paid by the next generation: $B_{t+1} = b_{t+1}A_{t+1} = \theta w_{t+1}L_{t+1}$ where b_t is the benefit per retiree in period t.

The implicit rate of return, γ, that individuals earn on their tax 'contributions' is defined by the ratio of the benefits that they receive to the taxes that they previously paid:

$$B_{t+1}/T_t = \theta w_{t+1}L_{t+1}/\theta w_t L_t = (1+g)(1+n) = 1+\gamma$$

since $1+n = L_{t+1}/L_t$ and $1+g = w_{t+1}/w_t$. The implicit rate of return is therefore equal to the rate of growth of real income.

If the workers of generation t had instead saved and invested T_t, their savings would have earned the real marginal product of capital, ρ. If there were no tax on capital income, the individual savers would also receive a return of ρ. However, even if a capital income tax reduces the net return to individual savers, the nation as a whole earns the entire pre-tax rate of return. I shall assume that the benefits of that tax revenue accrues to the generation of savers who own the capital.[4] Thus instead of receiving $B_{t+1} = (1+\gamma)T_t$ in return for their social security taxes, they would receive $(1+\rho)T_t$. The social security program therefore reduces the retirement income of the workers of period t by

$$(\rho-\gamma)T_t = (\rho-\gamma)\theta w_t L_t.$$

The present value of this loss as of the first period of these workers' lives is

$$(\rho-\gamma)\theta w_t L_t/(1+d)$$

where d is the rate at which individuals discount income between the two periods. If there is no capital income tax, individuals equate their rate of time preference to the marginal product of capital: $d = \rho$. A capital income tax at rate t lowers the *annual* marginal rate of return to individual savers[5] from r to $(1-t)r$ and therefore makes the net rate of return per *period* $\rho_N = [1+(1-t)r]^y-1$ where y is the number of years in a generation. I shall define an effective 'period tax rate' τ via the identity $\rho_N = (1-\tau)\rho$. Thus, with a capital income tax, the equality of the individuals' time preference and the net rate of return implies $d = (1-\tau)\rho$.

In the next generation the corresponding loss is

$$(\rho-\gamma)\theta_t w_{t+1}L_{t+1}/(1+d) = (\rho-\gamma)\theta(1+g)w_t(1+n)L_t/(1+d)$$
$$= (1+\gamma)(\rho-\gamma)\theta w_t L_t/(1+d).$$

Thus the generational loss grows at rate γ. If the program is introduced with workers of generation $t=0$ and continues forever,[6] the present value of the infinite stream of losses is given by

$$Z = \sum_{t=0}^{\infty} \frac{(\rho-\gamma)\theta W_t L_t}{(1+d)(1+\delta)^t} \tag{1}$$

where δ is the appropriate discount rate for the inter-generational aggregation of consumption.[7] Since

$$w_t L_t = (1+g)^t w_0 (1+n)^t L_0 = (1+\gamma)^t w_0 L_0$$

we have

$$Z = \frac{(\rho-\gamma)\theta w_0 L_0}{1+d} \sum_{t=0}^{\infty} \left(\frac{1+\gamma}{1+\delta}\right)^t. \qquad (2)$$

If the discount rate exceeds the growth rate ($\delta > \gamma$), the sum converges and the present value of the losses to all generations of workers is

$$Z = \left(\frac{1+\delta}{1+d} \quad \frac{\rho-\gamma}{\delta-\gamma}\right) \theta w_0 L_0. \qquad (3)$$

Although Z measures the loss to all generations of workers who participate in the program, it ignores the benefit to the initial generation of retirees who receive benefits without paying any tax. Their benefits are equal to the taxes paid by the first generation of workers, $\theta w_0 L_0$. The present-value net loss to all generations, including the first generation of retirees, is thus

$$N = Z - \theta w_0 L_0 = \left(\frac{1+\delta}{1+d} \quad \frac{\rho-\gamma}{\delta-\gamma} - 1\right) \theta w_0 L_0. \qquad (4)$$

The value of N depends critically on the value of δ, the social discount rate used for the inter-generational aggregation of consumption. There are two alternative theories of the appropriate definition of δ. The first theory equates the social inter-generational discount rate with the private intra-generation discount rate; that is, $\delta = d$. The rationale for this approach is that the generations are linked by bequests and that the preferences of the bequeathers are accepted as normatively valid. The alternative theory rejects the private discount rate as irrelevant for inter-generational comparisons and bases the social discount rate on the presumed decline in the marginal utility of income as the level of income grows. If *per capita* income grows at rate g and the elasticity of the individual marginal utility function is ϵ, the marginal rate of substitution of income in successive periods is $(1+g)^\epsilon$. Conventional assumptions put ϵ between one and three.[8]

Consider first the implication of equating the social discount rate and the private discount rate, $\delta=d$. In an economy with no capital income tax, the private discount rate should equal the marginal product of capital; thus $d=\rho$ and therefore $\delta=\rho$. Substituting these values into equation (4) implies $N=0$. Thus there is no net excess burden caused by the reduction in private saving if the economy has no capital income tax (or other savings distortion) and if the marginal product of capital is used to discount future income reductions.[9] In this unique case, the benefit to the initial generations of retirees who receive the unrequited transfer when the program is established just balances the infinite stream of losses sustained by all future generations.

If we continue to accept the equality of the social discount rate and the private discount rate but recognize the existence of a capital income tax, the welfare neutrality of the savings reduction disappears. With $\delta=d=(1-\tau)\rho$, equation (4) implies[10]

$$N = \left(\frac{\rho-\gamma}{(1-\tau)\rho-\gamma} - 1 \right) \theta w_0 L_0 = \frac{\tau\rho}{(1-\tau)\rho-\gamma} \theta w_0 L_0. \qquad (5)$$

It is clear that N is an increasing function of the tax rate, the marginal product of capital and the economy's rate of growth. A positive capital income tax rate implies that the marginal product of capital exceeds the rate of time preference and therefore that any change in the rate of saving has a first-order welfare effect.[11] The higher the marginal product of capital, the greater the welfare loss from any reduction in saving. A higher rate of growth of the economy means that the annual losses grow at a faster rate and therefore have a greater present value.

The net value presented in equation (4) can also be interpreted as the net gain of terminating an existing program in *any* year. Terminating the program implies that the retirees in the terminal period receive no benefits while the workers in that period and all future periods pay no tax and receive no benefits. If the terminating period is defined to be $t=0$, the net present value (as of $t=0$) of the welfare gain of termination is measured by N with $\theta w_0 L_0$ the amount of tax that would be collected in that period if the program were not terminated.

Although the absolute present value measure is directly relevant for assessing the desirability of starting or terminating a social security program, it is also interesting to restate this loss as a proportion of the present value of all taxes.[12] Since taxes at $t=0$ are $\theta w_0 L_0$ and benefits grow at the rate γ per period, the present value of taxes, discounting at rate δ, is

$$V = \frac{1+\delta}{\delta-\gamma} \theta w_0 L_0. \tag{6}$$

The ratio of the net loss to this present value of taxes is therefore

$$\frac{N}{V} = \frac{(1+\delta)(\rho-\gamma) - (1+d)(\delta-\gamma)}{(1+d)(1+\delta)(\delta-\gamma)}. \tag{7}$$

In the important special case where the private and social discount rates are equal ($\delta=d$), this implies

$$\frac{N}{V} = \frac{\rho-\delta}{1+\delta}. \tag{8}$$

It is interesting to compare this with the net loss to a typical worker per dollar of his or her tax payments. Since he (or she) receives a return of γ on his social security taxes rather than the total return of ρ,[13] his loss is $\rho-\gamma$. This loss is a reduction in his retirement income. Its present value as of the time that he works and pays tax is therefore $(\rho-\gamma)/(1+\rho)$. Since $\gamma > \delta$ is a necessary condition for the convergence of N and V, it is clear that N/V is smaller than the steady-state loss per dollar of tax revenue. This difference reflects the fact that N/V incorporates the extra benefit to the initial generation of retirees.

When the social and private discount rates are equal to the net-of-tax rate of return, $(1-\tau)\rho$, equation (7) can be written as

$$\frac{N}{V} = \frac{\tau\rho}{1+(1-\tau)\rho}. \tag{9}$$

The net loss per present-value dollar of social security taxes is equal to the tax revenue that is lost per dollar of forgone savings, discounted at the individual's net of tax return.

Some Illustrative Calculations

Some numerical calculations will indicate plausible magnitudes for the welfare losses derived in the previous section. To obtain values for γ, ρ and τ, I will use the experience of the US economy in the three decades beginning in 1950. I will assume that the length of a 'period' or generation is 30 years.

During the 30 years beginning in 1950, the average annual rate of growth of real personal income was 0.037, implying that $\gamma = (1.037)^{30} - 1 = 1.97$. The average pre-tax marginal product of capital in the US non-financial corporate sector was 0.114 (Feldstein et al. 1983), implying that $\rho = (1.114)^{30} - 1 = 24.50$. Finally, during the same period these corporations, their shareholders and their creditors paid approximately 68 per cent of their pre-tax capital income in taxes to federal, state and local governments (Feldstein et al. 1983). Since this average tax rate may exceed the corresponding marginal tax rate, 1 will make the conservative assumption that $t=0.50$. With $r=0.114$ and $t=0.50$

$$(1-\tau)\rho = [1+(1-t)r]^{30} - 1 = 4.28.$$

Since $\rho = 24.50$, $\tau = 0.825$.

Substituting these values into equation (5) (based on the assumption that the social and private discount rates are equal to each other and to the net-of-tax return, $(1-\tau)\rho$) implies that the net loss is $N=8.75\ \theta w_0 L_0$. The net welfare loss caused by the reduction in saving induced by the social security program is equal to 8.75 times the initial size of the program; that is, 8.75 times the unrequited benefits received by the first generation of retirees. Alternatively, this calculation implies that reducing the existing social security program by a fraction f, and thereby denying benefits of $f\theta w_T L_T$ to the 'current' generation of retirees, would generate a net welfare gain of 8.75 $f\theta w_T L_T$.

These losses and potential gains can be restated as a proportion of the present value of social security taxes by using equation (9). With $\tau\rho = 20.21$ and $(1-\tau)\rho = 4.28$, equation (9) implies $N/V = 3.83$; the net loss is 3.83 times the present value of the taxes. This surprisingly high ratio reflects the fact that the real pre-tax rate of return on the forgone investment is high relative to the discount rate and that this difference compounds substantially over the 30-year length of each period.[14]

Although these calculations are only illustrative, the parameter assumptions are not unrealistic and the derived values of N and N/V do indicate the substantial size of the potential welfare loss caused by the reduced savings that result from starting or continuing an unfunded social security pension program.

If we reject the assumption that the social discount rate is necessarily equal to the private discount rate and instead use the assumed diminishing marginal utility of consumption to calculate δ, we obtain $\delta = (1+g)^\epsilon - 1$ where g is the rate of growth of *per capita* real income and ϵ is the elasticity of the marginal utility schedule. During the three decades after 1950, the annual rate of growth of real *per capita* income was 0.023. Thus $1+g = (1.023)^{30} = 1.98$. It is clear from equation (2) that convergence to a finite value of N requires $\delta > \gamma = 1.97$ and therefore $\epsilon > 1.6$.

With $\epsilon = 2$, $\delta = 2.92$. Equation (4) implies that with $\delta = 2.92$ and $d = (1-\tau)\rho = 4.28$, $N = 16.61\ \theta w_0 L_0$, which is substantially greater than the value of N obtained by assuming that $\delta = (1-\tau)\rho$. Similarly $N/V = 4.24$ is larger than it was with the higher discount rate. To reduce N to $8.75\ \theta w_0 L_0$, δ must be equal to $(1-\tau)\rho = 4.28$. Since $(1+\delta) = (1+g)^\epsilon$, the elasticity of the marginal utility function must be at least 2.45.

Thus, both approaches to the selection of a discount rate indicate a very substantial value for the net welfare loss.

Finite Horizons

The derivations and calculations in the two previous sections all assume that the social security program goes on forever. There is never a 'last generation' that pays a social security tax but receives no benefit. In Samuelson's words, social security is 'a Ponzi game that works,'[15] at least in the sense that it continues to command political support even if each new generation incurs a welfare loss.[16]

It is important, however, to consider whether the qualitative results and the general order of magnitude of the losses depend critically on the assumption of an infinite horizon. As I noted earlier, terminating the program in year T involves a net gain that is exactly equal in magnitude to the net loss implies by starting a program in that period, say

$$G_T = \frac{\tau\rho}{(1-\tau)\rho-\gamma}\ \theta w_T L_T \tag{10}$$

in the special case in which $d = \delta = (1-\tau)\rho$. The present value of this termination gain (as of time $t=0$) must be offset against the loss calculated for the infinite horizon.

The present value of G_T as of time zero is $G = (1-\delta)^{-T}G_T = [1+(1-\tau)\rho]^{-T}G_T$. Thus

$$G = [1 + (1-\tau)\rho]^{-T}\frac{\tau\rho}{(1-\tau)\rho-\gamma}\theta w_0 L_0 (1+\gamma)^T \qquad (11)$$

or

$$G = \left(\frac{1+\gamma}{1+(1-\tau)\rho}\right)^T N. \qquad (12)$$

Since $\gamma < (1-\tau)\rho$, the offsetting gain is of decreasing relative importance as T increases.

If, for example, the program is terminated after three generations (90 years), $G = 0.18N$. The present-value loss of a program that lasts three generations is thus 82 per cent of the loss of an infinite program.

For plausible parameter values, the assumption of an infinite horizon does not alter the qualitative or general quantitative conclusions.

Conclusion

The analysis and calculations presented in this paper make it clear that a social security program that replaces an equal amount of private saving can impose a welfare loss whose present value is many times the size of the existing generation's benefit. The actual adverse welfare effect depends, of course, on the extent to which social security benefits do depress private saving as well as on the effect of social security programs on labor supply, retirement behavior, etc. Moreover, because some individuals behave myopically, the social security program not only reduces saving by less than the full amount of taxes but also provides income to those who might otherwise have too little in old age.

Evaluating the magnitude of the welfare loss caused by reduced saving is therefore just one part of the evaluation of the welfare effect of social security. A similar analysis is required to evaluate the effects of changes in retirement and labour supply. These adverse consequences must then be balanced against the favorable effect of providing retirement income for those who lacked the foresight to provide for themselves. The net welfare effect of variations from the current level of benefits could then be assessed as a basis for deciding the appropriateness of changing the existing program.

Notes

1 See, for example, Barro (1978), Barro and MacDonald (1979), Blinder et al. (1986), Darby (1979), Diamond and Hausman (1982), Feldstein (1974; 1977; 1980; 1982), Feldstein and Pellechio (1979), Kotlikoff (1979), and Munnell (1974).

2 Empirical estimates of the extent to which social security benefits reduce private saving vary but most of the estimates indicate that each dollar of social security wealth reduces private wealth accumulation by between 50 cents and one dollar.

3 Cass and Yaari (1967) show that if the economy's rate of growth exceeds its marginal product of capital, the substitution of social security for private saving raises welfare in all generations. This is an application of the familiar proposition that welfare can be unambiguously improved by reducing capital intensity in an economy whose capital intensity is greater than the Golden Rule level. Samuelson's economy without productive capital is a special case of the growth rate exceeding the productivity of capital.

4 This may be in the form of direct benefits for retirees, a lower tax rate on capital income, or an equivalent reduction in the labor income tax. If instead the revenue is used to reduce the tax burden on the next generation of workers, the analysis would differ only slightly from the one that follows in the text.

5 A capital income tax reduces the marginal return to individual savers even though the total return to savers as a whole is ρ.

6 The possibility of a finite termination date is discussed in section 3.

7 I shall return directly to the appropriate value of δ.

8 Irving Fisher (1892) and Ragnar Frisch (1932) purported to estimate ϵ by imposing certain separability assumptions and obtained $\epsilon=2$.

9 This conclusion also rests on the assumption that changes in the rate of saving do not alter the marginal product of capital or the marginal rate of substitution.

10 Recall that τ is defined so that $(1-\tau)\rho$ is the after-tax rate of return per period.

11 This is analogous to the fact that any tax change has a first-order welfare effect if there is a pre-existing distortionary tax.

12 Note that since taxes and benefits are equal in each period, the present

value of taxes is also the present value of benefits.
13 Recall that individuals may only receive the net-of-tax return $(1-\tau)\rho$ directly but also get the benefit of the tax revenue $\tau\rho$ indirectly.
14 Reducing the length of the period to 20 years lowers N and N/V but their values remain high: $N = 5.86\ \theta w_0 L_0$ and $N/V = 1.86$.
15 Ponzi was a famous Boston swindler whose chain letter scheme collapsed when further buyers could not be found.
16 If there were only two generations, the workers would vote to terminate the program and, because they are more numerous, would prevail. In reality, there is a distribution of ages and some of those who are not yet retired would be net losers if the program were terminated. The redistribution in the actual program further complicates the voting equilibrium. See Feldstein and Pellechio (1979b) for a brief discussion of these issues and some empirical estimates.

References

Atkinson, A. and Stiglitz, J. 1980: *Lectures on Public Economics*. New York: McGraw-Hill.
Barro, R. J. 1978: *The Impact of Social Security on Private Saving*. Washington: American Enterprise Institute.
Barro, R. and MacDonald, G. 1979: 'Social security and consumer spending in an international cross-section.' *Journal of Public Economics*.
Blinder, A., Gordon, R. and Wise, D. 1986: Life cycle savings and bequests: cross-sectional estimates of the life cycle model. In Franco Modigliani (ed.), *The Determinants of National Savings and Wealth*, London and New York: Macmillan.
Cass, D. and Yaari, M. 1967: 'Individual savings, aggregate capital accumulation, and efficient growth.' In K. Shell (ed.), *Essays on the Theory of Optimal Economic Growth*, Cambridge, Mass.: MIT, 233–68.
Darby, M. R. 1979: *The Effects of Social Security on Income and the Capital Stock*. Washington: American Enterprise Institute.
Diamond, P. A. and Hausman, J. 1982: *Individual Retirement and Savings Behavior Decisions*, presented at the Oxford Conference on Microdata and Public Economics, 27–30 June.
Feldstein, M. 1974: Social security, induced retirement, and aggregate capital accumulation. *Journal of Political Economy*, 82, 905–26.
—— 1977a: The social security fund and national capital accumulation. *Funding Pensions: The Issues and Implications for Financial Markets*. Boston: Federal Reserve Bank.
—— 1977b: Social security and private savings: international evidence in an extended life cycle model. In M. Feldstein and R. Inman (eds), *The Economics of Public Services*, London: Macmillan.

—— 1980: International differences in social security and saving. *Journal of Public Economics*, 14, 225–44.

—— 1982: Social security and private saving: reply'. *Journal of Political Economy*, 90, 630–42.

Feldstein, M. and Pellechio, A. 1979a: Social security and household wealth accumulation: new microeconomic evidence. *Review of Economics and Statistics*, 61, 361–8.

—— 1979b: Social security wealth: the impact of alternative inflation adjustments. In C. Campbell (ed.), *Financing Social Security*, Washington: American Enterprise Institute.

Feldstein, M., Poterba, J. and Dicks-Mireaux, L. 1981: 'The effective tax rate and the pre-tax rate of return.' *Journal of Public Economics*, 1983.

Fisher, I. 1892: *Mathematical Investigations in the Theory of Value and Prices*. Connecticut: Academy of Arts and Sciences.

Frisch, R. 1932: New methods of measuring marginal utility. In *Beiträge zur ökonomischen Theorie*, no. 3, Tübingen: J. C. B. Mohr.

Harberger, A. C. 1964: Taxation, resource allocation, and welfare. In J. Due (ed.), *The Role of Direct and Indirect Taxes in the Federal Revenue System*, Princeton, NJ: Princeton University.

Kotlikoff, L. J. 1979: Testing the theory of social security and life cycle accumulation. *American Economic Review*, 69, 396–410.

Munnell, A. H. 1974: *The Effect of Social Security on Personal Saving*. Cambridge, Mass.: Ballinger.

Samuelson, P. A. 1958: An exact consumption-loan model of interest with or without the social contrivance of money. *Journal of Political Economy*, 66, 467–82.

—— 1975: Optimal social security in a life-cycle growth model. *International Economic Review*, 16, 539–44.

2 The Federal Budget and Federal Insurance Programs

MICHAEL J. BOSKIN, BRAD BARHAM, KENNETH CONE AND SULE OZLER

No other economist in recent times has done as much as Arnold Harberger to professionalize the analysis of economic policy. His contributions to cost–benefit analysis are numerous and important enough to have become part of the working *modus operandi* and vocabulary of scores of economists analysing tax, trade, and government-spending programs. In addition to his analytical contribution, Professor Harberger has continually stressed the importance of reducing the dimensionality of public decision-making to rules that are relatively easy to implement. As a consequence, cost–benefit theory needs to be based on measurable economic variables.

While debates over analytical issues such as the appropriate social opportunity cost of public funds tends to dominate economists' discussions of cost–benefit analysis, more mundane, but equally important, measurement problems continually arise. We often take for granted that we can measure with some precision the expenditure in any given period of time on a particular public activity, and then go ahead to discuss various ways to estimate the present value of the benefits to compare with these costs. Unfortunately, there are many public activities for which estimating outlays, let alone true resource costs, is a non-trivial matter. This paper is devoted to the simple task of discussing one major class of such government outlays

This paper is based on research done for *The Real Federal Budget* by Michael J. Boskin, to be published in 1987. We thank seminar participants at Stanford University and NBER for suggestions, and the Center for Economic Policy Research at Stanford University, IBM and NBER for financial support of this research.

that are an important feature – whether overtly or covertly – of virtually all economies: namely, government insurance programs. In the United States, the government provides many types of explicit insurance, for example: guarantees to creditors of loan repayments by specific classes of borrowers; explicit (and also implicit) insurance of demand deposits in banks and thrifts; disaster insurance via direct outlays or *ex post* subsidized loans to the disaster victims; and co-insurance through the tax system for various types of casualty losses and large medical expenditures.[1]

The budgetary treatment of such insurance programs in the United States, as in the budgetary documents of most countries, can be highly misleading and inaccurate. We focus in this paper on explicit and implicit deposit insurance and loan guarantees, because they are among the largest government insurance programs, and because they contain a special feature less likely to be inherent in other types of insurance programs: the risks are highly correlated, leading to the possibility of extremely large payouts. In discussing the various complications in measuring outlays correctly for deposit insurance and loan guarantees, and comparing them with the existing treatment of these programs in the United States Budget, we pay tribute to Arnold Harberger's career of concern for careful cost–benefit analysis. We attempt no comparison of costs of deposit insurance or loan guarantees with the potential benefits. Indeed, we present only hypothetical examples of costs, focusing instead on conceptually proper measures of costs and their comparison with current budgetary treatment. Such a framework is obviously a necessary input into a more complete cost–benefit analysis of any federal insurance program, or any of its features, or to the analysis of a socially optimal program level and structure.

The severe financial solvency problem of many thrift institutions in recent years, the rapid increase in lending to less developed countries with potential for outright debt repudiation, and the ballooning agricultural debt crisis of American farmers are among the reasons for which deposit insurance and loan guarantees may have significant economic costs. Yet the range of potential budgetary impacts under various scenarios is, at best, ignored in the budget documents. Systematic development of a forward-looking bad debt reserve, or even an accurate statement of the full potential liabilities for these programs, has not yet been developed and included in the budget. There is no reasonable accrual accounting, no separate capital account and no adjustment of assets or liabilities to market value.

In order to aid understanding of these issues, we present a brief introduction to deposit insurance and loan guarantee programs, together with some data highlighting their recent problems. We then discuss the current treatment of deposit insurance and loan guarantees in various budget documents, and develop an analytically proper approach for incorporating improved information in the budget about these programs. We illustrate these points with important recent examples from the Federal Deposit Insurance Corporation, Federal Savings and Loan Insurance Corporation, and the Small Business Administration. We conclude with our suggestions for reform of the conceptual, measurement, and accounting treatment of federal insurance programs in the federal budget.

Introduction to Federal Insurance Programs: Crisis in the 1980s

Federal insurance programs and certain loan guarantee programs are in the midst of their deepest financial crisis since their inception in the 1930s. Loan losses in real estate, agriculture, energy, and less developed countries threaten the solvency of the two major deposit insurance programs, the Federal Deposit Insurance Corporation (FDIC) and the Federal Savings and Loan Insurance Corporation (FSLIC). At the same time, the agricultural debt crisis has already brought the Farm Credit System (FCS), a federally regulated and sponsored financial intermediary, to Congress for emergency financial relief. Finally, agricultural loan guarantees by the Farm Home Administration (FmHA), are also now in danger of massive default and substantial federal payouts. These are four of the major federal insurance programs in crisis in the 1980s.[2] Their bail-outs by the federal government will probably cost tens of billions of dollars and could well be an order of magnitude higher in a worse but not worse-case scenario. Budgetary treatment of these bail-outs has so far been backward-looking, and strangely silent on the subject of expected future losses.

FDIC and FSLIC

The overwhelming bulk of banks are members of the FDIC. Insurance is mandatory for national banks and state bank members of the Federal Reserve System. Insured banks pay insurance premiums calculated as an annual percentage of the bank's average deposit liability. The FDIC adjusts net payments to reflect recent aggregate insurance loss experience and to maintain the level of the insurance fund. The FDIC insures individual deposits up to $100,000.

Federal deposit insurance law provides several methods to protect depositors.

1. *The payoff case.* The FDIC pays for the insured portion of deposits and then reimburses itself by selling the assets of the closed bank and collecting on its outstanding loans.
2. *The deposit case.* The FDIC merges the failing bank into a sound one, usually by purchasing some of the bad assets of the failing bank at above market value, and thereby protects all depositors.
3. *The loan case.* The FDIC makes a loan to the ailing bank, so that it can continue operation. This method provides some protection for stockholders as well as complete protection for the depositors.[3]

The history of FDIC operations, including the 1984 Continental Illinois bail-out, shows that the FDIC has in fact protected all *deposits* thus providing 'implicit' insurance for officially uninsured funds.[4] Total deposits at insured banks were $1807 billion and $1974 billion for 1984 and 1985 respectively; whereas the insured amounts were $1390 billion and $1503 billion respectively. For the Federal Saving and Loan Insurance Corporation (FSLIC), total insured deposits for 1984–85 were $635 billion and $780 billion.[5]

Since the percentage of insured deposits at FDIC member banks[6] is about 75 percent, the provision of implicit insurance increases the maximum possible government payout by about 33 percent. Furthermore, these not explicitly insured deposits are heavily concentrated in a few large banks that are thinly capitalized and unusually exposed to certain highly correlated risks, especially in international loans. As a result, implicit insurance liabilities might substantially increase government payouts under certain conditions.

The two insuring agencies' financial resources consist of the insurance premiums they receive each year plus the interest earned on security holdings bought out of their previous earnings. For 1984–5 the FDIC's premium income was $1.3 billion and $1.5 billion, respectively. Income from other sources was $1.5 billion and $1.6 billion for the same period. For the FSLIC, premium income in 1984–5 was $0.6 billion, and $1.4 billion, while income from other sources was $0.7 billion and $0.5 billion.

In a crisis the agencies can also draw on the accumulated capital of their funds. Total assets of the FDIC in 1984 and 1985 were $22.2 billion and $24.6 billion respectively, while total assets of the FSLIC were $9.4 billion and $10.7 billion during those years. Thus, the asset to insured deposit ratios of these institutions were between one and two percent.

By law, both the FDIC and FSLIC have a statutory right to borrow from the Treasury, but the limits are $3 billion and less than $2 billion respectively. Since they are technically independent agencies, they could legally default on their liabilities without giving their creditors a direct claim on the US Treasury.

Until recently, premium revenues and liquidation receipts have always adequately covered payouts; at no time since 1934 had either FDIC or FSLIC required direct assistance from general government revenues. However, FSLIC's financial position eroded rapidly in the 1980s. By September 1986, its asset to insured deposit ratio had plummeted to 0.31 percent, with only $2.5 billion in usable funds against $844 billion of insured deposits. In a letter to House Banking Committee Chairman, Fernand J. St Germain, the Chairman of FSLIC, Edwin J. Gray, predicted that the fund's usable funds would fall below $1 billion by the end of 1986. Insolvency would force FSLIC to stop closing failing thrifts in 1987, unless a large-scale recapitalization plan was passed by Congress.[7]

The recapitalization bill could be huge. One Congressional bill in 1986 proposed a $25 billion injection over five years. However, known thrift institution problem cases threatened even larger payouts – over 252 thrifts with assets of $95 billion were currently being monitored by FSLIC. Of that total, 130 were considered in need of liquidation or sale to a healthy institution.

FSLIC, in all probability, will receive a large infusion from the Treasury via Congress sometime in 1987. Whether a similar fate awaits the FDIC depends largely on how the continuing international debt crisis is played out.[8] So far, the FDIC has avoided any serious solvency problems. However, as table 2.1 illustrates, between 1980 and 1984, the FDIC's recognized losses exceeded those between 1940 and 1979 by more than a factor of twenty. Clearly, there is little justification for assuming that the fund's history contains all the information relevant to the estimation of future payouts. Risks and the nature of insurance problems change over time. Another world recession could lead many third-world debtor nations to default on their loans, and the FDIC's financial position could quickly become similar to FSLIC's – insolvent and in need of government support.

Table 2.1 Basic FDIC data on a current-flow basis ($m)

Years	Disbursements	Principal recoveries	Losses
1940–9	143.4	137.1	6.3
1950–9	31.0	28.0	3.0
1960–9	122.1	112.9	7.9
1970–9	4640.0	4202.0	124.9
1980–4	8232.6	2360.4	3381.5

Source: FDIC, Annual Report, 1984

The Farm Credit System (FCS)

During the past fifteen years, the Farm Credit System, a government-sponsored financial intermediary, has become the largest creditor in US agricultural markets. Table 2.2 shows the market shares of agricultural lending and the general expansion of the FCS and other government programs in agricultural lending from 1970–84.

As a network of primary and secondary lenders, the Farm Credit System consists of:

1. twelve Federal Land Banks, which finance mortgages on farms

Table 2.2 Market shares of agricultural lending, 1970–1984 (percent of total). Note: data are for ends of years

Source of lending	1970	1975	1980	1984
Government programs: direct and sponsored	32.6	35.6	44.5	48.1
Farm Credit System	23.2	29.6	31.1	31.9
Farmers Home Administration	6.0	5.6	10.7	12.1
Commodity Credit Corporation	3.4	0.4	2.7	4.1
Private sources	67.4	64.4	55.5	51.9
Commercial banks	27.3	28.9	22.1	23.5
Individuals and others	29.8	28.2	26.3	22.5
Life insurance companies	10.3	7.3	7.1	5.9

Source: Economic Report of the President, 1986, p. 197

and rural real estate through 300 local Federal Land Bank Associations (FLBAs);
2. twelve Federal Intermediate Credit Banks which provide funds to 216 Producer Credit Associations (PCAs) for operating loans; and
3. twelve Banks for Cooperatives.

The FLBAs and PCAs are owned by the borrowers who must buy stock in the Associations in proportion to their loans. In turn, the FLBAs and PCAs hold stock in the larger regional banks. Thus, the FCS is considered privately held, but it maintains a special relationship to the federal government that has historically been reflected in its ability to raise funds in credit markets at five to ten basic points above the Treasury bill rate.

The FCS holds about $70 billion of the $210 billion outstanding agricultural debt in the mid 1980s. Along with the rest of agriculture, it is in the midst of a severe financial crisis. In 1985 alone, it reported a $2.7 billion loss, by far the largest annual deficit posted by a US financial institution. The US General Accounting Office (1986) estimates it will post a $2.9 billion loss for 1986.

The systems' resources are rapidly dwindling: it reported on 31 December 1985, $5.1 billion in additional non-accrual loans, or eight per cent of its total loans. In comparison, on 31 December 1984, FCS reported only $1.8 billion of loans as non-accrual, or 2.2 per cent of its loans. The system also had on 31 December 1985 an additional $928 million in other non-earning assets, primarily foreclosed farmland, and an additional $4 billion in substandard credits it labels 'high-risk' assets. By June 1986, non-accruals had grown to $7.6 billion and high-risk loans amounted to $4.7 billion. Operating losses in 1986 could deplete the system's surplus built up from prior years' earnings. Although total system capital would still be $9.6 billion according to US General Accounting Office estimates, bail-out estimates for FCS are of the order of $10–20 billion.[9]

It is crucial to note that these huge increases in the FCS crisis indicators reflect the system's first independent audit in its fifty-year history and a wrenching switch to 'generally acceptable accounting principles.' In 1985, Price Waterhouse's audit unmasked the severe deterioration in the system's loan portfolio.

As the system's insolvency was revealed to investors and creditors, FCS found itself paying as much as 130 basic points above the Treasury rate on credit markets. However, in late December 1985, Congress passed and the President signed a rescue measure giving

FCS access to Treasury funds on the condition that it reorganize itself and exhaust its own resources first. Although this bail-out has not yet involved Treasury outlays, Standard and Poors Corporation re-qualified the FCS as eligible investments for triple-A-rated structural financings. Standard and Poors said that 'The congressional bill represents an important expression of government commitment' to the system, 'and indicates that further support would be available if needed in the years ahead.'[10] Yields on FCS bonds have since narrowed to between 35 and 55 basis points above Treasury bill yields.

One of the intriguing features of the December 1985 Congressional measure was that it required healthy regions, such as the Northeast, to provide surplus funds to ailing ones, such as the Midwest Cornbelt, before the open line of credit from the Treasury could be accessed. This measure effectively taxes the successful regions 100 percent at the margin, which of course discourages the participation of successful farmers in the system. In fact, system gross loans have declined rapidly in 1985–6, from $83.5 billion at the end of 1984 to an estimated $63.7 billion at the end of 1986.[11] As a result, the FCS portfolio appears to be suffering from a serious decline in average loan quality.

Loan Guarantees

Loan guarantees are another type of federal insurance that grew to major proportions in the 1970s. Total outstanding guarantees rose from $24 billion in 1952 to $410 billion in 1985, an annual growth rate of nine percent. Annual growth sharply accelerated in the late 1970s; in the 1980s the growth rate was slowed by recession and tighter budget control.

Loan guarantee programs have historically been dominated by housing. In 1952, 97 percent of outstanding federal loan insurance was allocated to housing, primarily to the Federal Housing Administration programs. In the 1970s the Farmers Home Administration (FmHA), the Small Business Administration (SBA), international military and commerce, and student loans all became significant insurance programs and reduced housing's share of total outstanding guarantees to about 80 percent.

Defaults and high federal government payouts in the case of loan guarantees are largely concentrated in the programs that expanded in the 1970s, particularly in FmHA, foreign and military sales credits, SBA, and student loans. The FmHA is by far the largest of these, as it holds $28 billion of the nation's $210 billion farm debt, including estimates of $12 billion in bad loans.[12]

Summary of Federal Insurance Programs in Crisis

The relevance of budgetary treatment of the FDIC, FSLIC, FCS, and loan guarantees, particularly FmHA, is underlined by the current crisis in these programs. They will almost surely result in at least tens of billions of dollars in payouts over the next few years, yet so far that cost has been poorly reflected in the budget. In the following sections, we consider current methods of measuring the costs of these programs and contrast them to more appropriate methods at both a conceptual and empirical level. At the very least, the value of accurate measurement and accounting would have helped federal budget policy in the last two decades to compare the real costs of federal insurance programs with the benefits that they offered.

Current Treatment of the Cost of Four Major Insurance Programs in the Budget and Related Documents

Federal insurance programs are beginning to receive closer attention in the budget. However, the discussion and data are still quite inadequate for the purposes of estimating the costs of major programs, nor is there a serious effort to measure the costs of these programs in a forward-looking manner.

The US budget lists the current deposit insurance outlays as part of mortgage credit and thrift insurance (MCTI) under the general heading 'commerce and housing credit' (CHC). The annual *net* outlays of the agencies – the difference between receipts and expenses – is the *only* information given. The historical figures are not disaggregated by agencies; only the MCTI and CHC totals are listed for the past eight years. This section of the budget does provide disaggregated outlays for the recent fiscal year and outlay 'estimates' for the next four years. For example, the 1987 budget has the following information on outlays given in table 2.3. However, these data have at least two important shortcomings. First, they use realization rather than accrual accounting, make no separate allowance for capital expenditure, and thus provide a distorted picture of the actual budgetary impact of insurance programs. Second, they systematically underestimate future outlays. As late as FY1984, the

Table 2.3 Actual and estimated outlays for 1985–9

	Outlays ($m)				
	Actual	Estimates			
	1985	1986	1987	1988	1989
FDIC	−1942	−1658	−1900	−2150	−2400
FSLIC	615	457	−197	472	359

Source: US Budget, FY1987, part 5–59. *National Need: Commerce and Housing Credit*

appendix to the budget stated, 'The estimates for 1983 and 1984 in these statements make no provision for losses and expenses which might occur by reason of the closing of any bank after September 30, 1982, because there is no sound basis for predicting which insured banks, if any, will close after that date.'

Significant steps have been taken since FY1984, as more recent federal budgets, including FY1987, contain provisions for losses and expenses resulting from bank closures. Nevertheless, the tendency to underestimate future outlays seems to persist. At the end of 1985, for example, the FDIC had to increase their loan loss reserve by an additional $2.3 billion when some of the loan assets they had acquired in 1984 from Continental Illinois had to be written off and a record number of banks collapsed.

The appendix to the budget contains some information on these insurance agencies under the heading 'other independent agencies.' These data include insurance fund asset and liability positions as well as a breakdown of revenues and expenses for the recent fiscal year and estimates for the next two fiscal years. Again, these estimates make inadequate allowance for future insurance payouts.

Current budgetary treatment of the Farm Credit System and loan guarantees is similar to that of deposit insurance. Both credit activities are omitted from the unified budget, and potential outlays resulting from the government's role as an insurer are not recorded. As a privately held corporation, the FCS is by law treated as an off-budget program despite what is now its explicit legal right to draw on the Treasury. In the case of loan guarantees, net cash outlays are recorded only after a default or a purchase of an insured loan and its reissue as a government direct loan. Therefore, the implicit interest rate subsidies and the government's assumption of the default risk in these insurance programs are also omitted from the unified budget and at least explicitly from congressional decision-making. Treatment of the present consequences of current loan guarantees and Farm Credit System programs are left for future budgets; i.e., there is no accrual accounting in these two types of insurance programs either.

In 1980, the Carter administration introduced the Credit Budget as a means of controlling federal credit activity and focusing budgetary discussion on the gross levels of new commitments rather than net outlays from past credit programs. This action helped to improve the budgetary mechanism for restricting the level of new commitments. The Reagan administration sharpened the budgetary process further by making the Credit Budget subject to the same Congressional procedures and controls as normal outlays and by requiring that Congress be responsible for establishing aggregate limits on new insurance commitments for loan guarantees.

However, neither the presentation of costs of loan guarantee programs nor of activities of the government-sponsored financial intermediaries are integrated in the budget process. Some of the necessary steps for such an improvement in the budgetary process have already occurred. Special Analysis F reports on annual loan guarantee write-offs, and the Office of Management and Budget has begun to estimate the interest subsidy costs of these insured loans.[13]

Finally, the Treasury Department's 'Statement of Liabilities and Other Financial Commitments of the US' provides a schedule of the amount of federal insurance in force by agency. This represents an estimate of total insured deposits for each of the funds, and at least demonstrates an awareness of the potential federal payouts that can arise from the explicit insurance. However, as explained at the beginning of this chapter, the insuring agencies routinely protect deposits in excess of the official insurance limit. Hence, the Treasury figures probably underestimate the true total potential liability of the insurance system.[14] Of course, even an accurate estimate of the total system liability would provide no direct clue as to expected future payouts.

Given the above information we emphasize that the treatment of federal insurance in the budgetary documents is incomplete and inadequate. It is inconsistent with accrual accounting, separate current operating and capital accounts, and market valuation of assets and liabilities. We now propose a methodology for improving this treatment.

Federal Insurance Programs in the Budget: an Analytical Framework

An ideal accounting system conveys as precisely as possible the economic value or cost of each budget item. Because deposit insurance (a general case) represents a potential claim on future government revenue, we would like our accounting system to convey the expected net present value of that claim conditional on the best available information. Changes in future expected payouts, whether caused by changes in the value of total bank deposits and assets or by changes in the kinds of risks faced by the banking system, would then be recognized in the budget on an *accrual* basis, rather than at realization. Equation (1) presents a formal analytical framework for this type of accounting system:

$$V_\tau = \sum_{t=\tau}^{\infty} \frac{1}{(1+r)^{t-\tau}} \int_0^\infty E_t f(E_t|\phi_\tau) \, dE_t \tag{1}$$

where V_τ is the present discounted value of expected payouts as of the period τ (the loss reserve), τ is the reference period in which V_t is calculated, E_t is the insurance outlays in period t, ϕ_τ is the information set available in period τ, $f(E_t|\phi_\tau)$ is the density function for E_t conditional on information available in period τ, r is the discount rate, assumed constant for simplicity (although this is clearly unlikely in a severe financial crisis). The model represents a simple idea. The loan loss reserve appropriate for deposit insurance should equal the discounted present value of all future government insurance expenditures, times the probability of those payouts occurring, where the probabilities are calculated using all information available in period τ.[15] Any change in the information set $\phi\tau$, for example a change in the level of total deposits, or a change in the degree of risk carried by the banking sector, will give a new value to the conditional density function $f(E_t|\phi\tau)$, and hence will change the value of $V\tau$. Accrued government insurance expenditure between dates τ and $\tau + 1$ can then be represented by the change in the loss reserve, plus outlays during the period, or

$$G_\tau = V_{\tau+1} - V_\tau + E_\tau. \tag{2}$$

Government net investment in deposit insurance equals revenues net of expenditure, or

$$I_\tau = R_\tau - G_\tau \tag{3}$$

where $R\tau$ represents the insurance revenue collected between τ and $\tau + 1$. Note that current outlays E_τ are only part of the conceptual measure of both expenditure and investment. *Accrued* expenditures could be *negative* even when current outlays are large and positive, if $V_{\tau+1}$ fell to a sufficiently low level.

Note, however, that while the expected present value of accrued spending is a useful budget concept, these costs and benefits of the programs should not necessarily be simply added across programs. The modern theory of finance informs us that when there is risk involved in expenditures or revenues, the covariance between tax or program-specific costs and benefits and other sources of national income must be considered in valuing the net social benefits of a program.

Equation (4) breaks government payouts into three categories: legally required payments on insured deposits at failed banks (term 1), payouts by the insuring agency to uninsured depositors multiplied by the probability of such payments occurring (term 2), and government expenditures in support of the financial system over and above the first two categories (term 3).[16] Note that we have dropped the E-variable and now calculate expected outcomes based on the density function of bank *asset* returns.

$$V_\tau = \sum_{\tau=t}^{\infty} \frac{1}{(1+r)^{t-\tau}} \int_0^\infty E \sum_{i=0}^{N} \left(\max 0, L_{it} - A_{it} \frac{LI_{it}}{L_{it}} \right.$$

term 1

$$\left. + \rho(\bar{A}_t) \max 0, L_{it} - A_{it} \frac{(L_{it} - LI_{it})}{L_{it}} + P(\bar{A}_t)|g(\bar{A}_t|\phi_\tau) \, d\bar{A}_t \right) \tag{4}$$

term 2   term 3

where
L_{it} is the market value of total liabilities of bank i at time t,
A_{it} is the market value of total assets of bank i at time t,
LI_{it} is the total *insured* liabilities of bank i at time t (deposits less than \$100 thousand),
$\bar{A}_t$ is the vector of asset values at all banks at time t,
$g(\bar{A}_t|\phi_t)$ is the density function for $\bar{A}$ conditional on information available in period τ,

$\rho(\bar{A}_t)$ is the probability that the insuring agencies will make good on uninsured deposits, as a function of the total state of all bank assets at time t, and

$P(\bar{A}_t)$ are the quasi-insurance payouts over and above those made to depositors at failing banks, as a function of A_t.

There are basically two main problems with our current budget accounting system. First, the existing system concerns itself only with *current* cash flows instead of estimated expected payouts.[17] In the next section we discuss why this is not at all adequate. Second, problems in the financial system sometimes induce government outlays not officially reported as insurance losses, which term 3 captures in equation (4). For example, the All Saver's Certificate program provided a tax subsidy for the thrift industry that reduced deposit insurance payouts. Such *ad hoc* programs may substitute for explicit insurance or may exceed the requirements of deposit intermediaries. These programs will usually show up elsewhere in the budget – often on a realization basis – although some, like the All Saver's Certificate program, do not show up at all.[18] We do not necessarily have to add these programs to deposit insurance outlays for budget reporting, but we should treat them analogously and discuss them together with the explicit insurance system.

The Federal Reserve's expenditures in support of the financial system are also treated in a misleading way under our current accounting system: the great bulk of the Federal Reserve banks' net earnings are turned over to the US Treasury. Since the FED is legally a private corporation owned by the member banks, its profits are treated as part of corporate sector profits. The FED's remittances to the Treasury are added to corporate income tax revenues. About 95–98 percent of the net earnings have been turned over to the Treasury in recent years. For the period 1980–2 these remittances were 11.7, 14.0, and 15.2 billion dollars respectively, whereas corporate income tax receipts were 64.6, 61.1, and 49.2 billion dollars. Hence, these remittances have been a large percentage of the corporate income tax revenue. Under the current accounting system, expenses incurred by the FED in support of the financial system will show up as a reduction of the FED's net earnings and therefore a *decline in corporate income tax receipts*. Nowhere in the budget will these expenses be added to government expenditures.[19]

Our current accounting system is also misleading in that it counts only the *deficit* of insurance programs as part of government expenditures. We should instead add program expenditures (measured on an accrual basis) to total government expenditures, and add insurance revenues to total revenues. The results of our current system can be very counter-intuitive. For example, the FDIC ran cash surpluses in 1980 and 1981, and thus reduced reported expenditures and deficits at a time when severe strains in international lending markets were greatly increasing expected future payouts.

Accrual Accounting for Federal Insurance Programs.   As discussed in the last section, the existing insurance accounting system concerns itself with current cash flows, as determined by the *history* of risk-taking and insurance payouts. The insuring agencies adjust premiums to compensate for past payouts and to keep the insurance fund at a constant proportion of total deposits. The backward-looking system, which provides no direct estimate of future payouts, can be justified only if the fund's history contains all information relevant to estimating future payouts.[20]

However, the history of insurance payouts is a poor predictor of the future, mainly because the insurance programs contain strongly correlated risks that generate small but finite probabilities of extremely large payouts. The government's tendency to pay *more* than its statutory obligation in times of crisis and the encouragement of risk-taking by government and the insurance programs both tend to exacerbate this problem.

To support this contention we will briefly discuss two recent episodes resulting from the current crisis in the thrift and banking industry. A parallel argument could be made for FCS and FmHA.

The thrift industry has a strategy of borrowing short and lending long. Mutual savings banks and savings-and-loan associations have traditionally financed housing purchases by making long-term fixed-rate loans. The industry has generally raised these funds by issuing short-term liabilities, principally pass-book deposits. This financial structure introduces a large component of systematic risk into the deposit insurance system and encourages the development of such risk.

Borrowing short and lending long creates an extremely risky portfolio by making the industry highly sensitive to interest rate fluctuations. A rise in rates reduces the value of long-term mortgages, without strongly affecting the value of short-term deposits. Since a change in interest rates will affect all thrift institutions simultaneously, the industry practice of borrowing short and lending long introduces a large component of systematic risk into the deposit insurance system.

By insuring thrift deposits, the federal government essentially sells an interest rate option, which increases in value as the industry's position becomes riskier.[21] Since the insurance premium is not adjusted on an institution-by-institution basis to reflect these risky practices, each thrift has an incentive to maximize its interest rate exposure. This perverse incentive structure may help to explain why the industry has continued to make fixed-rate mortgages, despite the advent of variable-rate mortgages. While the thrift crisis may have been partially caused by a policy surprise that upset market expectations based on 40 years of more stable interest rates, recent developments cannot solely be explained by industry ignorance of the risks involved.[22]

In fact, the perverse incentive structure has led insolvent or potentially insolvent thrifts to deepen federal exposure through high-risk real-estate loans. In many cases, this has led to substantially greater losses. The jury is still out, however, on whether the losses incurred from allowing many thrifts to operate through several years of insolvency based on a forecast that interest rate differentials would drop and help restore the net worth of the thrift industry will be costly or a cost saving.[23]

Crises often induce government policy makers to undertake expenditures exceeding statutory obligations. The thrift industry crisis provides a good example of this phenomenon. Widespread insolvency in the thrift industry led to a number of direct-aid programs, most notably the All Saver's Certificate program, and the Net Worth Certificate Act, that provided some help to *solvent* institutions, as well as to thrifts that would otherwise have failed. This type of program increases the degree of correlated payout risk in the system, since government outlays in a crisis become proportionately higher than normal outlays.[24] Such programs also increase the frequency of payouts in general, since events that might not cause bank failures can still lead to government expenditures.

The present international banking crisis provides another example of the potential error involved in assuming that the history of deposit insurance contains all information relevant to estimating future payouts.

Starting from almost nothing in 1965, US bank lending to less developed countries (LDCs') governments and to individuals whose debts were guaranteed by LDC governments reached a level of $357.4 billion in 1983. Such loans appeared to be quite safe throughout the 1970s and carried only small risk premiums.[25] However, the deep recession that commenced in 1981 and sharply reduced international trade, combined with the unusually high real interest rates that persisted from early 1982 have made repayment doubtful for a number of major borrowers.[26] In addition, the collapse of world oil prices has seriously harmed some important LDCs, particularly Mexico.

The current international lending situation clearly contains a high degree of correlated insurance risk. Loans that are large relative to the capital of the lending banks have been concentrated in the hands of a few borrowing countries whose economies show a high degree of correlation with each other.[27]

Furthermore, large banks carry out the bulk of international lending;[28] hence defaults on international loans would strike directly at the money center banks that form the core of the US financial system. In addition these banks have a high percentage of volatile uninsured funds. Any serious threat to the solvency of these banks could conceivably produce 'runs' that would badly disrupt the financial system.

Insurance *encourages* many kinds of risk-taking by insured intermediaries, since good outcomes accrue to the shareholders and borrowers, while government pays for the bad outcomes.[29] Therefore, the structure of deposit insurance *encourages* development of correlated risk, and increases the likelihood that a low-probability event (such as a sustained rise in real interest rates) will result in a large insurance payout.

For the purposes of accurate budget accounting we should make loss provisions equal to the expected value of total insurance outlays as soon as the risks occur. No accounting system will accurately predict specific payout levels, but we should at least recognize large changes in the risk exposure of insured institutions.

Our current accounting system sometimes fails to register expected future payouts even when such payouts have an extremely high probability of occurring. For example, the abrupt rise in inflation and interest rates that took place in 1979–81 made large numbers of savings and loans insolvent in a market value sense. Although this decline in value took place immediately as rates rose, industry accounting standards obscured the situation somewhat through the use of 'book-value'[30] accounting. Under these accounting rules an institution might appear to have positive net worth for several years after becoming fundamentally insolvent.[31] In this situation a backward-looking accounting system becomes seriously misleading, since future insurance payouts that are almost certain to occur as institutions gradually become insolvent, in book-value terms do not appear anywhere in the budget.

The FSLIC budget provides a case where simple accrual accounting would drastically improve the information transmitted by the budget. FSLIC reported a cash flow surplus of $588 million in 1982. However, 1982 witnessed a decline in long-term bond rates from 12.2 per cent in January to 8 per cent in December. This interest rate decline vastly improved the industry's financial position. Carron (1983) estimates that the net worth of the industry improved from $-57 billion at the beginning of the year to $-40 billion at the end, with a corresponding decline in expected future FSLIC payouts.[32] This expected decline, from the gigantic but unreported amounts accrued in the preceding years, surely swamped the reported surplus, and net investment was correspondingly understated.

A Hypothetical Example of Improved FDIC Budget Treatment

To illustrate our concerns further, we present a purely hypothetical example in table 2.4 of budget reporting and accounting for deposit insurance under our proposed procedures. We present 'hypothetical,' as well as actual, data for FY1982. The reported actual *net* outlays for FY1982 were $-1440 millions for the FDIC.

For expository convenience (although it is unlikely), suppose the accumulated reserves in the insurance funds at the start of the year were the appropriate loss reserves, V_τ. These were $14.9 billion for the FDIC. The analysis at the agency concludes that the LDC debt problem worsened sharply during the year, and a larger loss reserve is appropriate. The (hypothetically) estimated *change* in the present value of expected payouts amounts to a $10 billion increase for the FDIC. Again this figure is hypothetical but not necessarily

Table 2.4 Actual and 'hypothetical' data for FY1982 (in $m)

	Reported net current outlays $E_\tau - R_\tau$	Loss reserve $V_{\tau+1}$	V_τ	net change $V_{\tau+1} - V_\tau$	Estimated net investment $R_\tau - G_\tau$
Agency: FDIC	−1440	24,921	14,921	10,000	−8560

unreasonable in magnitude given events and the above estimates. The budget information would appear in Table 2.4.

Thus, the accumulated actual reserves would no longer (except by coincidence) reflect the estimated $V_{\tau+1}$. Various policies and accounting procedures could reconcile the difference. If we were optimistic that the values of $V\tau$ could be estimated accurately, the actual premiums charged could be adjusted (although we favor a name change to excise tax) accordingly. Note that the banks themselves often increase their loss reserves despite the simple proportionality rules used to set (and rebate) premiums. *Explicitly* recognizing these issues can help generate consideration of the appropriate nature and amounts of deposit insurance in view of its expected cost in the appropriations and regulatory processes of government.

Life Cycle of Loan Guarantees

In this section, we develop a life cycle approach to estimating the net spending equivalent (NSE) of a loan guarantee commitment and then apply it to a cohort of loans guaranteed by the Small Business Administration over the period 1969–77. Our analytical scheme for deriving the NSE of a new loan commitment requires some explanation.[33] The scheme depends on using historical data on the life cycle of loans in order to predict the NSE of new commitments. In the case of an insurance program, such as the FDIC, and more specifically, in the case of loans to less developed countries, where the risks of default across borrowers are highly correlated and very rare, a model based on historical experience can be misleading as a means of estimating or simulating contingencies.

The life cycle approach can be useful, however, for many classes of loans, such as student loans, small business loans, and housing loans, where the default risks may not be as highly correlated. The life cycle model could be strengthened by incorporating economic variables that affect the likelihood of loan losses, such as recessions, interest rate swings, and changes in land or commodity values. For example, loan loss estimates on energy industry commitments could be based on a variety of assumptions about the level of oil prices, so that the life cycle model would reflect more than just simple historical experience of energy loans.

A Simple Life Cycle Model

Our scheme for the life cycle of new loan guarantees begins with the new commitments made in the current period, labeled NC_0. The government will purchase a certain amount of these loans in each subsequent year t, P_t. The purchase price may be less than the original loan if partial repayment had occurred to the original lender. The government, now owning the loan, may be paid back some or all of the outstanding balance. For those loans that eventually default, the remaining unpaid balance must be charged off when the event is recognized, CO_τ. Thus, for each cohort of the loans, in general $CO \leq P \leq NC$. Furthermore, the ratio of present value of CO_τ to NC_0 gives the subsidy of spending ratio of the loan guarantee commitments from that cohort of loans, as the present discounted value of CO_τ is a net spending equivalent measure (NSE).

The derivation of the NSE is shown in equation (5) through (7). Suppose that in period 0, NC_0 new commitments are made for a term of τ periods. In each of the subsequent periods, the government will purchase a certain percentage of these commitments, $a_1, \ldots, a_\tau$. The government's purchase of the original guarantees in period t is

$$P_t = a_t(NC_0 - X_t) \tag{5}$$

where the X_t are the partial repayments to original lenders. Of P_t, some or all may be paid off by the borrower. Therefore, the present value of the charge-off in any future period t will be

$$CO_t = b_t \left[\left(\sum_{t=0}^{t} P_t \right) - X_t^* \right] \frac{1}{(1+r)^t} \tag{6}$$

where b_t is the percentage of purchases charged off in period t, and X_t^* is the repayment on this loan to the government. The present value of the charge-off for all periods $0, \ldots, \tau$, which equals the net spending equivalent commitments at period 0 (NSE_0) can thus be written as

$$NSE_0 = \sum_{t=0}^{\tau} CO_t = \sum_{t=0}^{\tau} b_t \left[\left(\sum_{t=0}^{t} P_t \right) - X_t^* \right] \frac{1}{(1+r)^t} \tag{7}$$

Given the estimates of the likelihood of purchase and charge-off, and the corresponding unpaid balances, these data can be entered into equation (7) and the NSE of new commitments for a given cohort of loans can be calculated.

Application to the Small Business Administration

The ratio of the present value of the charge-offs (the NSE_0) to new commitments, or NSE_0/NC_0, gives us the 'effective' default rate of a loan guarantee. With data from a cohort of 1969–77 Small Business Administration (SBA) loan guarantees,[34] we estimated a life cycle effective default rate of about 12.5 percent, which indicates that a new commitment of $100 million in SBA guarantees in 1969 would have cost the federal government $12.5 million in present-value terms.

In defense of the SBA, our impression from a survey of other loan guarantee programs is that their effective default rate of 12.5 percent was probably comparable with many other programs and significantly less than some programs, such as the Foreign Military Credit Sales, Rural Electrification Administration, and the Farm Home Administration. Furthermore, their careful administration and supervision of the loans made them one of the few agencies in which data were readily available for estimating a simple net spending equivalent.

The ability of the President, Congress and specific departments and agencies to make similar estimates on the basis of historical experience of each loan guarantee program would be a tremendously useful step toward evaluating the explicit costs of federal credit activity. Including these estimates explicitly in the budget process and the budget itself would render federal insurance programs comparable with the rest of government fiscal activity, and open meaningful and coherent debate about their benefits and their costs.

Conclusion

The current budgetary treatment of federal insurance programs is highly inadequate and potentially quite misleading. Spread among various reports of different agencies, this treatment fails to: (1) separate current and capital spending; (2) adjust book to market values; (3) report gross (rather than net) revenues and outlays; (4) recognize expected payouts as they accrue; or (5) report quasi-insurance outlays.

A conceptually proper budgetary treatment would recognize expected payouts as they accrue, adjust par to market values, provide for the expected future quasi-payouts outside the official funds, and report a comprehensive and consistent set of income statements and balance sheets. The vehicle of a more conceptually proper loss reserve would render all of this possible. While forecasting the probability of future outlays cannot be done with great precision in all cases, a range of alternatives are available. For example, losses expected from interest rate changes may be forecast conditional on various rate assumptions, with the alternative scenarios presented and compared with Administration and private interest rate forecasts. Losses already suffered in a market value sense can be estimated continually. Changes in future payouts due to international lending, caused by either growth of such loans or by changes in the probabilities of complete repayment (as opposed to rescheduling, rate concessions or default) can also be estimated for alternative scenarios.

The reporting across agencies should be made more comparable, and the assumption of small future failures to estimate outlays must be replaced with a sensible forward-looking reserve. Gross outlays and revenues should be brought directly into the main budget to provide a more accurate estimate of total government activity. Net investment or disinvestment should be expressly estimated and included in a separate capital account.

These changes will not be easy to implement for a variety of technical, bureaucratic and political reasons, but they will be well worth the effort. Not only will they provide us with more accurate, conceptually proper, and complete information, but they will also provide an impetus to review various policies from different points of view. Thus, the interaction of (potential) budget, tax, monetary, international trade and finance, and financial institution regulatory policy can be seen much more clearly. Of course, better information will only be a potential input into, not a guarantee of, improved decisions.

Notes

1 Social security, unemployment compensation, and pension benefit guarantees are other significant government insurance programs. For further discussion of the budgetary treatment of Social Security; see Boskin (1986).

2 Other Federal insurance programs of questionable solvency include the Pension Benefit Guarantee Corporation and Social Security. Here, we limit our focus, but we should remember that improving the budgetary treatment of these federal insurance programs is critical as well. Their costs may swamp the others discussed here. See Boskin (1986).

3 This authority was given to the FDIC in 1971. Even though it has been used infrequently, the amount disbursed by this method by the end of 1980 exceeded cumulative principal disbursements since inception in the payoff cases.

In a very few cases, the FDIC has opened its own bank, called a Deposit Insurance National Bank. This new bank has taken over the failed bank's deposits prior to either paying off deposits or merging the bank with a sound one. Another possibility is to reorganize a bank.

4 The FDIC abandoned the policy of implicit insurance in one important case in 1982 by allowing uninsured depositors to take substantial losses in the failure of the Penn Square Bank.

5 FDIC and FSLIC Annual Reports (1983, 1984) and verbal communications for 1985.

6 This has been 73.4, 75.0, and 76.9% for 1982, 1983, and 1984 respectively.

7 *New York Times*, 19 September 1986.

8 In an emergency, the Federal Reserve System could be the principal source of funds. The FED most notably followed this policy during the failure of the Franklin National Bank, by allowing that bank to borrow some $1.7 billion in the five months preceding its closure.

9 All figures came out from US General Accounting Office (1986, pp. 1–5), except the bail-out estimates, which are from various farm economists.

10 Standard and Poor's (1985).

11 US General Accounting Office (1986, p. 22). Members of the FSC are required to buy equity in the system with a small percentage of their loans. Solvent farmers fearing losses in equity and debt appear to have withdrawn from the system.

12 US General Accounting Office (1985). It is difficult to separate loan losses emanating from loan guarantees and direct loans, since many of the direct loans were sold to the Federal Financing Bank (FFB), an off-budget arm of the Treasury. In the process, the FmHA became the guarantor for the FFB and was recapitalized for the purposes of making additional loans.

13 See Budget of the United States Government, Special Analysis F (1987).

14 The market values of intermediate- and long-term bank liabilities vary as interest rates change. Hence the Treasury estimates should be adjusted to account for differences between par and market values.

15 For simplicity we assume here that expenditures in each period are independent of expenditures in other periods (once we condition on ϕ).

16 For simplicity, equation (4) assumes that (i) the government will always back the insured funds, rather than stopping payment when the funds are exhausted, and (ii) the market values of bank liabilities are known with certainty for all periods.

17 Of course for some purposes the current realizations are useful in and of themselves. The actual payout in some period, for instance, may affect capital markets beyond any anticipated net surplus already reported in previous budgets.

18 'Tax expenditures', as programs such as the All Saver's Certificate are called, provide a subsidy to participants by reducing their tax liabilities. Although tax expenditures reduce government revenues, they are not recorded explicitly in the Budget, as either expenditures or as revenue reductions. Rather, there is a separate statement of Tax Expenditures, the estimation of which is highly questionable (see Stiglitz and Boskin, 1977).

19 Of course, sometimes the FED infusions of cash are loans that may be repaid eventually, either by the ailing institution or one that acquires it. In that case the accrual and separate capital account issues come into play.

20 If we make a conceptual distinction between premium income and general tax revenues, the current accounting system has another justification. As long as the fund always covers payouts, and as long as premiums are always adjusted *ex post* to replenish the fund, then deposit insurance represents no expected drain on general tax revenues. Both assumptions are questionable, but the major problem with this argument is the assumption of a clear distinction between taxes and premiums. The *incidence* of these levies may differ, with deposit insurance premiums falling primarily on depositors and bank shareholders, but both represent sources of revenue for government expenditures.

21 Marcus and Shaked (1982) explore this issue in more detail.

22 Federal law prohibited thrift institutions from offering variable-rate loans prior to 1980 so we might argue the industry was *forced* to accept interest rate exposure. Without insurance, however, high-risk premiums on deposit interest rates and depositor panics when rates rose might well have forced regulators to relax these restrictions.

23 *Economic Report of the President* (1986, pp. 204–5).

24 Such programs may be socially beneficial in a crisis. Nevertheless they do tend to increase payouts.

25 Sachs (1982) reports an average premium over LIBOR of only 120 basis points in 1978, compared to 63 basis points for industrialized nations.

26 Changes in real interest rates directly affect the cash flow of LDC borrowers, since most international loans have floating rates pegged to LIBOR.

27 For example, Argentina, Brazil, Chile and Mexico together owed $61.7 billion to the nine largest US banks in December of 1983. Capital and subordinated debt at these banks totalled about $31.5 billion, according

to the Federal Financial Institutions Examination Council, Country Exposure Lending Survey, December 1981.

28 88 per cent of outstanding US bank loans to Argentina, Brazil, Chile and Mexico came from 24 banks as of December 1983.

29 From the point of view of an individual bank, deposit insurance works essentially like buying a put-option contract. See Marcus and Shaked (1982) for the discussion of put-option.

30 Book-value accounting allows a firm to amortize its losses by reporting only the difference between current interest income and expenditure, ignoring capital gains and losses.

31 We should note that the accounting standards matter only because the existence of deposit insurance converts bankruptcy from a market decision to a regulatory one. Without insurance an insolvent institution would face a 'run' by depositors, and would be forced to liquidate its assets at market value.

32 FSLIC provides enough detailed data on thrift portfolios to permit the making of accurate estimates of short-run insurance losses, conditional on interest rate assumptions. For example, Carron (1982) has performed such an analysis, and estimates cumulative thrift industry payouts through the end of 1984 at around $8 billion, with intermediate interest rate assumptions.

33 Boskin and Barham (1984) offer a more thorough discussion of loan guarantees.

34 The authors express their gratitude to Elisabeth Rhyne and former SBA Commissioner James Sanders for their assistance in obtaining the SBA data.

References

Black, F., Miller, M. and Posner, R. 1978: An approach to the regulation of bank holding companies. *Journal of Business*, 51, July.

Boskin, M. J. 1982: Federal government deficits: myths and realities. *American Economic Review*, May.

—— and Barham, R. 1984: Measurement and Conceptual Issues in Federal Budget Treatment of Loans and Loan Guarantees. Center for Economic Policy Research, Working Paper no. 11.

—— 1986: *Too Many Promises: The Uncertain Future of Social Security*. Dow Jones-Irwin.

—— 1987: *The Real Federal Budget*, Harvard University Press.

Carron, A. 1982: *The Plight of the Thrift Institutions*, Brookings.

—— 1983: *The Rescue of the Thrifts*, Brookings.

Eaton, J. and Gersovitz, M. 1981: Debt with potential repudiation: theoretical and empirical analysis. *Review of Economic Studies*, 43, 289–309.

Federal Deposit Insurance Corporation, *Annual Report*, selected years.

Federal Home Loan Bank Board, *Annual Report*, selected years, Washington, DC.

Friedman, M. and Schwartz, A. 1963: *A Monetary History of the United States*. Princeton University Press for NBER.

Marcus, A. and Shaked, I. 1982: The Valuation of FDIC Deposit Insurance: Empirical Estimates Using the Options Pricing Framework. Boston University School of Management Working Paper no. 21/82.

National Credit Union Share Insurance Fund, *Annual Financial Report*, Fiscal Year 1982, Washington, DC.

Penner, R. 1982: How Much is Owed by the Federal Government?. Carnegie–Rochester Conference Series in Public Policy.

Sachs, J. 1982: LDC Debt in the 1980's: Risks and Reforms. Working Paper no. 861, National Bureau of Economic Research, February.

—— and Cohen, D. 1982: LDC Borrowing with Default Risk. Working Paper no. 925, National Bureau of Economic Research, July.

Stiglitz, J. and Boskin, M. 1977: Some lessons from the new public finance. *American Economic Review*, February.

US Congress Joint Economic Committee 1983: The Federal Debt: On-Budget, Off-Budget and Contingent Liabilities, June.

US Congressional Budget Office 1983: An Analysis of the President's Credit Budget for Fiscal Year 1984, March (and various years).

US Department of the Treasury 1983: Statement of Liabilities and Other Financial Commitments of the United States Government as of September 30, 1982. Washington, DC.

US General Accounting Office 1986: *Farm Credit System: Analysis of Financial Condition*, September.

US Office of Management and Budget, *Budget of the United States Government*, various (fiscal) years.

——, *Budget of the United States Government, Appendix*, various years.

——, *Budget of the United States Government, Special Analyses*, various years.

3 Weighted-Average Discount Rates in Public Expenditure Analysis: a Generalization

ALAN J. AUERBACH

Introduction

The use of weighted-average discount rates in public expenditure evaluation dates back to the contributions of Diamond (1968) and Harberger (1972), who argued that the shadow cost of government investment funds depends on the extent to which the extraction of these funds displaces private consumption as opposed to private investment. This approach was formalized in a two-period general equilibrium model by Sandmo and Drèze (1971), whose framework has been utilized by subsequent authors to consider the effects of introducing various complications and distortions. Such contributions have focused on the impact on the weighted-average formula of labor market distortions (Marchand et al., 1985), the government budget constraint (Hägen, 1983) and, most recently, the presence of more than one output per period (Marchand and Pestieau, 1984).

The purpose of the current paper is to demonstrate that the basic weighted-average approach is valid in very general circumstances, with the weights corresponding to the relative displacement effects, *given* the particular set of instruments available to the government. The formulae derived apply under general assumptions about consumption and production. This approach facilitates an intuitive interpretation of the impact on appropriate shadow prices of various restrictions on government instruments, consumer preferences and the private sector's production technology. One of our key findings is that when first-period commodity taxes are subject to choice, it will be optimal, under certain conditions, for the public production sector to use *consumer* prices for valuing output. This corresponds to the use of the rate of time preference in a model with one output per period. Conditions under which such a policy is optimal were presented by Arrow (1966) and discussed further by Kay (1972), but the current results differ in that they derive from a model without the constraints on individual saving or rationality that were present in the previous results.

The Model

We consider an economy with n commodities, comprising all goods and factors in both periods. The private production vector y must satisfy the production function

$$f(y) = 0 \qquad (1)$$

where $f(\cdot)$ is assumed to be homogeneous of degree zero in its arguments. As usual, a negative element of y may be thought of as a factor input. Note that there is no separate production function for each period, nor does 'capital' appear explicitly in the production function, since it is purely an intermediate good. That is, capital is never purchased or sold by the production sector as a whole. It is produced by primary factors and used in the production of commodities.

Government production, z, obeys the production function

$$g(z) = 0 \qquad (2)$$

with no assumption made about the homogeneity of $g(\cdot)$. The private-sector constant-returns assumption is made to obviate the need to consider private-sector profits and their disposition, although under suitable assumptions (typically the taxation of all such profits) these situations generally yield the same government decsision rules about optimal distortions (see, e.g., Stiglitz and Dasgupta, 1971, or Auerbach, 1985).[1]

We assume government seeks to extract a vector of goods and services R from the private sector, and may do so through the use of lump sum taxes, T, and proportional commodity taxes, t (expressed in units rather than *ad valorem*). It may also set levels of government production, z. Our analysis will focus on the effects of the government not having access to different subsets of these instruments.

Households are represented in this model by a single, representative consumer with preferences generating the indirect utility function

$$V(p,\ I) \tag{3}$$

where p is the price vector for the n commodities facing the consumer and I is lump sum income. By the definition of the tax vector, t, we may then express producer prices as $q = p - t$. Because of the constant returns to scale assumption for the private sector, no pure profits exist, and hence lump sum income equals lump sum government transfers, or $I = -T$. If x is defined to be the vector of private purchases, then $x + R = y + z$, i.e., total consumption equals total production.

Using these definitions, we construct the Lagrangian that the government seeks to maximize through the choice of its available instruments:

$$L = V(p,\ -T) - \mu F(x + R - z) - \gamma g(z). \tag{4}$$

For the sake of generality, we assume that a subset M of the taxes may be chosen and that a subset K of the public production levels may be chosen with the remaining taxes and public production levels exogenously fixed. With no loss of generality we assume there are m elements in M, k elements in K, and index the commodities so that the taxable commodities are l through m and those for which production levels are set are l_1 through l_k. We derive first-order conditions with respect to the consumer prices rather than the taxes on the commodities. This procedure is valid as long as the matrix relating changes in p and t is of full rank (see Dixit, 1975, or Auerbach, 1985), which we assume to be the case. Because the units of $f(\cdot)$ and $g(\cdot)$ are arbitrary, we are free to scale the Lagrange multipliers μ and γ. We therefore assume $\gamma = \mu$ and that μ is set so that the gradient of the private production function is equal to the producer price vector, q, rather than simply proportional (as required by private-sector production efficiency).

Basic Results

The first-order conditions derived from (4) (in addition to the two production constraints) are:

(public production)

$$\mu(f_i - g_i) + \sum_{l \notin M} \frac{dp_l}{dz_i}\left(-\lambda x_l - \mu \sum_j f_j \frac{dx_j}{dp_l}\right) = 0 \quad (i \in K) \quad (5a)$$

(commodity taxes)

$$-\lambda x_i - \mu \sum_j f_j \frac{dx_j}{dp_i} + \sum_{l \notin M} \frac{dp_l}{dp_i}\left(-\lambda x_l - \mu \sum_j f_j \frac{dx_j}{dp_l}\right) = 0 \quad (i \in M)$$

$$(5b)$$

(lump sum taxes)

$$-\lambda + \mu \sum_j f_j \frac{dx_j}{dI} - \sum_{l \notin M} \frac{dp_l}{dI}\left(-\lambda x_l - \mu \sum_j f_j \frac{dx_j}{dP_l}\right) = 0 \quad (5c)$$

where p_l $(l \notin M)$ is implicitly a function of the government instruments and λ is the marginal utility of income, $\partial V/\partial I$. Using the Slutsky equation, the definition of z, the equality of q_i and f_i for all i, and the fact that $p'x = I$, we may simplify these expressions to obtain

$$f_i - g_i + \sum_{l \notin M} \frac{dp_l}{dz_i}\left(\alpha x_l + \sum_j t_j S_{jl}\right) = 0 \quad (i \in K) \quad (6a)$$

$$\alpha x_i + \sum_j t_j S_{ji} + \sum_{l \notin M} \frac{dp_l}{dp_i}\left(\alpha x_l + \sum_j t_j S_{jl}\right) = 0 \quad (i \in M) \quad (6b)$$

$$\alpha - \sum_{l \notin M} \frac{dp_l}{dI}\left(\alpha x_l + \sum_j t_j S_{jl}\right) = 0 \quad (6c)$$

where

$$\alpha = \left[\mu - \left(\lambda + \mu \sum_j t_j \frac{dx_j}{dI}\right)\right]\Big/\mu \quad (7)$$

is the marginal excess burden per dollar of revenue, measured by the normalized difference between the shadow cost attached to the government budget constraint and the 'social' marginal utility of income (as in Diamond, 1975).

To simplify expressions (6), we must solve for $p_{\check{M}}$, the price vector corresponding to those goods not in set M. Note that

$$\frac{dp_l}{dz_i} = \frac{dt_l}{dz_i} + \frac{dq_l}{dz_i} = \frac{df_l}{dz_i} = \sum_j f_{lj}\frac{dx_j}{dz_i} - f_{li} \quad l \notin M, i \in K. \tag{8}$$

Furthermore, in the neighborhood of the optimum, where these derivatives are being evaluated, changes in z_i have no first-order welfare effects, so

$$\frac{dx_j}{dz_i} = \left(\frac{dx_j}{dz_i}\right)^{comp} = \sum_{r \notin M} S_{jr}\frac{dp_r}{dz_i}. \tag{9}$$

Substitution of (9) into (8) yields conditions that may be stacked to obtain

$$P = (H_{MK}H_{\check{M}K})\binom{S_{K\check{M}}}{S_{\check{K}\check{M}}} P - H_{\check{M}K} \tag{10}$$

where P is the $(n-m) \times k$ matrix with elements dp_l/dz_i, and H_{ij} and S_{ij} are components of the Hessian and Slutsky matrices with rows indexed by set i and columns indexed by set j. Assuming invertibility, we obtain from (10)

$$P = (H_{\check{M}}.S._{\check{M}} - I) H_{\check{M}K} \tag{11}$$

where the notation '·' signifies that all elements $1, \ldots, n$ are represented.

In similar fashion, we may solve for the response of uncontrolled prices with respect to controlled ones:

$$\frac{dp_l}{dp_i} = \frac{df_l}{dp_i} = \sum_j f_{lj}\left(\sum_{r \notin M} S_{jr}\frac{dp_r}{dp_i} + S_{ji}\right) \quad i \in M, l \notin M \tag{12}$$

which may be stacked for $Q = (dp_l/dp_i)$:

$$Q = -(H_{\check{M}}.S._{\check{M}} - I)^{-1} H_{\check{M}}.S._{M} \tag{13}$$

where Q is $(n-m) \times m$.

Finally, solution for dp_I/dI yields

$$\frac{dp_I}{dI} = \frac{df_I}{dI} = \sum_j f_{Ij} \sum_{r \notin M} S_{jr} \frac{dp_r}{dI} \quad \text{all } I \notin M \quad (14)$$

which, when stacked, yields, for $U = (dp_I/dI)$,

$$U = H_{\bar{M}}.S._M U \qquad (15)$$

which, under the previous invertibility assumption, implies that $U = 0$.

With these solutions for P, Q and U, the first-order conditions (6) may be expressed more simply as

$$f_K - g_K + P'(\alpha x_{\bar{M}} + S_{\bar{M}} \cdot t) = 0 \qquad (16a)$$

$$\alpha x_M + S_M \cdot t + Q'(a x_{\bar{M}} + S_{\bar{M}} \cdot t) = 0 \qquad (16b)$$

$$\alpha = 0 \qquad (16c)$$

where the last condition is the usual one requiring the marginal excess burden of taxation to be zero when lump sum taxes are available. This condition is presented separately so that (16a) and (16b) can be analyzed independently for the case in which lump sum taxes are proscribed.

Other well known results may be derived from (16). If $\bar{M}$ is empty, (16b) is the normal Ramsey rule.[2] In this case, of course, (16a) reduces to the requirement of production efficiency, $f_K = g_K$, as first shown by Diamond and Mirrlees (1971). If $\bar{K}$ is empty, then $y'P' = 0$, since $y'H_{K\bar{M}} = 0$ by homogeneity of $f(\cdot)$. Hence, premultiplying (16a) by y' yields the result that $y'g. = y'f. = 0$; private-sector production should yield zero profits when evaluated at public shadow prices (Diamond and Mirrlees, 1976).

For the remainder of the paper, we shall be interested in expressions that can be derived from (16) for the case in which the goods $1, \ldots, n$ are dated, with the first n_1 produced in period 1 and the remaining n_2 $(= n-n_1)$ produced in period 2. In all cases, we take second-period taxes as given. This is meant to encompass the usual intertemporal distortions associated with capital income taxation that raise the issue of which discount rate is appropriate. We shall consider cases when $m=n_1$ (first-period taxes can be controlled) and m=0 (no taxes can be controlled). To examine this latter case, it will be necessary to permit lump sum taxes. For the sake of comparability, as well as simplicity, we shall do this throughout most of the paper.

The assumption of lump sum taxation allows the substitution of (16c) into (16a) and (16b) to obtain (using the definitions of P and Q and the symmetry of H and S):

$$f_K - g_K + H_{K\bar{M}}(S_{\bar{M}}.H._{\bar{M}} - I)^{-1}S_{\bar{M}}.t = 0 \qquad (17a)$$

$$S_M.t + S_M.H._{\bar{M}}(S_{\bar{M}}.H._{\bar{M}} - I)^{-1}S_{\bar{M}}.t = 0 \qquad (17b)$$

Expression (17) will form the basis for most further analysis.

In addition to allowing for different regimes of tax control, we shall also consider two possible regimes for public production decisions: $k = n$ (all production controlled) and $k = n_2$ (only second-period production controlled).

Weighted Average Discount Rates

We consider four possible regimes for K and M combined. If the sets N_1 and N_2 correspond to first and second-period production, then the regimes considered are:

1 $(K,M) = (N,N_1)$
2 $(K,M) = (N_2,N_1)$
3 $(K,M) = (N,\varnothing)$
4 $(K,M) = (N_2,\varnothing).$

Regime 1 corresponds to that in which both sets of first-period instruments (taxes and public production) may be adjusted; regime 4 represents the other extreme where only second-period public production may be controlled. Regimes 2 and 3 are intermediate, where either first-period taxes (regime 2) or first-period public production (regime 3) are controlled. In this section, we derive the basic shadow pricing rules for each regime based on the first-order conditions for public production. In a later section we will compare these results and show how they can be simplified for various special cases.

In all cases, our approach will be to derive expressions for the shadow prices of second-period public production relative to those for first-period production, in terms of private-sector prices and demand and supply elasticities. In doing so, we treat all commodities symmetrically. It would also be possible to single out a particular commodity as numeraire, and define the ratio of its shadow prices in the two periods to be 'the' social discount rate, breaking down relative prices between periods for all other commodities into first- and second-period prices relative to the numeraire commodity plus the social discount rate. While this approach is useful under certain circumstances, it would merely obscure the results when few restrictions are placed on production and there is no obvious choice for the numeraire commodity.

All production and first-period taxes controlled $(K, M) = (N, N_1)$

This is regime A. Under the assumption of lump sum taxation, the first-order conditions (from (17)) become:

$$f_{\cdot} = g_{\cdot} + H_{\cdot 2}(S_2.H_{\cdot 2} - I)^{-1}S_2.t = 0 \qquad (18a)$$

$$S_1.t + S_1.H_{\cdot 2}(S_2.H_{\cdot 2} - I)^{-1}S_2.t = 0. \qquad (18b)$$

Using only the production first-order conditions (18a), we obtain (see the appendix) the following expression for the optimal marginal product vector for public production in period 2:

$$g_2 = (S_{22} - H_{22}^{-1})^{-1}(S_{22}\Gamma g_l - H_{22}^{-1}f_2) \qquad (19)$$

where

$$\Gamma = -S_{22}^{-1}S_{21} \qquad (20)$$

Here, the second-period production vector g_2 is a matrix-weighted average of the vectors Γg_1 and f_2, with weights that sum to the identity matrix.

To interpret expression (19), note first that the matrix Γ, defined in (20), may be thought of as a generalized expression of relative consumer prices between periods 1 and 2. This follows from the envelope theorem, which implies that

$$S_{21}(f_1 + t_1) + S_{22}(f_2 + t_2) = 0.$$

Hence

$$(f_2 + t_2) = -S_{22}^{-1}S_{21}(f_1 + t_1) = \Gamma(f_1 + t_1).$$

Therefore, we may view the term Γg_1 as representing the consumer price vector in the weighted-average expression for g_2, with f_2 representing the producer price vector. This is most easily seen if we define the matrix θ implicitly by putting $f_2 = \theta g_1$. (This matrix is the producer price analogue of Γ.) Then we may rewrite (19) as

$$g_2 = (S_{22} - H_{22}^{-1})\,(S_{22}\Gamma - H_{22}^{-1}\theta)g_1 = \Sigma g_1 \qquad (21)$$

where the matrix Σ, defining the marginal rates of transformation between first- and second-period publicly produced goods, equals a matrix-weighted average, with weights summing to I, of the matrices defining private marginal rates of substitution in consumption, Γ, and production, θ. The weighting matrices S_{22} and $-H_{22}^{-1}$ correspond to generalized versions of compensated own demand and supply elasticities for second-period commodities,[3] analogous to the single-commodity results of Sandmo and Drèze (1971), who expressed the weights in terms of the relative displacements associated with government saving of first-period consumption and private investment, respectively.

Aside from the generalization to several commodities per period, this result also is different from previous results in that the relevant production discount rates in the private sector are based on a comparison of f_2 with g_1, not f_1. In general, the vectors g_1 and f_1 will differ, as it may be optimal for production *within* the first period to be distorted. Even when there is only a single commodity in the first period, there remains no additional normalization that would allow us to set the two first-period production prices equal. Thus, the producer discount rates based on a comparison of f_2 and f_1 are not directly relevant in the determination of public discount rates.

Second-period production and first-period taxes controlled
$((K,M) = (N_2, N_1))$

Under this regime, regime B, expressions (17) become

$$f_2 - g_2 + H_{22}(S_2.H._2 - I)^{-1}S_2.t = 0 \qquad (22a)$$

$$S_1.t + S_1.H._2(S_2.H._2 - I)^{-1}S_2.t = 0. \qquad (22b)$$

The first-order conditions for first-period taxes, equation (22b), are the same as in the previous case. Utilizing only the first-order condition for public production, equation (22a), we obtain (see the appendix for details of the derivation)

$$g_2 = [S_{22} - (I - S_{21}H_{12})H_{22}^{-1}]^{-1}[S_{22}\Gamma f_1 - (I - S_{21}H_{12})H_{22}^{-1}f_2]$$

(23)

where Γ is defined as before. This expression differs from (19) in two respects. First, the relevant first-period producer prices are now f_1, not g_1. This is not surprising, given that public production in the first period is not necessarily being set at optimal levels. The second difference is that the weight on producer prices now has an additional term, $S_{21}H_{12}H_{22}^{-1}$.

To interpret this expression, consider again the special case in which there is only one good per period. Here, $S_{21}H_{12}$ is the increased demand for second-period consumption associated with an increase in the price of first-period consumption resulting from an increase in second-period output. Thus, $(I - S_{21}H_{12})H_{22}^{-1}$ is the *net* increase in supply resulting when an increase in second-period prices increases second-period supply. Hence, $-(I - S_{21}H_{12})H_{22}^{-1}$ is the net second-period supply displaced when a government investment policy causes a unit decrease in the second-period price via a rise in interest rates associated with more public investment. With several commodities per period, the same intuition holds.

The new, indirect term appearing in the weighting matrix is a result of the government's assumed inability to control first-period consumer prices via optimal taxation.

All production and no taxes controlled $((K,M) = N,\varnothing))$

In this regime, regime C, only the production first-order conditions apply, and (17a) becomes

$$f_{\cdot} - g_{\cdot} + H(SH - I)^{-1}St = 0.$$

(24)

As shown in the appendix, this yields the following expression for g_2:

$$g_2 = [(S_{22} + H_{22}^{-1}H_{21}S_{12}) - H_{22}^{-1}]^{-1}$$
$$[(S_{22} + H_{22}^{-1}H_{21}S_{12})\Gamma g_1 - H_{22}^{-1}f_2].$$

(25)

As in regime A, the ability to control first-period public production means that it is the public production shadow prices for the first period, g_1, that are relevant in the determination of g_2. As in regime B, the lack of full control of first-period instruments introduces an additional term to the matrix weights, this time to the weight on the consumption price vector Γ. The extra term, $H_{22}{}^{-1}H_{21}S_{12}$, is simply the transpose of the extra term appearing in the production weight in case B, and may be interpreted as adjusting demand increases occurring when interest rates rise, for any increase in supply indirectly caused by changes in first-period prices.

The comparison of this result with that of the previous case is instructive. There, the lack of a first-period demand control introduced an indirect demand effect to the supply weight in the discount rate formula. Here, the lack of a first-period supply control introduces an indirect supply effect to the demand weight in the discount rate formula.

Second-period production and no taxes controlled $((K,M) = (N_2,\varnothing))$

Here (regime D), expression (17a) becomes

$$f_2 - g_2 + H_{22}(S_2.H._2 - I)^{-1}S_2.t = 0 \qquad (26)$$

which, as shown in the appendix, is equivalent to

$$g_2 = [(S_{22} + H_{22}{}^{-1}H_{21}S_{12} + \Delta) - H_{22}{}^{-1}]^{-1}$$
$$[(S_{22} + H_{22}{}^{-1}H_{21}S_{12} + \Delta)\Gamma f_1 - H_{22}{}^{-1}f_2] \qquad (27)$$

where

$$\Delta = H_{22}{}^{-1}[(H_{21}S_{11} + H_{22}S_{21})(H_{11}S_{11} + H_{12}S_{21} - I)^{-1}$$
$$(H_{11}S_{12} + H_{12}S_{22})]. \qquad (28)$$

The lack of ability to control any first-period instruments adds an additional term, Δ, to the weighting scheme. The fact that first-period public production is fixed means that, as in case B, it is the private first-period production prices f_1 that matter in the determination of g_2.

The term Δ is so complicated that it is difficult to provide any intuitive explanation of its economic role beyond the general statement that as the set of first-period instruments available to the government declines, the number of indirect effects that appear in the relevant definitions of private-sector demand and supply response increase, from none in case A to one involving only the cross-period supply and demand terms H_{12} and S_{21} in case B and H_{21} and S_{12} in case C, to one involving all these terms plus the first-period own supply and demand terms H_{11} and S_{11} in case D.

Simplification of the Basic Results

The examination of the four cases, A–D, shows that, even for completely general descriptions of production technology and preferences, the first-order conditions for constrained optimality in public production call for setting forward prices for second-period public production equal to a matrix-weighted average of the value placed on such production by private producers and consumers, with the weighting matrices summing to the identity matrix and corresponding to relative demand and supply displacements induced by an expansion of second-period production. For simplicity, we collect these four expressions here for regimes A–D (in order):

$$g_2 = (S_{22} - H_{22}^{-1})^{-1}(S_{22}\Gamma g_1 - H_{22}^{-1}f_2) \tag{29a}$$

$$g_2 = [S_{22} - (I - H_{21}S_{12})H_{22}^{-1}]^{-1}[S_{22}\Gamma f_1 - (I - H_{21}S_{12})H_{22}^{-1}f_2] \tag{29b}$$

$$g_2 = [(S_{22} + H_{22}^{-1}S_{21}H_{12}) - H_{22}^{-1}]^{-1}[(S_{22} + H_{22}^{-1}S_{21}H_{12})\Gamma g_1 - H_{22}^{-1}f_2] \tag{29c}$$

$$g_2 = [(S_{22} + H_{22}^{-1}S_{21}H_{12} + \Delta) - H_{22}^{-1}] \\ [(S_{22} + H_{22}^{-1}S_{21}H_{12} \\ + \Delta)\Gamma f_1 - H_{22}^{-1}f_2] \tag{29d}$$

where

$$\Gamma = -S_{22}^{-1}S_{21} \tag{30a}$$

$$\Delta = H_{22}^{-1}[(H_{21}S_{11} + H_{22}S_{21})(H_{11}S_{11} + H_{12}S_{21} - I)^{-1} \\ (H_{11}S_{12} + H_{12}S_{22})]. \tag{30b}$$

We now consider various special cases corresponding to assumptions frequently made in the literature.

One Capital Good

Capital does not appear directly in the production function, but the existence of a single, well-defined capital aggregate imposes certain restrictions nonetheless.

If a single capital aggregate, K, exists, then the private production function may be written as

$$h(K, y_2) = 0 \qquad K \equiv \phi(y_1) \tag{31}$$

where y_1 and y_2 are first-period and second-period commodity vectors. This restriction simply says that first-period production influences second-period production through a single factor, which we call capital.

By the implicit theorem, we may solve (31) for K (assuming the usual conditions are met) to obtain

$$K \equiv \phi(y_1) = \phi(y_2) \tag{32}$$

which means that the production function $f(\cdot)$ is additively separable in first- and second-period output. Hence, $H_{21} = 0$. This has the implication that, in regime A, when first-period public production is in the set of government instruments, it is optimal to set $g_1 = f_1$. This follows from expression (18a). Thus (29a) and (29b) may be written[4] as

$$g_2 = (H_{22}S_{22} - I)^{-1} (H_{22}S_{22}\Gamma f_1 - f_2) \tag{33}$$

and (29a) and (29c) may be written as

$$g_2 = (H_{22}S_{22} - I)^{-1} (H_{22}S_{22}g_1 - f_2). \tag{34}$$

The expression for regime D remains quite complicated unless S is also block-diagonal ($S_{21} = S_{12} = 0$), which would involve rather severe restrictions on preferences.

A Small Number of Second-Period Commodities $(n_1 \geqslant n_2)$

Up to this point, we have not used the first-order conditions for first-period taxes that apply in regimes A and B. They allow us to simplify the expressions for g_2.

Consider first regime A. Pre-multiplication of (18a) by S_1. and subtraction from (18b) yields the very simple expressions

$$S_1.[g. - (f. + t)] = 0 \tag{35a}$$

which can be simplified still further by the envelope theorem to

$$S_1.g. = 0. \tag{35b}$$

Expression (35b), which applies without restriction, says that public shadow prices should also satisfy the envelope condition. Using the fact[5] that $S_{11} = S_{12}S_{22}^{-1}S_{21}$, we may also write (35b) as

$$S_{12}S_{22}^{-1}S_2.g. = 0 \tag{36}$$

which, *if* the rank of S_{12}, $\rho(S_{12})$, is greater than or equal to n_2, implies that $S.g. = 0$. Combined with (35a), this would require that $Sg. = 0$, a condition met only by the consumer price vector (up to a choice of numeraire). In terms of the previous notation, $g_2 = \Gamma g_1$. All weight should be put on the relative consumer prices between first- and second-period commodities, Γ. Relative producer prices do not matter.

The requirement that $\rho(S_{12}) \geq n_2$ will normally be satisfied if and only if $n_1 \geq n_2$, in which case $\rho(S_{12}) = n_2$. Otherwise, $\rho(S_{12}) < n_2$, and the vector g may lie in a space of greater dimension. Such a restriction is less easily characterized.

A similar simplification exists even if first-period production cannot be set, in case B. To see this, note that expression (22b) may be rewritten, using the identity $S_{12}S_{22}^{-1}S_{21} = S_{11}$, the envelop theorem and the definition of Γ, as

$$S_{12}(\Gamma f_1 - f_2) = S_{12}(S_{22}^{-1}S_{21}H_{12} + H_{22})\Omega S_2.t \tag{37}$$

where

$$\Omega = (S_2.H._2 - I)^{-1}. \tag{38}$$

If $\rho(S_{12}) = n_2$, we may cancel S_{12} in (37) solve for Ω:

$$\Omega S_2.t = (S_{22}^{-1}S_{21}H_{12} + H_{22})^{-1}(\Gamma f_1 - f_2). \tag{39}$$

Substitution of (39) into (22a) yields

$$g_2 = (S_{22} + S_{21}H_{12}H_{22}^{-1})^{-1}[S_{22}\Gamma f_1 + S_{21}H_{12}H_{21}^{-1}f_2]. \tag{40}$$

Comparing (40) with (29b), we see that the effect of optimal taxation is to remove the *direct* supply effect H_{22}^{-1} from the supply weight in the solution for g_2. This is precisely what happened in case A, where the direct effect *was* the supply weight. In case B, there remains the indirect term $S_{21}H_{12}H_{22}^{-1}$. Given the results of the previous discussion, however, this term will be zero if there is a single capital good, once again leading to the use of consumer prices to value second-period output. If $H_{21} = 0$, then expression (40) becomes

$$g_2 = \Gamma f_1. \tag{41}$$

Expression (41) calls for full weight on consumption prices, Γ, in determining the marginal rate of transformation between first-period *private* production and second-period public production. As stressed above, the appropriate production margin does not involve first-period public production in this case, where such production is assumed to be fixed.

These results bear an interesting relationship to that of Diamond and Mirrlees (1976), who showed that the overall zero-shadow-profits condition applied to private output (mentioned above) implies public production efficency ($g. = f.$) if there exist sufficient public production activities to span the private output space. There, sufficient production instruments led to the use of producer prices in public production. Here, sufficient consumption instruments (taxes) lead to the use of consumer prices. Both conditions could be set simultaneously only at a Pareto-optimum. This would occur, in the current model, in the case of one output per period. Here, setting the first-period tax at the same proportional rate as the one already in place in the second period would remove both consumption and production distortions and $f_2/f_1 = (f_2 + t_2)/(f_1 + t_1)$. (Indeed, a first-best outcome could be achieved using first-period taxation regardless of the number of commodities under a uniform capital income tax.)

One First-Period Commodity ($n_1 = 1$)

Frequently, models posit the existence of only a single first-period commodity. This is a special case of case A, for not only can this commodity be considered to be the unique capital stock but, in addition, the stock is equal to the scalar y_1. Hence, not only H_{21}, but also H_{11} equals zero. It follows that Δ (as defined in (30b)) equals zero, so (29d) also collapses to (33). In this case, all four regimes call for the same weights to be used on consumer and producer prices.

Conclusions

The results in this chapter show that the weighted-average approach to public discount rates is valid in a variety of circumstances regarding the availability of government instruments. Aside from the direct demand and supply response to changes in second-period government production, S_{22} and H_{22}^{-1}, various indirect effects on demand and supply appear in the weights depending on the degree of government control. Among the chapter's other results are the following three.

(i) When public production may be controlled in the first period, the private marginal rates of transformation relevant to determination of the public discount rate are based on a comparison of second-period *private* producer prices and first-period *public* shadow prices.

(ii) Three distinct cases yield the same weights when there is a single capital good in private production. (The fourth case also calls for such weights when capital is the only good produced in the first period.) In this situation, only the direct demand and supply weights are relevant.

(iii) When first-period taxes are available, it may be optimal to use consumption prices as shadow prices.

Although these results, like previous ones in the literature, depend on the presence of lump sum taxation, they could be extended to account for the marginal excess burden of revenues that is present when lump sum taxes are not. For example, in case A, with $n_1 \geqslant n_2$, expression (35) would be replaced by

$$Sg = -\alpha S_{\cdot 1} S_{11}^{-1} x_1. \tag{42}$$

Combined with the fact that $S(f.+t) = 0$, this yields

$$Sg = S\left[\frac{(f_1 + t_1) - \alpha S_{11}^{-1} x_1}{f_2 + t_2} \right] \tag{43}$$

Letting

$$F_1 = \begin{bmatrix} f_1^1 + t_1^1 & & 0 \\ & \ddots & \\ 0 & & f_1^{n_1} + t_1^{n_1} \end{bmatrix}$$

$$\frac{x_1}{p_1} = \begin{bmatrix} -x_1^1/(f_1^1 + t_1^1) \\ \cdot \\ \cdot \\ \cdot \\ x_1^{n_1}/(f_1^n + t_1^n) \end{bmatrix}$$

expression (43) may also be written as

$$Sg. = S \begin{bmatrix} F_1[1 - \alpha S_{11}^{-1} \left(\dfrac{x_1}{p_1}\right)] \\ f_2 + t_2 \end{bmatrix} \tag{44}$$

which says that shadow prices should equal consumer prices, after first-period consumer prices have been adjusted for a term equal to the marginal dead-weight cost of revenue, α, multiplied by the inverse of the 'vector' elasticity of demand for first-period consumption, S_{11}^{-1} (x_1/p_1).

Appendix

In this appendix, we derive the various expressions for weighted-average discount rates presented within the chapter.

Cases A and B

For case B, the envelope theorem implies that (22a) may be re-written:

$$g_2 = f_2 + H_{22}(S_2.H._2 - I)^{-1}(-S_{21}f_1 - S_{22}f_2) \tag{A1}$$

which, given the fact that for two invertible matrices F and G, $F^{-1}G^{-1} = (GF)^{-1}$, is equivalent to

$$\begin{aligned} g_2 = & [S_{22} - (I - S_{21}H_{12})H_{22}^{-1}]^{-1}[-S_{21}f_1 \\ & - (I - S_{21}H_{12})H_{22}^{-1}f_2] = [S_{22} \\ & - (I - S_{21}H_{12})H_{22}^{-1}]^{-1}[S_{22}\Gamma f_1 \\ & - (I - S_{21}H_{12})H_{22}^{-1}f_2] \end{aligned} \tag{A2}$$

with the last step based on the definition $\Gamma = -S_{22}^{-1}S_{21}$. This is expression (23) in the text.

For case A, expression (18a) includes (22a) plus a condition relating g_1 and f_1, which we may solve for f_1 and substitute into (A2).

From (18a), we have

$$f_1 = g_1 - H_{12}\Omega(S_{21}t_1 + S_{22}t_2) \qquad (A3)$$
$$= g_1 - H_{12}\Omega(S_{21}f_1 + S_{22}f_2)$$

where, as before,

$$\Omega = (S_2.H._2 - I)^{-1}. \qquad (A4)$$

Collecting terms in f_1 and inverting to solve for f_1 yields

$$-S_{21}f_1 = S_{22}\Gamma f_1 = \chi S_{22}\, g_1 - \chi S_{21}H_{12}\Omega S_{22}f_2 \qquad (A5)$$

where

$$\chi = (I - S_{21}H_{12}\Omega)^{-1}. \qquad (A6)$$

Substituting (A5) into (A2), we obtain

$$g_2 = H_{22}\Omega\chi\{S_{22}\Gamma g_1 - [S_{21}H_{12}\Omega S_{22} + \chi^{-1}(I - S_{21}H_{12})H_{22}^{-1}]f_2\} \qquad (A7)$$

which, after a few steps of canceling terms, yields

$$g_2 = (S_{22} - H_{22}^{-1})\,(S_{22}\Gamma g_1 - H_{22}^{-1}f_2) \qquad (A8)$$

which is expression (19) in the text.

Cases C and D

For case C, expression (24) applies. It can be written as

$$g. = f. + (HS - I)^{-1}HSt \qquad (A9)$$

since $H(SH - I)^{-1} = (HS - I)^{-1}H$. (This is verified by pre-multiplying both sides by $(HS - I)$ and post-multiplying by $(SH - I)$.) Hence,

$$\mathbf{g}. = (\mathbf{f}. + \mathbf{t}) + (HS - I)^{-1}\mathbf{t}. \tag{A10}$$

Partitioning the matrix $(HS - I)$ in the following way:

$$(HS - I) = \begin{bmatrix} H_1.S._1 - I & H_1.S._2 \\ H_2.S._1 & H_2.S._2 - I \end{bmatrix} = \begin{bmatrix} B & C \\ D & E \end{bmatrix} \tag{A11}$$

we have, by the formula for matrix inversion (see any matrix theory text),

$$g_1 = (f_1 + t_1) + B - CE^{-1}D)^{-1} t_1 - B^{-1}C(E - DB^{-1}C)^{-1}t_2 \tag{A12a}$$

$$g_2 = (f_2 + t_2) - E^{-1}D(B - CE^{-1}D)^{-1}t_1 + (E - DB^{-1}C)^{-1}t_2. \tag{A12b}$$

For future use, note that in case D only expression (A12b) applies.

For case C, we pre-multiply (A12a) by $E^{-1}D$ and add to (A11b) to obtain

$$g_2 = E^{-1}[-Dg_1 + D(f_1 + t_1) + E(f_2 + t_2) + t_2] \tag{A13}$$
$$= E^{-1}[-Dg_1 + D(f_1 + t_1) + (E + I)(f_2 + t_2) - f_2].$$

However, by the envelope theorem, $D(f_1 + t_1) + (E + I)(f_2 + t_2) = 0$, so

$$g_2 = E^{-1}(-Dg_1 - f_2) = (H.S._2 - I)^{-1}\{H_2.S._1 g_1 - f_2\}. \tag{A14}$$

Multiplying the term in curly brackets by $H_{22}H_{22}^{-1}$ and using the definition of Γ, we obtain (25).

For case D, we collect terms in (A12b) and rewrite it as

$$\begin{aligned} g_2 = \ & [I + (E - DB^{-1}C)^{-1}](f_2 + t_2) \\ & - E^{-1}D(B - CE^{-1}D)^{-1}(f_1 + t_1) \\ & - (E - DB^{-1}C)^{-1}f_2 \\ & + E^{-1}D(B - CE^{-1}D)^{-1}f_1. \end{aligned} \tag{A15}$$

It may be shown (details available upon request) that the first two terms cancel. It may also be shown, using the properties of an inverse, that

$$E^{-1}D(B - CE^{-1}D)^{-1} = (E - DB^{-1}C)^{-1}DB^{-1}$$

so (A15) becomes

$$\mathbf{g}_2 = (E - DB^{-1}C)^{-1}\{DB^{-1}\mathbf{f}_1 - \mathbf{f}_2\}. \tag{A16}$$

It may also be shown that

$$DB^{-1} = -(E + I - DB^{-1}C)(E + I)^{-1}D$$

and that $-(E + I)^{-1}D = \Gamma$. Substituting these identities into (A16) and multiplying the term in curly brackets in (A16) by $H_{22}H_{22}^{-1}$ yields expression (27) in the text.

Notes

1 Previous authors, notably Sandmo and Drèze (1971), have assumed decreasing private returns in their analysis. With multiple inputs and outputs, lack of homogeneity would make the problem much more difficult.
2 This is also the case of $\tilde{M}$ has only one element, since a free normalization of taxes is possible in the absence of pure profits.
3 Note that the diagonal elements of H_{22} are dq_2^i/dy_2^i.
4 One cannot multiply through by $H_{22}H_{22}^{-1}$ as above since H_{22} is no longer invertible when $H_{21} = 0$.
5 This follows from the fact that the determinant of S is zero.

References

Arrow, K. J. 1966: Discounting and public investment criteria. In A. V. Kneese and S. C. Smith (eds), *Water Research*, Johns Hopkins. p. 13–32.

Auerbach, A. J. 1985: The theory of excess burden and optimal taxation. In A. J. Auerbach and M. S. Feldstein (eds), *Handbook of Public Economics*, 1, pp. 61–127.

Diamond, P. A. 1968: The opportunity cost of public investment: comment. *Quarterly Journal of Economics* 82, 682–8.

—— 1975: A many-person Ramsey rule. *Journal of Public Economics*, 4, 335–42.

—— and Mirrlees. J. A. 1971: Optimal taxation and public production I. *American Economic Review*, 61, 8–27.

—— and Mirrlees, J. A. 1976: Private constant returns to scale and public shadow prices. *Review of Economic Studies*, 43, 41–8.

Dixit, A. K. 1975: Welfare effects of tax and price changes. *Journal of Public Economics*, 4, 103–23.

Hägen, K. P. 1983: 'Optimal shadow prices and discount rates for budget-constrained firms.' *Journal of Public Economics*, 22, 27–48.

Harberger, A. C. 1972: 'The Opportunity costs of public investment financed by borrowing.' In R. Layard (ed.), *Cost-Benefit Analysis*, Penguin. pp. 303–10.

Kay, J. A. 1972: Social discount rates. *Journal of Public Economics*, 1, 359–78.

Marchand, M., Mintz, J. and Pestieau, P. 1985: Public Production and Shadow Pricing in a Model of Disequilibrium in Labor and Capital Markets. *Journal of Economic Theory*, 36, pp. 237–56.

Marchand, M. and Pestieau, P. 1984: Discount rates and shadow prices for public investment. *Journal of Public Economics*, 24, 153–69.

Sandmo, A. and Drèze, J. H. 1971: Discount rate for public investment in closed and open economies. *Economica*, 38, 395–412.

Stiglitz, J. E. and Dasgupta, P. 1971: Differential taxation, public goods and economic efficiency. *Review of Economic Studies*, 38, 151–74.

4 Taxation and the Size and Composition of the Capital Stock: an Asset Price Approach

LAWRENCE H. SUMMERS

The importance of taxation in determining the size and composition of the nation's capital stock is by now widely recognized. Taxes affect both individuals' incentives to save, and the allocation of savings among alternative forms of investment. These effects have been extensively studied within the context of general equilibrium models of the type developed by Harberger (1962), and elaborated in the work of Shoven and others.[1]

These models have been used to estimate the welfare loss that arises from tax wedges, which causes the pre-tax marginal product of capital in different sectors to diverge, and to analyse the long-run effects of tax reforms on real wages and rates of return. However, general equilibrium models are not well suited to analysing the short- and intermediate-run response of the economy to changes in tax policy. They assume that there are no costs of adjustment impeding the accumulation or reallocation of capital. As a consequence, sectoral marginal products of capital are always equated. This means that there is essentially no scope for variation in the asset price of existing capital goods. Studies of tax incidence within this framework focus on the effects of tax changes on the after-tax rate of return, because the constancy of the relative price of capital goods precludes any wealth effects.

I am grateful to Andrei Shleifer for valuable research assistance.

The implausibility of these assumptions may be seen by noting that they imply that corporate shareowners would not gain relative to homeowners from increases in the tax burdens on residential capital and reductions in the tax burdens on corporate capital. More generally, standard general equilibrium models have the counterfactual implication that all owners of capital should have the same preferences about tax policy, since all capital will be equally affected. Capitalists would have no reason to oppose systematically taxes on their own industry. This is because the standard approach to tax incidence ignores an important aspect of the actual economy's response to such a tax change. We return to the example of a reduction in corporate taxes. In the short run, the price of existing corporate capital would rise, and of existing homes would fall, as investors reallocated their portfolios. The price changes would capitalize the expected present value of the effects of the tax reform on future returns, conferring windfall gains on the owners of corporate capital, and losses on homeowners. These price changes would act as signals to the suppliers of new capital, calling forth more plant and equipment and fewer homes, until their relative prices were again equated to their relative long-run marginal costs of production.

The extreme volatility of asset prices in the American economy suggests that these 'capitalization' effects are of substantial importance. The ratio of the market value of corporate capital to its replacement cost has varied by a factor of more than two over the last 15 years. The relative price of the stock of owner-occupied housing has increased very substantially. Bulow and Summers (1984) point to evidence of substantial volatility in the prices of specific used capital goods. Even more extreme volatility has been observed in the relative price of non-reproducible assets such as land, gold, and Rembrandts. Such relative price changes represent important transfers of wealth, and must be considered if the incidence of tax changes is to be accurately assessed.

A second type of example suggests the importance of focusing on asset prices in examining tax incidence. Investment can be stimulated by reducing the corporate tax rate or by the use of incentives for new investment such as the investment tax credit or accelerated depreciation. In the long run, these two types may be designed to have very similar effects, but their incidence will differ dramatically. Because the former policy benefits old as well as new capital, it will confer a windfall gain on the owners of capital at the time at which reform is announced. On the other hand, investment incentives may actually confer a windfall loss on the holders of existing capital. This distinction cannot be captured within the standard general equilibrium model, but requires a framework in which the distinction between new and old capital is a meaningful one.

This paper develops a general equilibrium model in which costs of adjustment are incorporated, so that it is possible to examine jointly the short-run effects of tax policy on asset prices and the long-run effect on patterns of capital accumulation. The model is intended to provide a realistic guide to the likely responses of the American economy to tax reforms and so it is calibrated to econometric estimates of the relevant parameters and to data from the National Income Accounts. The model is solved using the method of multiple shooting developed by Lipton et al. (1982).

While the model is somewhat stylized in that it incorporates only three types of capital – corporate plant and equipment, owner-occupied housing and land – it is capable of examining the wealth effects of tax reforms on economic behavior. Consider, for example, the effects of compensated reductions in the corporate tax rate. This reform is normally analysed in terms of its effects on firms' invest-ment incentives, but it has another potentially large effect. Such a tax reform will raise stock market values instantaneously as investors capitalize subsequent tax savings. The resulting increase in wealth will increase consumption tending to increase required rates of return on all assets.

The advantages of the asset price approach to the evaluation of tax reforms taken here are discussed in detail in Summers (1985). The only parameters in the model that are estimated statistically pertain to tastes or technology and so can be assumed to be invariant with respect to the choice of policy rule. Thus the estimates pre-sented here are not vulnerable to the Lucas critique of econometric policy evaluation exercises. Because of its forward-looking character, the model developed here can easily be used to examine the effects of policy announcements and the differential impacts of temporary and permanent tax reforms.

The model developed in this chapter is used to examine the effects of indexing the tax system and of various types of tax reform. The effects of inflation working through the tax system have been extensively studied. Typically, researchers have closed their models by making an arbitrary assumption about the response of interest rates to inflation. The general equilibrium character of the model developed here makes it possible to derive the response of inflation to interest rates endogenously. Changes in depreciation provisions continue to be a major issue in US tax reform debates. The model presented here can be used to trace the effects of policies that benefit new but not old capital investments.

The paper is organized as follows. The next section describes a simple model illustrating the asset price approach to the analysis of investment incentives and lays out the general structure of the model used in this paper. In the following section, the corporate sector of the model is described. The markets for housing and land, along with the consumption function, are discussed in the next section after that. The section following that considers the long-run steady-state effects of changes in inflation and in tax policy. The effects of inflation and tax reforms on asset prices and on short-run economic performance are taken up in the penultimate section. A final section concludes the paper by discussing the implications of the analysis for current tax policy debates.

Asset Prices and Investment

An Illustrative Model

This section begins by presenting a very simple partial-equilibrium model in which the effects of tax policy on asset prices and investment may be analysed graphically. The model is a simplified version of the framework used in the analysis by Summers (1981c) of the tax returns and corporate investment, and the analysis by Poterba (1984) of the effect of inflation on the price of owner-occupied housing. Assume that there is one type of capital that is supplied elastically because of either internal or external adjustment costs. That is

$$\dot{K} = I(P_K) \qquad I' \geqslant 0, I(1) = 0 \qquad (1)$$

where P_K is the price of capital goods relative to consumption goods. Note that $\dot{K}$ can be negative because of depreciation. Assume further that the capital good K is used in some production process where it earns a total return $F'(K)K$ and that $F''(K)$ is negative. Finally assume that all returns are paid out and that investors require some fixed rate of return, ρ, to induce them to hold the capital assets. The returns to holding a unit of capital come in the form of rents $F'(K)$ and capital gains, so

$$\rho = F'(K)/P_K + \dot{P}_K/P_K . \qquad (2)$$

Equations (1) and (2) describe the dynamics of the adjustment of the quantity and price of capital. The phase diagram is depicted in figure 4.1. Equilibrium occurs at the intersection of the two schedules at the point where $F'(K) = \rho$. Note that the system displays saddle-point stability. Except along a unique path marked by the dark arrows, the system will not converge. Only along this path does the supply of investment exactly validate the future returns capitalized into the market price of capital goods. Such saddle-point stability is characteristic of asset price models. It implies that at any point in time, the stock of capital and assumption of saddle-point stability uniquely determine the asset price of capital.

The phase diagram in figure 4.1 can be used to examine the effects of various types of tax changes. In figure 4.2 the effect of a tax on the asset's marginal produce is considered. Such a tax does not affect its supply curve, so the $\dot{K}=0$ locus does not shift. The reduction in after-tax returns leads to a leftward shift in $\dot{P}_K = 0$ locus. Since an increase in the tax rate has no immediate effect on the capital stock, the market price of capital drops from E_1 to B. As capital is decumulated, the marginal product of capital rises and the system converges from B to E_2 where P_K again equals its equilibrium value. Note that after the first instant investors always receive a fixed return ρ as reduced rents are made up for by capital gains as equilibrium is restored. The position of the adjustment path depends on the elasticity of supply of the capital good. If the elasticity is substantial, adjustment is rapid, so the tax change has little effect on the asset price of capital. If the supply of capital is

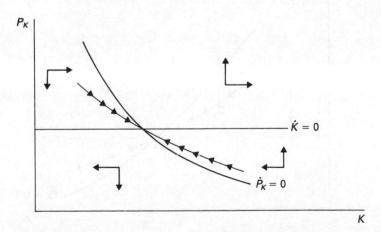

Figure 4.1 Dynamics of investment and market valuation

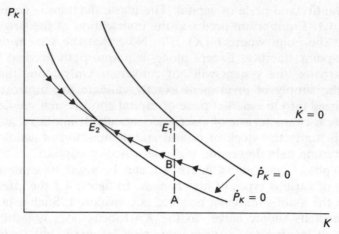

Figure 4.2　Response to a tax increase

relatively inelastic, there is a larger movement in the price of capital. In the limiting case, where the supply of capital is completely inelastic, the relative price of capital declines to point A along the $\dot{P}_K = 0$ locus.

The effect of a subsidy to new capital investment that does not apply to existing capital, such as accelerated depreciation or the investment tax credit, is depicted in figure 4.3. This shifts the $\dot{K} =$

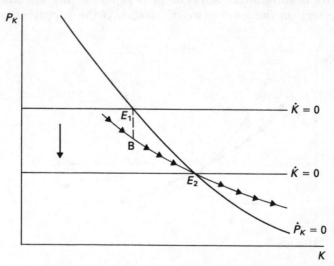

Figure 4.3　Effect of an investment subsidy

0 schedule but has no effect on the return from owing capital and so does not affect the $\dot{P}_K = 0$ locus. Such a subsidy leads to an increase in long-run capital intensity but reduces the market value of existing capital goods. This illustrates that tax measures that encourage investment may hurt existing asset holders. The magnitude of the loss will depend upon the elasticity of the supply of capital. If it is high owners of existing capital will suffer a loss close to the subsidy rate. If not, they will continue to earn rents during the period of transition so the loss will be smaller.

This result may at first seem counter-intuitive. It occurs because the subsidy reduces the price of new capital, which is a substitute for existing capital. The adverse effect of a reduction in new car prices on used-car prices illustrates the effect considered here.

Note that effects of tax policy in this model depend only on the production function and the supply curve for capital goods. These parameters are technological, and so their estimation is not dependent on the assumption of a stable policy regime. This is not the case for standard approaches based on estimated investment equations. The asset price approach can also be used to examine the effects of policy announcements, and the differential effects of permanent and temporary policies.

The General Equilibrium Model

This paper constructs a general equilibrium perfect-foresight growth model in which asset market prices and investment decisions are determined in a manner parallel to that illustrated here. There are two important advantages of this approach over standard general equilibrium models, which assume perfect capital mobility.

First, models that recognize that stocks of capital adjust slowly are likely to provide much more realistic estimates of the consequences of tax measures over the policy-relevant horizon. A second virtue of this approach is that it provides a more satisfactory approach to the analysis of tax incidence. Without introducing adjustment costs of some type it is not possible to account for the variations in the price of existing assets relative to replacement costs, which account for most of variation in the return received by asset holders.

Note also that because it provides a basis for evaluating the windfall gains and losses from tax return, the model here can be used to address questions of horizontal equity. The importance of the announcement effects of tax policies on asset values from the perspective of equity is stressed in Feldstein (1976), who stresses the desirability of reforms that do not confer windfalls. The present model provides a basis for considering policies directed at this objective.

Taking account of adjustment costs entails other sacrifices. It is not computationally feasible to solve multi-sector models with more than a very small number of capital goods. This means that the model must be much more aggregative than many of those surveyed in Shoven and Whalley (1984). As in general equilibrium models, there is no explicit treatment of uncertainty, or effort to model the effects of taxation on corporate financial policy. Considerable attention is however devoted to modelling the effects of the non-indexation of the tax system.

The modelling of each sector is treated in subsequent sections. Here the general structure of the model is described. It is assumed that physical output is homogeneous and is produced according to an aggregate production function $F(K,L) + F_T T$ where T is the economy's land endowment, and F_T are the rents generated on land. The assumption that land enters the production function in an additively separable way is maintained only for convenience and does not affect the qualitative results. Output takes two forms: the basic good X which is consumed and used as physical capital, and H, housing capital which produces housing services. The composition of output depends on the relative price P_H of housing in terms of X. The production function may thus be written as

$$G(X,IH) = F(K,L) + F_T T = Y \tag{3}$$

where IH represents the production of housing capital. Producers maximize profits by setting

$$G_{IH}/G_X = P_H. \tag{4}$$

This generates an upward-sloping supply schedule of housing capital.

There are three physical assets in the model: capital K, houses H, and land T. The last is inelastically supplied. The supply of the housing depends on its relative price as shown in (4). Investment in plant and equipment K is assumed to incur adjustment costs, so it depends on Tobin's q-ratio of the market value of capital to its replacement cost. This ratio is adjusted for the effects of taxes on the cost of acquiring new capital goods. This is described in more detail in the next section.

The simplest possible model of portfolio equilibrium is assumed. The three forms of physical capital are treated as perfect substitutes up to risk premiums, which cause their after-tax returns to differ by fixed amounts. However, the value of the rental services provided by the housing stock is assumed to be a decreasing function of the quantity of housing capital. Bonds are also treated as perfect substitutes for capital. Money does not explicitly enter the model. Implicitly, it is assumed to be demanded inelastically. Exogenous changes in the rate of inflation should be thought of as coming from movements in the rate of money growth.

The Corporate Sector

In the model all physical output is assumed to be produced in the corporate sector. As already noted, it is assumed that investment in the corporate sector involves internal adjustment costs. The determinants of corporate investment and the market valuation of the corporate sector are modelled using the approach developed by Summers (1981c).

The model is based on a q-theory of investment linking the level of investment to the q-ratio of the market value of the corporate capital stock to its replacement cost. The essential insight underlying Tobin's theory is that in a taxless world firms invest as long as each dollar spent purchasing capital raises the market value of the firm by more than one dollar. Tobin assumes that, to a good approximation, the market value of an additional unit of capital equals the average market value of the existing capital stock – that is, average q, measured as the ratio of the market value of the capital stock to its replacement cost, is a good proxy for the value of the marginal q as an additional dollar of investment. It is natural then to assume that the rate of investment is an increasing function of q.

I draw on earlier work by others, especially Hayashi (1982), to show that under certain circumstances there is an exact correspondence between average q as measured in the conventional way, and the shadow price of capital, or 'marginal q', associated with dynamic optimization of a firm's value in the presence of adjustment costs. This correspondence can be used as a basis for econometric estimation of the adjustment cost function. While the discussion is carried on within a perfect-foresight context, Poterba and Summers (1983) show that the conclusions are valid in the presence of technological uncertainty, and uncertainty about future factor prices. The calibration of the corporate sector of the general equilibrium model is then discussed.

I begin by examining how individuals value corporate stock and then turn to the decision problem facing a firm. Throughout it is assumed that firms neither issue new equity nor repurchase existing shares.[2] Hence share prices are proportional to the outstanding value of a firm's equity. The required return, ρ, is the sum of capital gains and dividends net of tax. It follows that

$$(\rho + \pi)V_t = (1 - c)\dot{V}_t + (1 - \theta)\text{Div}_t = i(1-\theta) + \delta_K \qquad (5)$$

where c is the capital gains tax rate on an accrual basis and θ is the personal tax rate on interest and dividend income, π is the rate of inflation and δ_K is the equity risk premium. All investors are assumed to have the same tax rates.[3]

The second equality is an arbitrage condition linking the return on stocks and bonds. Imposing a transversality condition ruling out eternal speculative bubbles and integrating this differential equation yields an expression for V_t:

$$V_t = \int_t^\infty \frac{(1 - \theta)}{(1 - c)} \text{Div}_s \left(\exp \int_t^s \frac{-(\rho + \pi)}{(1 - c)} \, du \right) ds. \qquad (6)$$

Each firm is assumed to produce with constant returns to scale and to be perfectly competitive in all markets, taking as given the price of its output, the wage, and the rate of return required by investors. These competitive assumptions, together with the requirement that capital is homogeneous, are essential to the derivation of the linkage between market valuation and investment incentives that is discussed below.

The typical firm seeks to choose an investment and financial policy to maximize equation (6) subject to the constraints given by its initial capital stock, by a requirement that the sources of funds equal the uses, and the requirement that the firm maintain debt equal to a fixed fraction, b, of the capital stock.[4]

A crucial feature of the model is that there is a cost to changing the capital stock. Without this cost, the size of the firm would be indeterminate because of the constant returns to scale and the assumption of perfect competition. The cost of installing additional capital rises with the rate of capital accumulation, thereby preventing jumps in the demand for capital. The cost function is taken to be convex and linearly homogeneous in investment and capital.

Under these conditions, dividends can be derived as after-tax profits minus investment expenses.[5] Thus,

$$\text{Div} = (pF(K,L) - wL - pbiK)(1 - \tau) - [1 - \text{ITC} - b$$
$$+ (1 - \tau)\phi]pI + \tau D + pbK(\pi - \delta^R), \tag{7}$$

where K and L are factor inputs, p is the overall price level, $F(K,L)$ the production function, w the wage rate, i the nominal interest rate, τ the corporate tax rate, ITC the investment tax credit, ϕ the adjustment cost function, assumed to be convex, I the investment, δ^R the rate of economic depreciation of the capital stock and D_K the value of currently allowable depreciation allowances.

The calculation of D_t assumes that the rate of depreciation used for tax purposes reflects accelerated depreciation and that tax depreciation is based on historical cost. Adjustment costs are considered expenses and ineligible for the investment tax credit. If these costs are taken to represent managerial effort, or interference with concurrent production, the assumption made here is appropriate. Treating adjustment expenses as investment under the tax law would not importantly alter the results.

Combining equations (6) and (7) and separating the terms reflecting the value of depreciation allowances on existing capital, B, and future acquisitions, Z, yields an expression for the market value of a firm's equity at time t:

$$V_t = \int_{J_t}^{\infty} \{(pF(K,L) - wL - pbKi)(1 - \tau)$$
$$- [1 - \text{ITC} - Z - b + (1 - \tau)\phi]pI + pbK(\pi - \delta^R)\}$$
$$[(1 - \theta/(1 - c)]\,\mu_s\,ds + B_t\,.$$

All the tax parameters can be arbitrary functions of time. For the purpose of exposition the following symbols are introduced:

$$\mu_s = \exp\int -\frac{(\rho + \pi)}{(1 - c)}\,du \tag{9a}$$

$$B_t = \int_t^\infty \tau_s \delta^T \mu_s \frac{(1-\theta)}{(1-c)} \, \text{KDEP}_t \, [\exp(-\delta^T)\,(s-t)] \, ds \qquad (9b)$$

$$Z_s = \int_t^\infty \tau \, \delta^T \frac{\mu_u}{\mu_s} [\exp(-\delta^T)\,(u-s)] \, du. \qquad (9c)$$

The variable B_t represents the present value of depreciation allowances on existing capital,[6] and Z_s is the present value, evaluated at time s, of the depreciation allowances on a dollar of new investment.

In maximizing equation (8), the firm can ignore B_t because it is independent of any current or future decisions. The constraint that capital accumulation equals net investment faced by the firm in maximizing (8) is

$$\dot{K}_s = I_s - \delta^R K_s. \qquad (10)$$

This dynamic optimization problem can be solved using the Pontryagin maximum principle. A shadow price, $\lambda(t)$, is introduced for the constraint given by (10). It can be interpreted as marginal q, the change in a firm's value resulting from a unit increment to the capital stock. The first-order conditions for optimality are[7]

$$F_L = w/P \qquad (11a)$$

$$1 - \text{ITC} - Z - b + \phi(1-\tau) + \frac{I}{K}\phi'(1-\tau) = \frac{\lambda(1-c)}{p(1-\theta)} \qquad (11b)$$

$$\dot{\lambda} = \lambda \left(\frac{(\rho+\pi)}{(1-c)} + \delta^R \right) \left[(pF_K - bi)\,(1-\tau) \right.$$

$$\left. - p\left(\frac{I}{K}\right)^2 (1-\tau)\phi + b\,(\pi - \delta^R) \right] \frac{(1-\theta)}{(1-c)} \qquad (11c)$$

The first-order condition, equation (11a), implies that labor is hired until its marginal product and wage are equal. Equation (11b) characterizes the investment function; it implicitly defines a function linking investment to the real shadow price of capital, λ/p, the tax parameters, and the costs of adjustment. This equation has an intuitive explanation. The right-hand side is the shadow price of additional capital goods, which is equal to their marginal cost in after-tax corporate dollars on the left-hand side.

The third first-order condition, (11c) describes the evolution of the shadow price, λ. It guarantees that the shadow price equals the present value of the future marginal products of a unit of capital. In this model, capital investment is productive in terms of output and, because of the form of the adjustment cost function, in reducing the cost of subsequent investment.

Equation (9b) is of no operational significance as a theory of investment unless an observable counterpart to the shadow price, λ/p, can be obtained. Hayashi has shown in a similar model with a less elaborate tax system how the shadow price is linked to the market valuation of existing capital.

This link can be demonstrated as follows. Note that $V_t - B_t$ given by equation (8) is homogeneous in K_t – that is, a doubling of K_t together with the optimal doubling of investment and labor in every subsequent period will double $V_t - B_t$. This is a consequence of the constant-returns-to-scale production function and the homogeneity of the adjustment cost function. It follows directly that

$$V_t^* - B_t = \gamma_t K_t \tag{12}$$

where V_t^* is the stock market's value at time t when the optimal path is followed. In other words, the maximized value of the firm at time t minus the value of depreciation allowances on existing capital is proportional to the value of its initial capital stock. The maximum principle implies that

$$dV_t^*/dK_1 = \lambda_t. \tag{13}$$

This is what is meant by the assertion that λ is the shadow price of new investment, or marginal q. Combining equations (12) and (13) demonstrates that

$$\lambda_t = (V_t^* - B_t/p_t K_t. \tag{14}$$

This expression provides an observable counterpart for the shadow price of new investment if it is assumed that the firm maximizes value so that $V_t = V_t^*$. It implies that the investment function can be written as

$$\frac{I}{K} = h\left(\frac{(V - B)(1 - c)/pK\,(1 - \theta) - 1 + b + \text{ITC} + Z}{1 - \tau}\right) = h(Q). \tag{15}$$

where Q is the tax-adjusted q and $h(\cdot) = [\phi + (I/K)\phi']^{-1}$.

The various adjustments in Q for the effects of taxes may be understood quite easily. The term $b + \text{ITC} + Z$ reflects the reduction in the effective purchase price of new capital goods caused by debt finance, the investment tax credit and the presence of depreciation allowances. Since depreciation allowances of new capital purchases are reflected in Z, it is necessary to subtract out the present value B of remaining depreciation allowances of existing capital goods. The term $(1 - c)/(1 - \theta)$ results from the assumption that marginal equity investments are financed out of retentions rather than new share issues. Firms should retain earnings until the point where the marginal dollar of retentions raises market value by only $(1 - \theta)/(1 - c)$ dollars since dividends are taxed more heavily than capital gains. Finally, the term $(1 - \tau)$ in the denominator of (13) arises from the assumption that adjustment costs are expensed, so adjustment is less expensive as the corporate tax rises. These adjustments are discussed more extensively in Summers (1981a).

It is not difficult to verify that if the adjustment cost function takes the form

$$\frac{I}{K} = \frac{\beta}{2}\left(\frac{I}{K} - \gamma\right)^2 \bigg/ \frac{I}{K}. \tag{16}$$

The relationship between investment and tax-adjusted Q will take the particularly simple form

$$I/K = h^{-1}(Q) = \alpha + (1/\beta)\,Q. \tag{17}$$

The empirical estimates of Q-investment equations in my earlier paper are used as a basis for estimating the parameters of the adjustment cost function. The estimated Q-investment relation for the period 1931–78 obtained using instrumental variables was:[8]

$$\frac{I}{K} = \frac{0.076}{(0.012)} + \frac{0.051Q}{(0.013)}. \tag{18}$$

This implies that the adjustment cost function is given by

$$A = 19.61\left(\frac{I}{K} - 0.076\right)^2 K \text{ for } \frac{I}{K} \geq 0.076$$
$$A = 0 \qquad\qquad\qquad \text{for } \frac{I}{K} \geq 0.088. \tag{19}$$

In all the analysis here firms will be operating in the range where adjustment costs are positive.

The remaining assumptions about the corporate sector are drawn from Summers (1981a). It is assumed that production of gross output is given by a Cobb–Douglas production function. The assumption is quite common in literature on investment and is consistent with the constancy of factor shares despite the changing ratio of capital to output. The share of capital in the production function is taken to be 0.25. This is quite close to the observed value in the non-financial corporate sector. Effective labor supply, which is taken to be exogenously determined, is assumed to grow at three per cent a year. Because of the focus on long-run issues, full employment is assumed. It is assumed that b, the fraction of new investment financed with debt, is 0.25. I assumed that the risk premium on equity is eight per cent. This is the difference between the after-tax required return on equity and debt. It is consistent with the average real pre-tax return of 8.7 per cent for stocks and 0.0 per cent for Treasury bills reported by Ibbotson (1984).

The tax parameters are chosen to mirror closely the current US tax system. The initial values are $\tau = 0.46$, $\theta = 0.35$, $c = 0.05$, ITC $= 0.056$ and $\delta\tau = 0.17$,[9] where $\delta\tau$ is the rate of depreciation for tax purposes on the capital stock. One additional complication is introduced in the simulations: firms are assumed to pay corporate income taxes on FIFO inventory profits. The magnitude of this tax as a fraction of output is estimated as the product of the corporate tax rate and the ratio of the inventory valuation adjustment of the non-financial corporate sector to its gross output. From this procedure one can conclude that each point of inflation raises corporate taxes by 0.17 per cent of output.

Land, Housing and Consumption

This section describes the general equilibrium structure of the model, considering the other asset markets, and then the remaining components of aggregate demand, consumption and government spending. The benchmark steady state used in the simulations of tax return effects is then presented. The risk-adjusted returns on all assets are assumed to be equal. Nominal bonds in the model are a purely inside asset. Their real after-tax return is given by $i(1 - \theta) - \pi$. All the risk premiums here refer to after-tax spreads between the return on other assets and on nominal bonds. The tax rate on interest income is taken to be equal to the dividend tax rate of 0.35.

This assumption is defended in Feldstein and Summers (1979) and Summers (1981a).

Land

In order that the model can have a steady state it is assumed that effective land grows at the same rate as the labor force. The asset land is assumed to represent all inelastically supplied assets such as exhaustible resources, antiques and gold as well as actual land. Land is assumed to yield *per capita* rents equal to FT each year. In the benchmark steady state of the model these rents represent three per cent of GNP. The risk premium on land is somewhat arbitrarily taken to equal 0.06. For simplicity it is assumed that the rental income and capital gains from land are untaxed. This gives rise to the portfolio equilibrium equation for land:

$$\rho = \frac{FT}{P_T} + \frac{\dot{P}_T}{P_T} = i(1 - \theta) - \pi + \delta_T. \tag{20}$$

This equation characterizes the evolution of the price of land. It demonstrates that in general tax measures that affect the required after-tax rate of return will affect prices of land. Note that it implies that if $di/d\pi = 1$ the steady state value of land prices will rise with inflation. This is the essential point of the analysis by Feldstein (1981c, d). This conclusion depends critically on the assumption made about the response of interest rates to inflation. The same tax effects that affect the pricing of land should also affect the pricing of bonds. If interest rates rise so that $di/d\pi = 1/(1 - \theta)$ there will be no effect of inflation on the price of land.

Housing

I begin by considering housing as a portfolio asset and then consider the production of housing capital. In the model all housing is owner-occupied. The return in owning houses comes in the form untaxed implicit rents and capital gains. Capital gains taxes on owner-occupied housing are neglected because the rollover provisions, the exemption for aged sellers, and the absence of constructive realization at death render them negligible.

The implicit rental on a unit of housing capital is assumed to be a decreasing function of the total supply of housing capital. In particular it takes the form

$$R(H) = KH^{1/}\eta \, H_0 \tag{21}$$

where η is the price elasticity of the demand for housing services. In order to induce investors to hold the existing stock of housing, it is necessary that the portfolio equilibrium condition

$$\frac{R(H)}{P_H} + \frac{\dot{P}_H}{P_H} = P(1 - \theta) - \pi + \delta_H \tag{22}$$

be satisfied, where δ_H reflects depreciation, property taxes, and any risk premium associated with home ownership. This equation holds that the rental return on housing plus the real capital gain must equal the cost of housing capital. Following the microeconometric evidence of Rosen (1979), the value of η is taken to equal -1. The value of δ_H is set at 0.06 in the simulations reported below. Individuals' consumption of housing services is treated as $P(H)H$ in calculating total consumption.

Note that in this model the deductibility of nominal interest payments is *not* the source of the tax advantage enjoyed by owner-occupied housing. Individuals can borrow to finance purchases of any asset so interest deductibility does not uniquely benefit housing. Rather, the source of the tax advantage to housing in this model is the fact that imputed rents escape taxation. This distinction is stressed in Summers (1981a).

The supply of housing is determined by profit maximization as in equation (4). Increases in its relative price P_H increase supply. Poterba (1984) estimates that price elasticity of the production of new owner-occupied housing is 2.0. This estimate is used here as a basis for calibrating the function G in equation (3). I assume this function takes the form

$$G(X,IH) = X + h_0 IH^{h_1} \tag{23}$$

where both forms of output are measured per unit of labor inputs. This implies that the supply for new housing is given by

$$IH = h_1 P_H \, 1/(h_1 - 1). \tag{24}$$

The value of h_1 is set equal to 1.5, so the supply elasticity of housing equals 2.0. The remaining constant h_0 is set so that, in the benchmark steady state, housing accounts for 40 per cent of the capital stock. This comports approximately with information in the

Federal Reserve Board's National Balance Sheets. Finally it is assumed that housing depreciates at four per cent a year. This estimate reflects the inclusion of maintenance costs.

Consumption

The remaining part of the model to be described is the determination of aggregate consumption. In Summers (1981c; 1982). I emphasize the importance of 'human wealth effects'. Increases in the rate of return may tend to increase saving because they reduce the present value of future labor earnings. These effects play an important role in the consumption function postulated here. It is assumed that consumption C is proportional to full wealth, which equals the sum of the present value of future labor incomes and the market value of existing corporate capital, housing and land. That is

$$C = C_0 \, (\text{HW} + bK + P_H H + P_T T) \tag{25}$$

where HW represents human wealth and all variables are expressed in *per capita* terms. This expression can be derived rigorously if an infinite-horizon logarithmic utility function is assumed. In general the marginal propensity to consume out of wealth will depend on the rate of return as discussed in Summers (1982). Limited sensitivity analysis suggested that allowing for these effects would not significantly alter the simulation results.

Human wealth, HW, represents the present value of future labor income after taxes. A 20.5 per cent tax rate on labor income is assumed. The discount rate is taken to include a risk premium δ_{HW} reflecting uncertainty about future labor income. Blanchard (1985) presents an elegant derivation of a consumption function of the type used here. It follows that HW evolves according to the pseudo-arbitrage equation:

$$\frac{YL}{\text{HW}} + \frac{\dot{\text{HW}}}{\text{HW}} = i(1 - \theta) - \pi + \delta_{\text{HW}}. \tag{26}$$

Human wealth like the other assets in the model will jump in response to changes in future tax policy.

The marginal propensity to consume C_0 is chosen so that the average propensity to save out of disposable income in the model's benchmark steady state is 0.05. This corresponds closely with actual economic experience.

The model is closed with an income–expenditure identity. It takes the form

$$C + IK + IH + \text{Gov} + A = F(K,L) + F_T + R(H)H. \qquad (27)$$

The level of government spending, Gov, is set equal to 25 per cent of GNP in the benchmark steady state. The term A reflects adjustment costs.

The characteristics of the model's benchmark steady state are displayed in table 4.1. The model was calibrated so that its steady state characteristics would be similar to those of the American economy, if inflation continues. An eight percent inflation rate is assumed. The shares of consumption, investment and government

Table 4.1 Characteristics of the benchmark steady state. (Note: this model is described in the text)

Composition of national income	Capital assets
$\dfrac{C}{Y} = 0.60$	$\dfrac{K}{Y} = 0.867$
$\dfrac{IK}{Y} = 0.11$	$\dfrac{KH}{Y} = 0.867$
$\dfrac{IH}{Y} = 0.04$	$\dfrac{T}{Y} = 0.434$
$\dfrac{\text{Gov}}{Y} = 0.24$	$\dfrac{(K + KH + T)}{Y} = 2.17$
$\dfrac{A}{Y} = 0.01$	$\dfrac{HW}{Y} = 12.4$

Financial markets	
$i = 0.100$	$\dfrac{\text{Div}}{V} = 0.062$
$i - \pi = 0.02$	$\dfrac{V}{K} + \beta = 1.02$
$i(1 - \theta) - \pi = -0.015$	

spending correspond almost exactly to the average actual shares in the economy over the 1970s. In the benchmark steady state, corporate capital accounts for two-fifths of total wealth, housing comprises two-fifths, and the remaining fifth is land. In the actual economy, at the end of 1979, the replacement value of the corporate capital stock was $1852.8 billion, owner-occupied housing totalled $1690 billion and non-corporate land was $890 billion. The last figure does not include the value of exhaustible resources, Rembrandts and other inelastically supplied assets. The major omission here is the $932.9 billion of non-corporate non-residential capital.

In equilibrium, the model is calibrated so that the dividend price ratio is 0.062. This earnings-price ratio is 0.098. In line with recent, but not very recent, experience, the real pre-tax interest rate is two per cent. Given the 35 per cent tax rate on interest income discussed above, this implies a real after-tax return on bonds of −1.5 per cent. The equilibrium value of Tobin's q-measure is 1.02. This is a coincidence reflecting the offsetting effects of tax parameters and the need for the market to be above its 'no-investment equilibrium' value by enough to induce replacement investment and normal growth of the capital stock.

The parameters have been chosen so that the government's budget is balanced assuming that no debt is outstanding. The tax reforms considered below will in general cause changes in government revenue. In the simulations it is assumed that the tax rate on labor income is varied to offset these revenue effects so that the government's budget constraint is always satisfied.

The model may be solved by recognizing that it contains three state variables, the stock of corporate capital K, of housing H, and the value of depreciation allowances on remaining capital B_t. The model has five forward-looking prices or co-state variables. These are V_t, the value of the stock market; V/P_H, the housing price; P_t, the relative price of land; HW, human wealth; and Z_t, the present value of depreciation allowances. The income–expenditure identity, equation (26) holds as a constraint across the five asset prices.

In formal terms, systems of this type are two-point boundary-value problems. In order to solve them uniquely, it is necessary to specify initial conditions for the state variable and terminal conditions for the asset price variables. The latter simply involve specifying transversality conditions ensuring the model's convergence. Solution of models of this type, which need to integrate both forwards and backwards, is numerically difficult. It can be accomplished using the method of multiple shooting as described by Lipton et al. (1982). The program described there is used in the calculations reported in this paper.

Steady-State Effects of Tax Reforms

This section uses the model described in the preceding sections to examine the long-run steady-state effects of various tax reforms. A discussion of transition paths and the effects of tax reforms on asset prices is provided in the next section.

Table 4.2 considers the long-run effects of changes in the rate of inflation. The results show clearly that inflation has a large negative effect on corporate capital accumulation. An increase in the rate of inflation from 8 to 12 per cent would, for example, reduce the steady-state capital stock by 9.2 per cent. The level of the stock market in the long-run steady-state is about nine per cent lower than in the presence of eight per cent inflation. The results of the calculation of the effects of zero per cent inflation and four per cent inflation suggest comparable effects of inflation on corporate capital accumulation. Since the model is structured so that inflation is neutral apart from tax effects, the zero-inflation steady state also indicates the effect of indexing the tax system.

A striking feature of the results is the insensitivity of the required rate of return on bonds, $i(i - \theta) - \pi$ with respect to the rate of inflation. This implies that to a very good approximation $di/d\pi - 1.5$. The demand for output in this model is very elastic with respect to the real interest rate, so shocks to the inflation rate are accommodated with only negligible variations in real interest rates.

Table 4.2 Steady-state tax effects of inflation. (Note: calculations are described in the text)

	$\pi = 0$	$\pi = 0.04$	$\pi = 0.12$
$i(1-\theta) - \pi$	− 0.015	− 0.015	−0.015
% ΔK	25.0	11.3	−9.2
% ΔK	27.6	11.6	−9.0
% ΔKH	−2.2	− 0.8	0.6
% ΔP_H	−1.0	− 0.4	0.3
% ΔP_T	−2.0	0.1	0.6
% ΔY	5.6	2.6	−2.2
% ΔC	3.9	1.9	−2.0

This finding suggests that contrary to the implications of the discussion of Feldstein and Summers (1978), the key determinant of the sensitivity of interest rates to inflation is the marginal tax rate on individual interest income, rather than the marginal tax rate on corporations. In terms of the analysis presented there, the long-run supply of funds to the corporate sector appears to be very elastic relative to the maximum potential interest rate (MPIR) schedule, so its movement with inflation determines the equilibrium relation between interest rates and inflation.

An important implication of this analysis is that analyses of the effects of inflation and taxes that assume $di/d\pi = 1$ are likely to be misleading. The standard argument that corporations benefit from the deductibility of nominal rather than real interest payments depends on the *ad hoc* assumption that nominal interest rates only adjust to inflation to a limited extent. The conclusion here should not be surprising. The gain corporations realize from the deductibility of nominal interest payments is largely offset by the loss their debtholders incur. Inflation subsidizes corporate investment only to the extent that $\tau > \theta$.

Increases in inflation slightly reduce the equilibrium real after-tax interest rate because of the reduced demand for investment. This raises the equilibrium price of land and housing, and raises by a small amount the steady-state level of housing consumption. In the model, these effects are very small. Indexation of the tax system reduces land prices by only about 2.0 per cent. The absence of a strong positive relation between inflation and the prices of land and housing is a consequence of the fact that $di/d\pi > 1$ which in turn results from the high elasticity of savings with respect to the real rate of return in the model. This high elasticity causes the ratio of wealth-to-labor income to decline with increases in the rate of inflation, if real after-tax interest rates decline at all. If a savings function were postulated that did not have this property, it would be necessary for the change in the market value of stocks of housing and land to equal the change in the stock market. In this greater changes in the rate of return on housing and land prices would be observed. A savings function with a lower interest elasticity could be introduced into the model by assuming that some consumers were liquidity-constrained, or by assuming a lower elasticity of substitution between present and future consumption.

The steady-state effects of various statutory tax reforms are considered in table 4.3. The second column considers an acceleration of tax depreciation roughly comparable with the American ACRS

Table 4.3 Long-run effects of alternative tax reforms

	Bench-mark	Acceleration of tax depreciation[a]	Elimination of corporate income tax	Elimination of capital gains tax	Elimination of dividend tax	Elimina-tion of interest income tax
i	0.100	0.101	0.105	0.100	0.102	0.065
$i - \pi$	0.02	0.021	0.025	0.02	0.02	−0.015
$i(1 - \theta) - \pi$	−0.015	−0.014	−0.012	−0.015	−0.013	−0.015
% ΔK	—	12.4	16.8	10.7	−1.5	4.5
% ΔV	—	5.5	86.5	3.2	51.7	4.6
% ΔKH	—	−0.9	−4.7	−0.5	−1.6	−0.4
% ΔP_H	—	−0.4	−0.24	−0.3	0.8	−0.2
% ΔP_T	—	4.0	−7.4	−0.7	−2.2	−0.5
% ΔY	—	3.1	3.2	2.0	−0.3	1.1
% ΔC	—	2.2	2.2	1.6	0	0.8

[a] The assumed acceleration of depreciation is a doubling of effective tax lives by raising the exponential rate of tax depreciation from 0.17 to 0.33.

program as enacted in 1981. The rate of tax depreciation is assumed to rise from 17 per cent a year to 33 per cent a year. This probably understates the actual acceleration of depreciation because most investment may be treated as equipment for tax purposes, and because double-declining balance depreciation is permitted.

As one would expect the results suggest that accelerating depreciation allowances would significantly increase long-run capital intensity. The predicted increase of 12.4 per cent is sufficient to raise steady-state GNP by 3.1 per cent and real wages by 2.5 per cent. The fact that the real after-tax rate of return rises by only 10 basis points in equilibrium means that a substantial fraction of the long-run benefit from accelerated depreciation falls on workers rather than the owners of capital. Because the increased demand for business investment bids up interest rates, there is again some crowding out of housing investment and land. This effect is small. The total reduction in the value of land and the housing stocks is only about one-eighth of the increase in the capital stock.

The third column considers the effects of eliminating the corporate income tax. This is predicted to have only a slightly greater impact on long-run capital intensity than the acceleration of depreciation. However its other effects are quite different. Where accelerating depreciation reduces the effective purchase price of new capital goods, elimination of corporate income taxes raises the effective purchase price because of the expensing of adjustment costs and the presence of accelerated depreciation. For this reason, the ratio of the value of the stock market to the stock or corporate capital rises a great deal when the corporate income tax is removed. This increase also reflects the fact that the elimination of the corporate tax applies to the return on old as well as new capital.

The substantial increase in wealth caused by the change in the value of the market relative to the corporate capital stock raises consumption, thus bidding up interest rates. While elimination of the corporate income tax spurs only slightly more corporate investment than acceleration of depreciation, it crowds out almost six times as much housing investment. It also reduces land prices by 7.4 per cent. The effects on market value shown here reveal that the long-run incidence of eliminating the corporate income tax is very different to that of accelerating depreciation allowances.

The fourth column of the table examines the effects of eliminating capital gains taxation. Recall that in the model only corporate capital is subject to capital gains taxation. This reform has a significant effect on capital formation despite its relatively small impact on the stock market. The reason for this involves the assumption that all equity investment is financed from retentions rather than new equity issues. Reductions in the capital gains tax raise the effective price of new capital goods, because they increase the tax penalty to paying dividends. Because this type of return has only small wealth effects, it has only a negligible impact on the prices of housing and land.

The dividend tax reduction considered in the fifth section has what may seem to be a paradoxical effect. It actually reduces the long-run capital stock by about 1.5 per cent. This result arises because of the assumption that equity investment is financed out of retained earnings. Reductions in dividend taxes raise the cost of capital by an amount just sufficient to offset the increased return to shareholders. Thus they are neutral with respect to new investment. The reduction in dividend taxes does however have a wealth effect, as it raises the equilibrium value of the stock market. This increases consumption raising demand and the interest rate, in turn reducing capital intensity. The increased interest rate slightly reduces the price of land and houses.

There is obviously an important moral for policy here. In so far as marginal investment is financed out of retentions, reductions in tax rates on high-bracket individuals are likely to confer windfalls without spurring significant amounts of new investment. This conclusion is supported by the simulation in the sixth column of the effects of eliminating the interest income tax. This encourages corporate investments slightly and discourages investment in housing and land. The result occurs because corporations deduct interest payments at the 46 per cent rate while households deduct them at a lesser rate. If interest rates adjusted to the change in θ by only enough to keep the real after-tax individual return on bonds constant, corporations would gain because of their reduced borrowing costs, and no one else would lose – so the income expenditure identity would not be satisfied. Hence the real return rises slightly but not enough to offset all the stimulus to corporate investment.

Steady-state calculations of the type reported here are only approximate guides in analysing tax policy. The next section considers the transition path of the economy following several alternative tax reforms. Particular attention is devoted to the windfall effects arising from asset revaluations following tax changes.

The Transition Path Following Tax Reforms

In table 4.4, the transition path of the economy following full indexation of the tax system is considered. The windfall effect conferred on existing shareholders from indexation is about ten per cent. Capital losses of about five per cent would be suffered by the owners of land and capital. A notable feature of the results is the large capital gain that long-term bond-owners would realize. While no long-term bonds are explicitly included in the model, a yield can be calculated by applying a term-structure relation to the sequence of short-term interest rates. The yield on a 20-year bond would fall by about 3.5 points if the tax system were indexed, implying a capital gain of over 30 per cent. Of course a similar loss is realized by the bond-issuer.

These windfall gains and losses occur because the adjustment path of the economy following this type of tax change is quite slow. The impact effect of indexing the tax system is estimated to be an 11.1 per cent increase in the rate of investment in plant and equipment and an 8.34 per cent decline in the rate of housing investment.

Table 4.4   Effects of full indexation of the tax system. (Note: all items except Δi refer to percentage changes from the benchmark steady state described in Table 4.1. Because of the round-off errors the calculations are not precise)

Year	%ΔV	%ΔP_H	%ΔP_T	%ΔK	%ΔIK	%ΔKH	%ΔIH	Δi
1	10.3	−4.85	−5.53	0	11.1	0	−8.34	−3.4
2	12.1	−4.53	−5.12	1.56	12.0	−0.334	−8.34	−3.4
3	13.8	−4.21	−4.89	2.89	12.8	−0.667	−8.34	−3.5
4	15.3	−3.90	−4.67	7.22	13.7	−1.00	−8.34	−3.5
5	16.5	−3.79	−4.45	5.56	14.5	−1.34	−8.34	−3.6
10	20.7	−2.63	−3.56	10.9	17.9	−2.23	−5.56	−3.7
15	23.1	−1.90	−2.89	14.9	19.7	−2.67	−2.78	−3.8
20	24.2	−1.48	−2.45	17.9	21.4	−2.78	−2.78	−3.9
50	27.6	−0.95	−2.00	25.6	25.6	−2.28	−2.78	−4.1

Only half of the adjustment in the corporate capital stock is completed within two years. The adjustment in the housing stock is somewhat more rapid.

An interesting feature of the results is the behavior of interest rates. Following the indexation of the tax system, the real after-tax short-term interest rate rises. This occurs because the demand for goods and services arises immediately as consumers and investors take account of reductions in future tax liabilities. In the short run, output is fixed and so real interest rates are bid up. In the longer run, capital is accumulated and the rate of interest declines until the real after-tax rate of return returns to its original level. This path of interest rates implies that there is significant short-run crowding-out following indexation, but much less in the long run.

In tables 4.5 and 4.6, the incidence of eliminating the comparable tax system and using accelerated depreciation are examined. Both have quite similar long-run effects on capital intensity in the corporate sector. However, their incidence effects are very different. The elimination of the corporate income tax causes corporate shareholders to receive a windfall excess return of 76.2 per cent when the tax reform is announced. Significant capital losses are suffered by the owners of houses and land. On the other hand, the windfall from accelerating depreciation is an increase of less than one per cent in the value of the stock market and much smaller reductions in the value of housing and land.

The differences point up the importance of taking an asset price approach to the analysis of tax incidence. Traditional approaches

Table 4.5 Effects of elimination of the corporate income tax. (Note: all items except Δi refer to percentage changes from the benchmark steady state described in Table 4.1. Because of the round-off errors the calculations are not precise)

Year	%ΔV	%ΔP_H	%ΔP_T	%ΔK	%ΔIK	%ΔKH	%ΔIH	Δi
1	76.2	−7.0	−8.67	0	7.69	0	−13.9	1.10
2	76.8	−6.65	−8.23	1.00	7.69	−0.556	−13.9	1.10
3	77.4	−6.02	−8.00	1.89	8.55	−0.100	−11.2	1.10
4	77.9	−5.59	−7.78	2.78	9.40	−1.45	−11.2	1.00
5	78.5	−5.56	−7.56	3.56	9.40	−1.89	−11.2	1.00
10	80.7	−4.44	−6.89	7.00	11.1	−3.34	−8.34	0.090
15	82.4	−3.59	−6.45	9.56	12.8	−4.12	−8.34	0.080
20	83.5	−3.27	−6.23	11.4	13.7	−4.56	−5.56	0.070
50	86.1	−2.43	−6.00	16.1	16.2	−4.78	−5.56	0.050

Table 4.6 Effects of acceleration of depreciation allowances. (Note: all items except Δi refer to percentage changes from the benchmark steady state described in table 4.1. Because of the round-off errors the calculations are not precise)

Year	%ΔV	%ΔP_H	%ΔP_T	%ΔK	%ΔIK	%ΔKH	%ΔIH	Δi
1	0.16	−2.42	−2.00	0	5.98	0	−5.56	+0.5
2	1.15	−2.21	−1.56	0.778	5.98	−0.223	−5.56	+0.4
3	1.43	−2.11	−1.56	1.55	6.84	−0.334	−2.78	+0.4
4	1.72	−1.90	−1.33	2.27	6.84	−0.556	−2.78	+0.4
5	2.01	−1.80	−1.33	2.78	7.69	−0.667	−2.78	+0.4
10	3.15	−1.16	−0.667	5.44	8.55	−1.00	−2.78	+0.3
15	3.87	−0.843	−0.445	7.44	9.40	−1.22	−2.78	+0.7
20	4.44	−0.632	−0.223	9.00	11.1	−1.22	0	+0.7
50	5.56	−0.316	−0.445	12.44	12.8	−0.889	0	+0.1

would convert an acceleration of depreciation allowances into a reduction in the effective tax rate, and then focus on differences in the steady-state rate of return to capital. They would reveal only very small differences between the effects of the two types of tax reform considered here, and miss entirely the windfall effect of reducing the corporate income tax. The source of the difference between the two policies is their differential effect on the value of used capital as explained in the preceding section. Note that the analysis here suggests that there is nothing paradoxical about the failure of the stock market to respond strongly to the recently enacted tax package. It may also help to explain the tendency for business to support statutory rate reduction as a preferred form of tax relief.

These results show that corporate tax changes have important effects on interest rates. The pattern of response is similar in both simulations. Following expansionary policy, the interest rate rises and then returns toward its equilibrium level as capital is accumulated. In the case of corporate tax elimination, the effect is very substantial as long-term bond-holders would suffer losses of over 10 per cent.

The implications of the results for tax incidence are very different in the long and short run. The short-run incidence is reflected in the windfall gains and losses discussed in the preceding section. The long-run effect of tax reforms appears to be primarily on the real wage.

A surprising feature of all the simulations is the relative unimportance of induced changes in land and housing prices, arising from inflation or changes in tax policy. The cause is the insensitivity of interest rate to tax changes. This in turn is a consequence of the form of the consumption function, which makes savings highly interest-elastic. If savings were more inelastic, taxes would have a greater impact on interest rates and larger spillover effects on other asset prices. Another way of generating larger effects on other asset prices would be to postulate lower-risk premiums. This would cause changes in interest to have larger effects on asset prices. In the absence of data on the 'dividend yield' of houses and land, it is difficult to see how to check the validity of the assumptions made here.

Conclusions

The simulations of the model may shed some light on recent economic experience. The model predicts the observed negative relationship between changes in stock market values and the rate of inflation, as well as the positive relationship between inflation and housing and land prices. These predictions, based on tax effects, first made in the 1970s, have stood up very well during the disinflation of early 1980s. Real stock prices have risen dramatically whereas real housing prices have actually declined. The composition of capital investment between residential and non-residential investment has also fluctuated as predicted by the model presented here.

In no sense can this model be interpreted as a descriptive theory of stock market prices, other asset prices or investment. It is clear that forces other than changes in the tax law account for most of the variations in these variables. Tax factors may help to explain their movements, but they are only a small part of the story. In analogy to a regression equation, their coefficients are large and significant but the R^2 is very low. The model does reveal one very striking anomaly – the behavior of interest rates in the face of rising inflation. The model yields the conclusion that inflation should raise interest rates by far more than point for point. The calculations indicate that each extra percentage point of inflation should raise nominal interest rates by close to 150 basic points. This is a prediction about the effects of long-run changes in the underlying inflation rate, caused by changes in the rate of money growth, not high-frequency movements in inflation. In Summers (1983), I show that this prediction is not borne out.

This anomaly raises important doubts about analysis of the effects of inflation and its interactions with the tax system. In what sense can this model be interpreted as demonstrating that the interaction of inflation and taxes partially explains the downturn in the stock market and the level of investment during the 1970s? The negative relationship between inflation and these variables in the model is predicated on an assumed increase in interest rates. If behavior more like the actual reality is inserted into the model, and interest rates are assumed to rise point for point with inflation, the implication would be an increase in the stock market and investment. This is the essential point of the analyses of Gordon (1982) and Hendershott (1981).

There is clearly more than one way to look at the question. I believe that a general equilibrium model of the type used here is the 'right' way to examine inflation–taxation interactions. It provides a way of examining the 'pure' effects of changes in the rate of inflation unaccompanied by other real shocks. The failure of interest rates to rise more fully with inflation presumably reflects either some form of inflation illusion or a historical correlation between rates of inflation and real shocks. In neither case would it be appropriate to ignore the forces affecting interest rates in considering the behavior of asset prices or investment. The usual procedure of estimating or postulating an inflation–interest-rate relationship and then using it as a basis for analysing tax effects involves an odd hybrid of theory and evidence. If the goal is to examine tax effects only, a general equilibrium model of the type used here is appropriate. If the objective is describing the actual behavior of the economy, it is necessary to model the full effects of whatever accounts for the absence of a stronger relationship between inflation and nominal interest rates.

The results here have implications for the analysis of statutory tax reform. Perhaps most importantly, they illustrate the importance of recognizing adjustment costs. The half-life of the adjustment of the capital stock following shocks is over a decade in the simulations reported here. Because of these substantial lags in the adjustment of the capital stock, tax reforms have important wealth effects. They confer large windfalls on the owners of different types of capital assets. For example, the simulations suggest that eliminating the corporate income tax would confer a windfall excess return of over 70 per cent on the owners of corporate stock. Measures that benefit only new capital such as the investment tax credit are likely to involve much smaller windfalls.

The finding that adjustment costs are large enough to lead to such sluggish behavior of investment may at first seem very surprising. Without such sluggishness, it is impossible to explain the observed volatility in asset prices. Regardless of the sources of the extremely volatile valuation of existing capital, there would only be small effects on stock market prices as long as new capital was very elastically supplied. The puzzle of market volatility that has followed in the wake of Shiller (1981) has an extra piece – explaining why q is not maintained at a more constant level by the elastic supply of new capital goods. An important priority for future research must be determining the nature of the adjustment costs that lead to the sluggish response of investment to tax changes.

A second major conclusion that comes from the analysis is the sensitivity of the supply of funds to the corporate sector to the rate of return. Because of the high elasticity of overall savings with respect to the rate of return, and the reallocation of investors' portfolios, changes in business taxation have only very small effects on interest rates. Eliminating the corporate income tax for example, which would raise the after-tax marginal product of corporate capital by about five per cent in the short run, is estimated to increase interest rates by 1.1 points in the short run and only 0.5 points in the long run. This finding is consistent with the empirical evidence in Feldstein and Summers (1978) suggesting that changes in tax policy have only very small effects on long-term bond rates. It implies that analyses of the effects of business tax incentives can to a first approximation omit the crowding-out effect of rising interest rates.

The model in this paper should be regarded as a preliminary empirical application of an asset price approach to investment. The model presented here can and will be refined much further along a variety of dimensions. These include increasing the number of sectors so that the capital assets in the model exhaust those in the economy. In addition, more exact calibration of the model to National Income Accounts data will be attempted. Perhaps more important, it is necessary to explore the effects of alternative consumption functions. The introduction of liquidity constraints, which would sharply reduce the importance of 'human wealth' effects, might well increase the sensitivity of interest rates to changes in tax policy.

At a somewhat greater remove, models of this type could be used to examine the welfare consequences of alternative tax policies. If we were able to assume that all assets were perfect substitutes, and had the same required rate of return, it would not be difficult to use an inter-temporal utility function to compute the effects of tax reform on lifetime utility, and then to compute compensating or equivalent variations. The difficulty comes when risk is introduced. Welfare analysis becomes impossible when *ad hoc* risk premiums enter the model. A more adequate treatment of uncertainty does not appear to be feasible at this point. Additional valuable extensions might include a more satisfactory treatment of corporate financial policy, and recognition of heterogeneity among consumers.

It would clearly also be possible to use the model developed in this paper to examine the effects of changes in the level of government spending, or the introduction of public debt. The effects of anticipated changes in monetary policy might also be considered.

The analysis here does demonstrate the importance of incorporating adjustment costs and the resulting variations in asset prices into models of the effects of taxation. It also suggests that in the presence of a tax system anything like that of the United States, inflation is likely to be far from neutral.

Notes

1 These studies include Shoven (1976), Fullerton et al. (1980), and Fullerton and Gordon (1981). For a summary of the now large literature on

general equilibrium modelling, see Shoven and Whalley (1984).

2 The formulation employed here is based on the '$q<1$' model of the effects of dividend taxation developed by Auerbach (1979). It is adopted for the sake of comparability with my earlier work. Poterba and Summers (1984) provide some evidence in favor of the alternative '$q=1$' model of the effects of dividend taxation.

3 Feldstein (1980a) considers a model in which tax rates vary among shareholders.

4 Note that if the postulated debt ratio corresponds to an optimum, the envelope theorem insures that ignoring the endogeneity of financial policy will not introduce error in estimation of the effects of small changes in tax policy.

5 The assumption here is that all marginal equity finance comes from retained earnings. This follows from the assumption of a constant number of shares made earlier. It accounts for some of the apparently paradoxical results described below. The last term reflects the net receipts from issuance of new debt (withdrawals) necessary to maintain the ratio of debt to capital as the capital stock depreciates and the price level rises.

6 KDEP$_t$ refers to the depreciable capital stock at time t. It differs from K_t because of historical cost and accelerated depreciation.

7 Similar first-order conditions with different assumptions about tax effects can be found in Hayashi (1982).

8 I use the instrumental variables estimate rather than the OLS estimate as in the simulations in my earlier paper. The equation reported here is equation (4–8) on page 92 of Summers (1981a). It implies a somewhat lower and more plausible value for adjustment costs than do the estimates in my earlier paper.

9 The basis for these estimates is discussed in Appendix B of Summers (1981a).

References

Auerbach, A. 1979: Share valuation and corporate equity policy. *Journal of Public Economics*, II, 291–305.

Blanchard, O. J. 1985: Debt, deficits and finite horizons. *Journal of Political Economy*, 92, 2, 223–47.

Bulow, J. I. and Summers, L. H. 1984: The taxation of risky assets. *Journal of Political Economy*, 92, 1, 20–39.

Federal Reserve System, Board of Governors, Flow of Funds Section, Division of Research and Statistics, 1980: Balance sheets for the U.S. economy, unpublished data mimeo, June.

Feldstein, M. 1976: On the theory of tax reform. *Journal of Public Economics*, 15, July, 77–104.

—— 1980a: Inflation and the stock market. *American Economic Review*, 70, 5, 839–47.

—— 1980b: Inflation, tax rules and the stock market. *Journal of Monetary Economics*, 14, 3, 309–17.

—— 1980c: Inflation, tax rules and the prices of land. *Journal of Public Economics*.

—— and Summers, L. H. 1978: Inflation, tax rules, and the long-term interest rate. *Brookings Papers on Economic Activity*, 1, 61–99.

—— and Summers, L. H. 1979: Inflation and the taxation of capital income in the corporate sector. *National Tax Journal*, December, 445–470.

Fullerton, D. and Gordon, R. 1983: A re-examination of tax distortions in general equilibrium models. In M. Feldstein (ed.), *Behavioral Simulation Methods in Tax Policy Analysis*, Chicago: University of Chicago Press, 369–462.

Fullerton, D., King, A. T., Shoven, J. and Whalley, J. 1981: Static and dynamic resource allocation effects of corporate and personal tax integration in the U.S.: a general equilibrium approach. *American Economic Review*.

Gordon, R. 1982: Inflation, taxation and corporate behavior. *Quarterly Journal of Economics*, 99, 2, 313–27.

Harberger, A. C. 1962: The incidence of the corporate income tax. *Journal of Political Economy*, 70, 215–40.

Hayashi, F. 1982: Tobin's marginal q and average q: a neoclassical interpretation. *Econometrica*, 50, 1, 213–24.

Hendershott, P. H. 1981: The decline in aggregate share values: inflation and taxation of the returns from equities and owner-occupied housing. *American Economic Review*, 909–22.

Ibbotson, R. G. 1984: *Stocks, Bonds, Bills and Inflation: 1984 Yearbook*. Chicago: Ibbotson Associates.

Ibbotson, R. G. and Sinquefield, R. A. 1976: Stocks, bonds, bills, and inflation: year-by-year historical returns (1926–1974). *Journal of Business*, 49, 11–47.

Lipton, D., Poterba, J., Sachs and Summers, L. H. 1982: Multiple shooting in rational expectations models. *Econometrica*, 50, 5, 1329–33.

Lucas, R. E. Jr. 1976: Econometric policy evaluation: a critique. *The Phillips Curve and Labor Markets*, Carnegie–Rochester Conference Series on Public Policy. Amsterdam: North-Holland, 1, 19–46.

Poterba, J. 1984: Inflation, income taxes and owner-occupied housing, *Quarterly Journal of Economics*, 99, 4, 729–52.

—— and Summers, L. H. 1983: Dividend taxes, corporate investment, and 'Q'. *Journal of Public Economics*, 22, 135–67.

—— and Summers, L. H. 1984: The economic effects of dividend taxation. In E. Altman and M. Subrahmanyan (eds), *Recent Advances in Corporate Finance*, Homewood, Ill.: Dow-Jones Irwin.

Rosen, H. S. 1979: Housing decisions and the U.S. income tax: an econometric analysis. *Journal of Public Economics*, February, 1–23.

Shiller, R. J. 1981: Do stock prices move too much to be justified by subsequent changes in dividends? *American Economic Review*, 71, 421–36.

Shoven, J. B. 1976: The incidence and efficiency effects of taxes on income from capital. *Journal of Political Economy*, 1261–83.

—— and Whalley, J. 1984: Applied general-equilibrium models of taxation and international trade. *Journal of Economic Literature*.

Summers, L. H. 1981a: Inflation, the stock market and owner-occupied housing. *American Economic Review*, 71, 2, 429–34.

—— 1981b: Taxation and capital accumulation in a life cycle growth model. *American Economic Review*.

—— 1981c: Taxation and corporate investment: a *Q* theory approach. *Brookings Papers on Economic Activity*, 1, 67–127.

—— 1982: Taxation, the rate of return and private savings. NBER Working Paper 995.

—— 1983: The non-adjustment of nominal interest rates: a study of the Fisher effect. In James Tobin (ed.), *Prices and Quantities*, Brookings, 201–41.

—— 1985: The asset price approach to the analysis of capital income taxation. In G. R. Feiwil (ed.), *Issues in Contemporary Macroeconomics and Distribution*, London: Macmillan.

5 The Welfare Cost of Resource Taxation

MARC S. ROBINSON

Introduction

The appropriate tax treatment of extractive resources has been extensively and heatedly debated over the last 30 years. Much of the discussion has centered on the wisdom of maintaining the many special tax provisions that affect resource industries, such as the percentage depletion allowance, expensing for intangible drilling costs, severance taxes, and the crude oil windfall profits tax.[1] The arguments are not over trivial amounts: the windfall profits tax alone was scheduled to raise \$227.7 billion in net revenues in the 1980s.[2] The magnitude of the revenues involved suggests that efficiency considerations are significant. For this reason, the welfare cost of such taxes should be analysed, especially since there are special features to resource production.

The central feature of extractive resources for the purposes of this analysis is their exhaustibility – that is, fixed (although possibly unknown) supply at a given cost of exploration and extraction. Among the implications of exhaustibility are that the value of the resource is greater than the cost of extraction – along both the competitive equilibrium and socially optimal time paths of extraction

I would like to thank Michael Boskin, Timothy Bresnahan, Ken Cone, John Shoven, Larry Summers, and various seminar participants for helpful comments on an earlier version and Neil Bruce for useful suggestions on the current version. The Institute for Energy Studies and the Center for Economic Policy Research provided financial support. None deserve any of the blame.

– and that inter-temporal choice is an essential part of the production decision.[3]

The theoretical literature on the taxation of exhaustible resources notes that the scarcity rent – the difference between the value and cost of production – can be taxed without loss in allocative efficiency.[4] Levying such a tax requires either the ability to tax directly the owners of the mineral rights, or an exact knowledge of the cost structure of the industry and the freedom to change tax rates over time. In practice, these requirements may be difficult to satisfy, at least if private ownership of the mineral is maintained.[5]

Since many countries, including the USA, have taxes that alter the inter-temporal extraction path, the effect of these taxes should be considered. Various papers address this point, but stop after determining the effect of a particular tax on the time path of production. For example, Dasgupta and Heal (1979) note that a constant-rate sales tax or a profits tax result in slower initial extraction rates than the undistorted equilibrium, while the percentage depletion allowance results in more rapid usage.[6]

The omission of any welfare cost calculation from the analysis is serious. Most other taxes cause distortions. The welfare cost for resource taxes per dollar of revenue should be compared with alternative means of raising revenue.[7] Should exhaustible resources be taxed more or less heavily than conventional commodities?

To address this question, it will be shown that the principles of applied welfare economics elucidated by Harberger (1971) can be extended to exhaustible resource taxation. Earlier efforts, such as that by Arrow and Kalt (1979), ignored the inter-temporal decisions facing producers. Despite the complexity of the producer's optimization problem, the welfare cost of a distortionary tax can be expressed in a simple form.

The welfare cost of a tax on resource production in a single period, in the absence of other distortions, is described in the following section. The welfare cost of multi-period taxes is then considered, whereupon a number of complications, such as capital taxes, are discussed.

The analysis suggests that taxes on exhaustible resources have relatively low welfare costs, even if they distort the time path of production, so long as they are permanent. We review these conclusions and discuss the possible extensions.

Welfare Costs of a Temporary Tax

In this section, the welfare cost of a one-period tax on the production of an exhaustible resource is analysed. As is usual in public finance literature, the welfare cost of a tax is the loss in utility from a tax over and above what would have occurred if the same revenue had been raised in a lump sum manner.

The principal difficulty in analysing the welfare cost of exhaustible resource taxation is that the value of the resource to consumers and society is greater than the cost of exploration and extraction at the margin. This would seem to violate one of the three basic postulates of applied welfare economics: 'the competitive supply price for a given unit measures the value of that unit to the supplier.'[8] In fact, the postulate still holds for resources, as demonstrated below.

The difference between price and cost is the scarcity rent which reflects the opportunity cost of producing the resource today, rather than in the future. This opportunity cost is a cost to society, as well as to resource owners. That is the essence of theorems that prove that the socially optimal time path of extraction is the same as that chosen in competitive equilibrium, so long as the social discount rate is the same as the private rate, property rights are secure, and uncertainty is absent.[9]

The conventional supply curve for an exhaustible resource measures, for competitive producers, the opportunity cost of the production. Applying the three basic postulates, the welfare cost of a *one-period* tax can be straightforwardly found. In the absence of any other distortions in the economy, a tax T_j^* on the exhaustible resource j in period t leads to the change in welfare

$$\Delta W = \int_{T_j=0}^{T_j^*} e^{-rt} T_j \frac{\partial X_t^j}{\partial T_j} dT_j \tag{1}$$

where r is the discount rate (assumed constant for notational convenience) and X_t^j is the quantity produced of resource j in period t.[10] That is, the welfare cost is the standard triangle.

It is true that the imposition of the tax will cause an outward shift in the supply of the resource in future periods, as producers adjust to a new equilibrium path. Under the assumption of no other distortions, the welfare change is unaffected by such responses, as with any other demand or supply shifts. What matters on the supply side is the general equilibrium response of production in period t to the imposition of the tax.

It is important to note that the welfare cost in equation (1) is *not* the difference between the value and the extraction (or even extraction plus exploration) cost of the lost production in period t. Typically, this lost production will not be lost forever. Indeed, under certain assumptions, cumulative production of the exhaustible resource woud be unaffected by the tax.

At least a portion of the lost scarcity rent will be recovered, from the perspective of both producers in period t and society. Because of the pecuniary externality created by the shifting of production, the scarcity rent of producers in other periods will generally fall. It is possible for the present value of the scarcity rent to all resource owners to fall by more than the full amount of the tax.

These results are formalized in the following theorems. It is assumed that producers are competitive and maximize the present value of profits on the resource. Costs for any unit are known, occur in the period of production and are independent of the period of production and the pattern of extraction. Demand in any period is a non-increasing, continuous function of the price in that period only, although it need not be stationary. These assumptions will be maintained in all theorems in the next two sections. The tax is levied only on the resource produced in period t.

Theorem 1.   Consider the resource produced in period t prior to the tax, X_t. Let $c_t^{\max}$ be the highest cost of production of any units in X_t. If price, $P_{t'}$, is greater than $c_t^{\max}$ for all $t' > t$ or if

$$\sum_{t'=t+1}^{\infty} X_{t'} \geq X_t$$

then all of the resource that would have been produced in period t in the absence of the tax will be produced eventually despite the tax.

Proof.   If costs are certain, producers can choose which period to produce, and extraction costs do not depend on time or the extraction pattern – the price of the resource will be rising over time whenever production occurs and the lowest-cost units will be produced first.[11] If p_t' is greater than $c_t^{\max}$ along the original production path for all $t' > t$, all of the original producers in period t could make positive profits even if demand in period t were 0, by the assumption that demand is continuous in every period and independent over time.

The tax will not cause any resource production to be shifted from periods before t to periods after t, nor will it increase cumulative resource production. Since any production originally scheduled for periods after t has costs no less than c_t^{max}, producers in period t cannot be undersold. Therefore, they will eventually produce, even if the tax stops production in period t.

A similar argument applies whenever cumulative production originally scheduled after period t is greater than production in period t. All of the period-t producers could make positive profits by postponing production, so, regardless of the tax, they will eventually produce. Q.E.D.

Theorem 1 states that producers originally scheduled to produce in period t will eventually produce, even with the tax. It is still possible that some high-cost production (originally planned for sometime *after t*) will be lost once the tax is imposed. The conditions in theorem 2 are sufficient to rule out this possibility.

Theorem 2. If $X_{t'} = 0$ for all $t' > T$, with $X_T > 0$ and T finite, and if $D(0) = p^*$ for all $t' \geq T$ along the original production path, then cumulative production will be unaffected.

Proof. These conditions would hold in equilibrium if, for example, there was a backstop technology that was a perfect substitute in elastic supply. Under these conditions, all of the resource with cost less than or equal to p^* will be produced without the tax, since it will be profitable and the producers are competitive. With the tax, all of the resource scheduled for production could be profitably produced even if production in period t were stopped. By the continuity of demand, all production with cost less than p^* will eventually be profitable to produce. Since the tax would not make any other production profitable, cumulative production would be the same with or without the tax. Q.E.D.

The following theorem shows that it is possible for the present value of the total scarcity rent to fall by more than the full amount of the tax.

Theorem 3. If extraction costs are zero, and demand is stationary with constant elasticity greater than one, then the present value of the scarcity rent will fall by more than the full amount of the tax.

Proof. Under these conditions, the competitive production path is the same as the unique production path of the monopolist.[12] Since the price set by the monopolist maximizes the present value of the scarcity rent, any change in the price path will lower the revenue collected. Yet the imposition of a tax in period t will change the production and price paths. Total receipts including taxes paid, will fall. Therefore, the present value of the scarcity rent will fall by more than the amount of the tax. Q.E.D.

The welfare cost of a single-period production tax is the difference between the value of lost production in that period and the value of the factors used in the production in their best alternative use. In the case of the exhaustible resource, that alternative use is probably production at some other time.

Welfare Cost of a Permanent Tax

If a tax is levied on resource production in more than one period, equation (1) needs to be modified even if there are no other distortions. More than one market is distorted, since resource markets at different dates are affected by the tax.

Consider a tax imposed in period t on production of an exhaustible resource with a tax already having been imposed on the resource in some other period. Again applying the three postulates, this case is equivalent to a tax on any good in the presence of pre-existing tax distortions in other markets. The notation of Harberger (1971) needs to be modified only slightly. The change in welfare is

$$\Delta W = \int_{T_t=0}^{T_t^*} e^{-rt}\, T_t \frac{\partial X_t}{\partial T_t}\, dT_t + \int_{T_t=0}^{T_t^*} \sum_{t' \neq t} e^{-rt'} \frac{\partial X_{t'}}{\partial T_t}\, dT_t \qquad (2)$$

where $T_{t'}$ is the tax imposed on the resource in period t'. As pointed out by Harberger,[13] this is equal to the standard welfare cost triangle, which reduces welfare, plus, when the $T_{t'}$ is constant, the term

$$\sum_{t' \neq t} T_{t'}\, \Delta X_{t'}$$

where $\Delta X_{t'}$ is the change in the equilibrium quantity of $X_{t'}$ caused by the tax T_t.

The general equilibrium welfare cost of a tax in period t will be larger or smaller than the welfare cost triangle according to whether $\Delta X_{t'}$ is negative or positive. Fortunately, in the case of an exhaustible resource, the sign is usually known. At least when demand at different times is independent, imposition of a tax in period t will increase production at other times and, therefore, reduce the distortion caused by the taxes in other periods. The welfare cost of imposing a tax on an exhaustible resource, when the only other distortions are taxes in other periods, will be smaller than the conventional triangle.

The following theorem formalizes this result. Once again, costs are assumed to be known, independent of time and extraction patterns, and incurred when production occurs. The quantity demanded is a non-increasing, continuous function of current price only, although it need not be stationary. Producers can choose which period to produce.

Theorem 4.   (i) The welfare cost of taxing exhaustible resource production in period t is less than or equal to the expression in equation (1); that is

$$\Delta W \geq \int_{T_t=0}^{T_t^*} e^{-rt} \, T_t \frac{\partial X_t}{\partial T_t} \, dT_t \qquad (3)$$

whenever the only other distortions in the economy are taxes on resource production in other periods.

(ii) The inequality in equation (3) is strict if the resource has a constant extraction cost and demand is strictly decreasing in all periods, and if $X_t > 0$ and $X_{t'} > 0$ for some t' that had a tax on the resource.

Proof.   The proof for part (i) requires showing that imposition of a tax in period t will not decrease production in any other period. The tax shifts demand downward in period t from the point of view of the producer and, by the assumption of independence of demand, no other demand curve is shifted. Production in period t will not increase, since the relative attractiveness of producing then has been decreased. Production will not decrease in any other period since the present value of the scarcity rent on the total stock cannot increase. A reduction in the quantity produced in any period except t would imply that producers had a more favorable opportunity in some other period. Since no demand curves have shifted up and demand in period $t' \neq t$ is unchanged, this is not possible. Since production will not decrease in any such period t', all of the $\Delta X_{t'}$ are non-negative. Therefore, the second term in equation (2) is non-negative and equation (3) follows.

If extraction costs are identical, as assumed in part (ii), and producers are competitive, the present value of the scarcity rent must be the same in all periods in which production occurs. If demand is a decreasing function of price in period t, imposition of the tax will reduce the price received by producers at the production prevailing before the tax. Production in period t will unambiguously decrease. Since demand in other periods is not perfectly elastic, the price received by at least some producers must fall. If the scarcity rent is reduced for some producers, it must be lower for all of them in equilbrium, if the extraction costs are the same. This means that price must fall in every period in which production occurs. If demand is continuous and decreasing, this can only happen if production increases in every period except t in which production previously took place. Since at least one such period had a pre-existing tax distortion by assumption, at least one of the $\Delta X_{t'}$ must be strictly positive. Since, as argued above, all of the $\Delta X_{t'}$ are non-negative, the second term of equation (2) is strictly positive. Q.E.D.

The intuition behind theorem 4 can be stated differently. There is a fundamental inelasticity associated with an exhaustible resource. While production will shift among different periods, the existence of the scarcity rent means that the elasticity of ultimate production of a particular unit is substantially less than the elasticity of its supply in any single period. A multi-period tax takes advantage of this ultimate inelasticity and captures more of the scarcity rent.

Theorem 4 has a number of policy implications. Holding the response to each individual tax constant, production taxes on an exhaustible resource in several periods have a lower welfare cost per dollar of revenue raised than similar taxes on unrelated markets. Moreover, adding additional periods of taxation increases the advantage over the same number of unrelated markets, *ceteris paribus*, since additional reductions in the distortions caused by taxes on resource production in other periods occur.

One way to think of a permanent tax on an exhaustible resource is to imagine a tax imposed on a single period t, then on some other period t', then in period t'', and so on, until a tax is imposed in every period. Each of these taxes generates a welfare cost triangle similar to the first term in equation (2). Each tax, other than the first, generates rectangles similar to the second term of equation (2). In general, the size of these triangles and rectangles will depend on the order in which the taxes are imposed in the thought experiment, although the sum of their areas – the total welfare cost of the permanent tax – will be the same.

The important point is that the total welfare cost of a permanent tax will be less than the sum of the triangles in this thought experiment. By theorem 4, all of the rectangles increase welfare.

A welfare cost calculation that was based on the supply response to one-period changes in, for example, demand would be appropriate for a single-period tax. It would overstate the welfare cost of a permanent tax. Such a calculation ignores the gains resulting from a reduction in the welfare cost caused by distortions in other periods. The elasticity of supply is greater for a one-period or temporary tax than it is for a permanent tax.

This suggests that, in the absence of any other evidence, exhaustible resources should be taxed more heavily than other commodities. Permanent taxes on exhaustible resources will tend to have a lower welfare cost per dollar of additional revenue than equivalent taxes on commodities that had the same sum of triangles in similar thought experiments. The ideal permanent tax on resource production would, of course, be a first-best tax. Tax rates in different periods could be manipulated so as to cause no change in the production path. The importance of theorem 4 is that, even if such a first-best tax is not feasible, the welfare cost of permanent resource production taxes will tend to be lower than equivalent taxes. Permanent resource production taxes have some of the characteristics of a first-best tax.

Until now, it has been assumed that there are no other distortions in the economy. In the following section, this assumption is relaxed.

The Welfare Cost of Resource Taxation when there are other distortions

Conceptually, the analysis of the welfare cost of resource taxation in the presence of other distortions is no different to what it would be if the tax were on an ordinary commodity. Imposition of a resource tax causes an adjustment in the general equilibrium, shifting supply and demand curves in other markets, including those that are distorted. Those shifts that exacerbate the distortion increase the welfare cost, while those that mitigate distortions lower the cost.[14]

A particularly important set of distortions in the economy is caused by taxes on capital. Resource markets are connected with capital markets in interesting ways. Capital and many exhaustible resources, such as oil and natural gas, are factors of production, so demand for each is connected through the production function. Secondly, capital formation and resource production inherently involve inter-temporal decisions.

The effect of a resource tax (as compared with a lump sum tax) on capital formation depends largely on whether capital and the resource are substitutes or complements. If they are substitutes, the marginal product of capital will rise (fall) in periods where resource use decreases (increases). If they are complements, the reverse is true.

Ignoring other indirect effects of the resource tax and, for the moment, inter-temporal issues, the welfare cost of the resource tax will not be much different from that calculated in previous sections when cumulative resource production is unaffected. The shifting of resource production among periods will increase the marginal product of capital in some periods and reduce it in others, with corresponding impact on savings in the preceding period. With cumulative resource production unchanged and a constant tax on capital, the rectangles of welfare gain and loss due to these shifts in saving will approximately cancel out.

If cumulative resource production is reduced, the sum of the rectangles due to the shifts in savings will probably be negative (positive) if the resource and capital are complements (substitutes). In the case they are complements, there will be more periods when saving is reduced than when it is increased, and so the distortion caused by the capital tax will probably be worse. In this case, the welfare cost calculated using equation (2) would be an under-estimate.

If the resource tax is unexpected, the adjustments to equation (2) as a result of the capital tax depend on the effect of the resource tax on the *timing*, as well as the level, of resource extraction. Timing is important since the initial capital stock cannot be adjusted in response to the changes in the marginal product of capital.

For example, constant-rate sales tax postpones production of the exhaustible resource. If the resource and capital are complements (substitutes), this will increase (decrease) the marginal product of capital in the future. Saving will tend to increase (decrease), and the distortion of the capital tax will be reduced (increased). The welfare cost calculated using equation (2) will need to be reduced (increased), even if cumulative production is unaffected.

Conclusions

The three basic postulates of applied welfare economics, when applied to the problem of exhaustible resources, yield some surprising insights. Despite the complicated inter-temporal adjustments that it induces, the welfare cost of a one-period tax on resource production can be calculated knowing only the elasticity of resource supply and demand in that period. It will be less than the difference between price and extraction cost on the lost production, since the production will not be lost forever. The same thing is true for temporary price controls. Resource producers may bear more than 100 per cent of the burden of the tax, although resource producers in a particular period will not.

A permanent tax on an exhaustible resource will have a smaller welfare loss per dollar of revenue raised than a temporary tax, since the elasticity of supply is smaller with the permanent tax in general equilibrium. Using single-period supply and demand, elasticities will tend to overestimate the welfare cost of a permanent tax.

In the presence of capital taxes, little modification needs to be made for a resource tax that is anticipated and causes no loss in cumulative production. When capital taxes must be taken into account, the sign of the derivative of the marginal product of capital with respect to the level of the resource is critically important. For an unexpected resource tax, the effect on the timing of resource production is also significant.

The most important policy implication relates to whether exhaustible resources should be taxed more or less heavily than other goods. The answer for a one-period tax depends purely on the relative magnitudes of the supply and demand elasticities for the resource and for other goods. The interaction among resource supply curves in different periods causes a permanent tax on resource production, even if it is distortionary, to have some of the characteristics of a first-best tax. This leads to a presumption that the permanent tax on resource production has a smaller welfare cost per dollar of revenue than taxes on ordinary commodities. This presumption needs to be verified with careful empirical analysis of resource supply and demand elasticities.

Before 1970, resource industries faced much lower tax rates than other industries. Since then, resources have borne an increasing tax burden, with the partial elimination of the percentage depletion allowance, the increase in severance taxes, and the imposition of the crude oil windfall profits tax.[15] The analysis in this paper indicates that this may have been a move in the right direction.

Notes

1 The US Treasury Department (1984) proposed eliminating expensing for intangible drilling costs, and percentage depletion, and rapidly phasing out the windfall profits tax as part of its tax reform proposal. After this generated an outcry, President Reagan's plan retreated in all three areas. For an earlier debate, see Harberger (1955), McDonald (1961; 1964), and Steiner (1963).

2 The windfall profits tax is scheduled to phase out over a 33-month period beginning in January 1988 or in the month after cumulative revenues reach $227.3 billion, whichever is later. In any event, the phase-out will begin no later than January 1991 (Arthur Anderson and Co., 1980).

3 Among many proofs of this, see Stiglitz (1974a, b) and Sweeney (1977).

4 See Dasgupta and Heal (1979), especially ch. 12.

5 Even if the government owns the resource it may not capture the full resource rent when there is uncertainty (see Robinson, 1984).

6 See also Sweeney (1977), Dasgupta et al. (1980), and Jacobsen (1979).

7 Stiglitz (1975) attempts a calculation of the optimal tax, on oil, in a static model with resource owners earning rents. Wright (1977) shows that Stigler made both calculation and conceptual errors. Gamponia and Mendelsohn (1985) analyse a property tax on a resource using simulation techniques, rather than theory. Boskin and Robinson (1985) consider optimal energy taxation, but focus on static issues.

8 Harberger (1971, p. 786).

9 See Sweeney (1977).

10 This is similar to equation (1.7) of Harberger (1971).

11 See Griffin and Steele (1980) and Dasgupta and Heal (1979).

12 See Stiglitz (1976) and Weinstein and Zeckhauser (1975).

13 Harberger (1971, p. 790).

14 Harberger (1971) uses an elegant expression

$$\Delta W = \int_{Z=0}^{Z^*} \sum_i D_i(Z) \frac{\partial X_i}{\partial Z} \, dZ$$

where D_i represents the excess of marginal social benefit over marginal social cost and Z is the policy variable.

15 Fullerton and Henderson (1983) and Auerbach (1983) find the effective marginal tax rate on investment in plant and equipment in energy industries to be approximately the same as in other sectors. Gravelle (1982), on the other hand, finds a much lower effective marginal tax rate on energy. The strong assumptions used make all of these studies, useful as they are, open to question.

References

Arrow, K. J. and Kalt, J. 1979: *Petroleum Price Regulation: Should We Decontrol?*. Washington: American Enterprise Institute.

Arthur Anderson and Co. 1980: *Tax News Briefs*, no. 80–2, March.

Auerbach, A. 1983: The corporate income tax. *Brookings Papers on Economic Activity*, 2, 451–505.

Boskin, M. J. and Robinson, M. S. 1985: Energy taxes and optimal tax theory. *Energy Journal*, 6, Special Tax Issue, 1–15.

Brannon, G. M. (ed.) 1975: *Studies in Energy Tax Policy*. Cambridge, Mass.: Ballinger.

Dasgupta, P. S. and Heal, G. M. 1979: *Economic Theory and Exhaustible Resources*. Welwyn, Herts.: Nisbet–Cambridge.

Dasgupta, P. S., Heal, G. M. and Stiglitz, J. E. 1980: The taxation of natural resources. *NBER Working Paper*, June.

Fullerton, D. and Henderson, V. 1983: Incentive effects of taxes on income from capital. The Urban Institute, unpublished mimeo. September.

Gamponia, V. and Mendelsohn, R. 1985: The taxation of natural resources. *Quarterly Journal of Economics*, C, 165–82.

Gravelle, J. 1982: Effects of the 1981 depreciation provisions on the taxation of income from business capital. *National Tax Journal*, 35, 1–20.

Griffin, J. M. and Steele, H. 1980: *Energy Economics and Policy*. New York: Academic Press.

Harberger, A. C. 1955: The taxation of mineral industries. In *Federal Tax Policy for Economic Growth*, US Congress, Joint Committee on the Economic Report, November, 430–49.

—— 1971: Three basic postulates of applied welfare economics. *Journal of Economic Literature*, 9, 785–97.

Jacobsen, L. 1979: Stanford University, unpublished doctoral dissertation.

McDonald, S. L. 1961: Percentage depletion and the allocation of resources: the case of oil and gas. *National Tax Journal*, 14, 323–6.

—— 1964: The non-neutrality of corporate income taxation: a reply to Professor Steiner. *National Tax Journal*, 17, 101–4.

Robinson, M. 1984: Oil lease auctions: reconciling economic theory with practice. *UCLA Working Paper* no. 292, September.

Steiner, P. O. 1963: The non-neutrality of corporate income taxation – with and without percentage depletion. *National Tax Journal*, 16, 238–51.

Stiglitz, J. 1974a: Growth with exhaustible natural resources: the competitive economy. *Review of Economic Studies*, symposium, 123–38.

—— 1974b: Growth and exhaustible natural resources: efficient and optimal growth paths. *Review of Economic Studies*, symposium, 139–52.

—— 1975: The efficiency of market prices in long run allocations in the oil industry. In Brannon, G. M. (ed.), *Studies in Energy Tax Policy*, Cambridge, Mass.: Ballinger, 55–100.

—— 1976: Monopoly and the rate of extraction of exhaustible resources. *American Economic Review*, 66, 655–61.

Sweeney, J. L. 1977: Economics of depletable resources: market forces and inter-temporal bias. *Review of Economic Studies*, 44, 125–42.

US Department of the Treasury, 1984: *Tax Reform for Fairness, Simplicity and Economic Growth*. Washington: US Government Printing Office, November.

Weinstein, M. and Zeckhauser, R. 1975: Optimal production of a depletable resource. *Quarterly Journal of Economics*, 89, 371–92.

Wright, B. D. 1977: Harvard University, unpublished doctoral dissertation.

—— 1980: The cost of tax-induced energy conservation. *Bell Journal of Economics*, 11, 84–107.

6 The Value-Added Tax: the Efficiency Cost of Achieving Progressivity by using Exemptions

CHARLES L. BALLARD AND JOHN B. SHOVEN

Introduction

In the decade following the Second World War, some of the nations of Western Europe began to adopt value-added taxes (VATs). Since then, the VAT has continued to grow in importance. More nations have adopted the tax, and the rates of tax have increased substantially in many nations. Given the increased popularity of the VAT, it is not surprising that some have advocated adopting a VAT in the United States. Even though the US Department of the Treasury decided not to call for adoption of a VAT in its recent report, some members of Congress are interested in the VAT as a means to raise revenue (see Birnbaum, 1985).

This paper examines the efficiency properties of introducing a VAT in the United States. In particular, we compute the efficiency–equity trade-off offered by a VAT, using an applied general equilibrium model of the US economy and tax system. We examine simulations in which the VAT revenues are used to scale back the personal income tax. We look at both a uniform-rate VAT

This work was supported by United States Treasury Department, Contract no. OS–84–1657, and by Stanford University's Center for Economic Policy Research. The views expressed in it, however, are those of the authors only. The authors would like to thank John Karl Scholz for his extremely able assistance.

and one that has a pattern of differentiated rates similar to those existing in Europe. The major research question we address is how much progressivity can be achieved with differentiated rates, and at what cost in terms of economic efficiency. We also report on the differences between a consumption-type and an income-type VAT.

In the next section we describe the structure of the model. We devote special attention to a linear expenditure system of demands. This is a new feature of the model, developed especially for our work on VATs. In the following section we report our simulation results. In the final section we attempt to draw conclusions from the analysis about the efficiency characteristics of alternative VAT forms and particularly about the use of differentiated rates to achieve progressivity.

Description of the Model

Arnold Harberger has exerted an immense influence on the field of economics known as computational general equilibrium analysis. Harberger did not use the same computational procedures that we use in this model, but a great number of the assumptions he uses in his 1962 and 1966 papers are incorporated here. We use the price of labor services as the numeraire in the model. We adopt Harberger's units convention, namely, that a physical unit of a good or factor is the amount that sells for one dollar in the initial equilibrium. Within any one period, we adopt Harberger's assumption on the time frame: the period is sufficiently long to allow capital to be allocated freely among sectors, but sufficiently short that the aggregate quantity of capital is fixed. In addition, our model retains the flavor of Harberger's analysis in that it uses assumptions of perfect competition throughout.

Our model is described in detail in Ballard et al. (1985a). We provide a brief description here. The model is a medium-scale computational general equilibrium model, calibrated to 1973 data for the United States. It combines a treatment of the entire US (federal, state, and local) tax system with competitive consumer and producer behavior. For each tax policy considered, such as the introduction of a VAT, equilibrium prices and quantities are determined. The counter-factual equilibrium (or path of equilibria) is compared with the no-policy-change equilibrium situation. The model can adjust other taxes endogenously so as to maintain total government revenue. The key elasticities in the model are the labor supply elasticity (which, for our standard cases, is set at 0.15) and the elasticity of saving with respect to the real interest rate (set at 0.4). The total endowment of labor grows at an exogenous rate of 2.89 per cent per year. In the base case (i.e., with no policy change), the model grows from the 1973 benchmark data in a steady-state manner.

We identify 19 producer goods industries, 16 consumer expenditure items, and 12 consumer types which are classified by income range. These are shown in table 6.1. Capital and labor services are the primary factor inputs used by industry, and these are owned by consumer groups in different proportions. These two factors are mobile between industries, and their use is dictated by the zero-profit conditions of perfectly competitive markets.

The model requires the assembly of a comprehensive and consistent microeconomic data set. Such a data set is essential for general equilibrium analysis of taxation policy. This data set provides information on factor use and factor taxes by industry, intermediate use of products, outputs of both producer and consumer goods, purchases of consumer goods by household type, incomes by source and by household type, income taxes paid, and several other items such as business investment and foreign trade. The complete 1973 data set used to calibrate the model is derived from five major sources. These include the July 1976 *Survey of Current Business*, unpublished worksheets of the US Commerce Department's National Income Division, the Commerce Department's Bureau of Economic Analysis Input/Output tables, the US Labor Department's 1973 *Consumer Expenditure Survey*, and the US Treasury Department's Merged Tax File.

In order to generate a consistent data set, a number of adjustments are made. All data on industry and government uses of factors are accepted as given, while the data on consumer factor incomes and expenditures are correspondingly adjusted. Tax receipts, transfers and government endowments are accepted as given, and government expenditures are adjusted in order to yield a balanced budget. Similar adjustments ensure that supply equals demand for all goods and factors, and that trade is balanced.

The fully consistent data set defines a single-period benchmark equilibrium in transactions terms. These observations on values are then separated into prices and quantities by making the Harberger assumption that a physical unit of a good or factor is the amount that sells for one dollar. All benchmark equilibrium prices are thus $1 and the observed values are the benchmark quantities.

Table 6.1 Classification of industries, consumer expenditures, and consumer goods in the model

Industries	Consumer expenditures
1 Agriculture, forestry, and fisheries	1 Food
2 Mining	2 Alcoholic beverages
3 Crude petroleum and gas	3 Tobacco
4 Contract construction	4 Utilities
5 Food and tobacco	5 Housing
6 Textiles, apparel, and leather products	6 Furnishings
7 Paper and printing	7 Appliances
8 Petroleum refining	8 Clothing and jewelry
9 Chemicals and rubber	9 Transportation
10 Lumber, furniture, stone, clay and glass	10 Motor vehicles, tires, and auto repair
11 Metals, machinery, miscellaneous manufacturing	11 Services
12 Transportation equipment	12 Financial services
13 Motor vehicles	13 Reading, recreation, miscellaneous
14 Transportation, communications, and utilities	14 Non-durable, non-food household items
15 Trade	15 Gasoline and other fuels
16 Finance and insurance	
17 Real estate	
18 Services	
19 Government enterprise	

Consumer groups (households classified by $thousand of 1973 gross income)

1	0–3	5	6–7	9	12–15
2	3–4	6	7–8	10	15–20
3	4–5	7	8–10	11	20–25
4	5–6	8	10–12	12	25+

The equilibrium conditions of the model are then used to determine the behavioral equation parameters consistent with the benchmark data set. This procedure calibrates the model to the benchmark data, in the sense that the benchmark data can be reproduced as an equilibrium solution to the model before any policy changes are considered. In order to implement this procedure, we specify the elasticities of substitution between capital and labor in each industry on the basis of econometric estimates in the literature. Factor employments by industry are used to derive production function weights, and expenditure data are used to derive utility function weights. This calibration procedure ensures that, given the benchmark data, the various agents' behaviors are mutually consistent before we evaluate policy changes.

Each industry produces a single producer good from a combination of capital services, labor services, and the outputs of other industries. Factor-input decisions are assumed to be made on the basis of cost minimization, and these decisions are affected by the tax system since taxes alter the relative producer prices of inputs for each industry.

The use of primary factors by each industry is described by a separate constant elasticity of substitution (CES) production function. The intermediate use of products by industries is described by a conventional fixed-coefficient input–output matrix. This matrix is derived from published 1972 input–output data for the United States which is updated to 1973. No substitution between primary factors and intermediate inputs is permitted.

A number of taxation instruments are treated as production taxes and directly affect industry costs. The corporate income tax, corporate franchise tax, and the property tax are in combination treated as *ad valorem* taxes on the use of capital services. The Social Security tax, unemployment insurance taxes, and public workmen's compensation taxes are treated as *ad valorem* taxes on the use of labor services. In making these choices on the modeling of factor taxes, we follow in the Harberger tradition.

In addition to taxes on the use of primary factors, the model includes taxes on the intermediate use of producer goods by industry and taxes on outputs of producer goods. Intermediate input taxes include the registration fees paid on motor vehicles for business use. Producer output taxes include the federal manufacturers' excise taxes paid on purchases for intermediate or final use.

The income of each consumer group in any period is determined by the ownership of labor and capital services and receipt of transfer income, such as Social Security payments, from the government. Demands for consumer goods, savings, and leisure are assumed to be generated by utility maximization subject to the household budget constraint.

In the standard version of the model (with Cobb–Douglas demands), the nested utility function is given by

$$U\left(H\left(\prod_{i=1}^{15} X_i^{\lambda_i}, L\right), C_f\right) \tag{1}$$

where H is a constant elasticity of substitution (CES) function determining the allocation of current expenditures between consumption goods X_i and leisure L, while the purchase decisions on the X_i are determined by a Cobb–Douglas sub-utility function as shown. U is another CES function, determining the allocation of income between those current expenditures and expected future consumption C_f. The demand for C_f results in a derived demand for savings.

Demands for the 19 producer goods are derived from the demands for the 16 consumer expenditure items using a transition matrix, Z. An element z_{ij} of this matrix is the amount of producer good i needed to produce one unit of consumer expenditure item j. The distinction we make between producer and consumer goods enables us to use simultaneously national accounts data on a producer good classification and the 1972–3 Consumer Expenditure Survey defined for consumer goods.

The 16th consumer expenditure item in savings, and the Z-matrix permits us to treat it like other goods. We assume that the demand for savings depends upon the current rate of return on capital, given by the current price of capital services relative to the purchase price of new capital goods. We thus assume myopic expectations in the sense that the current rental and purchase price of capital is expected to prevail in all future periods. Actual patterns of investment good purchases are the basis for constructing the column of the transition matrix that converts the consumer's demand for savings into demands for producer goods. This treatment assumes an equality between savings and investment. Savings of one period result in an equiproportional increase in the capital service endowment of households, where the conversion between net investment and capital service units uses a real net-of-tax rate of return of four per cent.

Progressive personal income taxes are incorporated by a sequence of linear tax functions, one for each consumer. With a negative intercept and a marginal tax rate applied to all income, we can replicate observed 1973 tax payments and still apply the proportional marginal rate to changes in income. State and local income taxes are modelled as percentage surcharge taxes applied to the federal levy.

Government purchases are derived from a Cobb–Douglas demand function defined over producer goods. Government real expenditures are assumed to equal tax receipts less transfers. Thus, we assume that the government budget is balanced. The foreign trade sector receives a simple treatment in order to close the model. By assuming that the net value of exports less imports for each producer

good remains constant, we can calculate the net-quantity transactions at any given vector of producer prices and transform domestic demands to market demands.

Next, we shall review the differences between the standard version
of the model (with Cobb–Douglas demands for the 15 consumer
goods) and the new version (with Stone–Geary or linear expenditure
system demands). In the Cobb–Douglas version of the model, the
demand functions are given by

$$X_i = \alpha_i I_x / P_i \qquad \text{for all } i = 1, \ldots, 15 \qquad (2)$$

where X_i is the demand for good i, α_i is the income available for
allocation among the 15 consumer goods, and P_i is the price of good
i. If we substitute the demand functions (2) into the utility function,
we get the indirect utility function:

$$V_X = \prod_{i=1}^{15} \left(\frac{\alpha_i I_x}{P_i} \right)^{\alpha_i}. \qquad (3)$$

Next, we can easily isolate and solve for I_X. The income solution
of the indirect utility function is I_X, the expenditure function:

$$I_X = V_X \prod_{i=1}^{15} \left(\frac{P_i}{\alpha_i} \right)^{\alpha_i} \qquad \sum_{i=1}^{15} \alpha_i = 1.0. \qquad (4)$$

Since the Cobb–Douglas utility function is homothetic, we have
the special property that income spent on X (I_X) equals the maximized value of X (V_X) multiplied by the ideal price index, P_X:

$$P_X = \prod_{i=1}^{15} \left(\frac{P_i}{\alpha_i} \right)^{\alpha_i}. \qquad (5)$$

This ideal price index goes directly into the next stage of the
maximization process.

Rather than using the Cobb–Douglas formulation of the standard
model, we adopt a Stone–Geary linear expenditure system (LES)
inner nest. This presents the following problem: since the
Stone–Geary utility function is not homothetic, the helpful properties discussed above do not apply. However, the Stone–Geary function *is* homothetic with respect to a 'displaced origin.' This is the

property that we exploit in using the Stone–Geary function as the inner nest.

Let us define γ_i as the ith component of the displaced origin or as the minimum required level of consumption for commodity i, and let us further define Γ as the sum of the values of the requirements:

$$\Gamma = \sum_{i=1}^{15} P_i \gamma_i. \tag{6}$$

The Stone–Geary demand functions are given by

$$X_i = \gamma_i + \beta_i (I_X - \Gamma)/P_i \tag{7}$$

where β_i is the marginal propensity to consume commodity i out of discretionary income.

The Stone–Geary utility function is

$$U_X = \prod_{i=1}^{15} (X_i - \gamma_i)^{\beta_i} \qquad \sum_{i=1}^{15} \beta_i = 1.0 \,. \tag{8}$$

We substitute the demand functions into the utility function (8) to get the indirect utility function:

$$V_X = \prod_{i=1}^{14} \left[\beta_i \left(\frac{I_X - \Gamma}{P_i} \right) \right]^{\beta_i} \tag{9}$$

or

$$V_X = (I_X - \Gamma) \prod_{i=1}^{15} \left(\frac{\beta_i}{P_i} \right)^{\beta_i}. \tag{9'}$$

Now we can solve for I:

$$V_X = A I_X - A \Gamma \tag{10}$$

where

$$A = \prod_{i=1}^{15} \left(\frac{\beta_i}{P_i} \right)^{\beta_i}. \tag{11}$$

Solving (10) for I_X, gives us

$$I_X = V_X/A + \Gamma. \tag{12}$$

Equation (12) is crucial to our problem. Clearly the maximized value of utility, V_X, cannot be multiplied by any ideal price index to get I_X. In fact, the ideal price index for the Stone–Geary function is quite messy. However, *if* we ignore Γ, we have a homothetic relationship between discretionary income, I_{XD}, and the indirect utility from consumption in excess of the requirements

$$I_{XD} = I_X - \Gamma = V_X \prod_{i=1}^{15} \left(\frac{P_i}{\beta_i}\right)^{\beta_i}. \tag{13}$$

Equation (13) has *exactly* the same form as equation (4) for the ordinary Cobb–Douglas function (except that presumably the αs and βs differ).

This suggests that we can use the ideal price index for the Cobb–Douglas form (equation (5)), appropriately modified to include the Stone–Geary weights. The ideal price index (for *discretionary* consumption) is

$$P_{XD} = \prod_{i=1}^{15} \left(\frac{P_i}{\beta_i}\right)^{\beta_i}. \tag{14}$$

We use P_{XD} as the price for the composite of discretionary consumption in the next, higher stage of the maximization process. This maximization procedure will give us, ultimately, a full set of prices, quantities and utilities, just as in the standard version of the model. To do welfare evaluation, we will have a stream of discretionary H from the base case and revised case, and a set of Γ from the base case and revised case. Our welfare measure would consist of two parts. The first would compare discretionary H in the base with discretionary H in the revised case. The second would compare the Γs.

Simulation Results

The first type of VAT that we model is an ideal-consumption VAT, where the tax base is the value of current-period production less investment. All expenditures/goods (other than leisure) are taxed at a uniform rate. We also model an ideal income-type VAT. Under an income-type VAT, firms are only allowed to deduct the value of depreciation in the current production period. Thus, the tax base equals the sum of consumption plus net investment. In each case, we consider destination-based taxes. This has no effect on the results (see Goulder et al. (1983) for a discussion of the equivalence between origin-based and destination-based taxes).

Against these two idealized VATs we model a more politically realistic 'mean European VAT.' The primary distinguishing characteristics of the European VATs are the consumption base, the destination basis, and differentiated rate structure. Thus, we model a destination-based, consumption-type VAT with rates ranging from 0 to 15 per cent. The rate structure is given in table 6.2. With this structure, we can determine the magnitude of the distortions in consumption decisions, caused by a differentiated rate structure. We can also determine which groups win and which lose from such a structure.

We perform a set of simulations in which we reduce the personal income tax by the size necessary to offset a 5, 10, and 15 per cent consumption- and income-type VAT. We do the same with the differentiated VAT (which raises the same amount of revenue as a 6.52 per cent flat consumption-type VAT). We report on the long-

Table 6.2   Rates of value-added tax for the 'mean European VAT'

Commodity group	Percentage rate
Food	5
Alcoholic beverages	15
Tobacco	15
Utilities	5
Housing	0
Furnishings	15
Appliances	15
Clothing and jewelry	15
Transportation	5
Motor vehicles, tires, and auto repair	15
Services	0
Financial services	0
Reading, recreation and miscellaneous	10
Non-durable, non-food household items	10
Gasoline and other fuels	15

run, steady-state effects. These simulations are very sensitive to the manner in which the income tax is scaled. We perform simulations reducing the income tax using additive replacement and multiplicative replacement. Additive replacement refers to additive changes to marginal income tax rates. That is, the same number of percentage points are added to all household marginal income tax rates. Lower-income households have a larger percentage tax change than wealthy households under additive replacement. Under multiplicative replacement, revenues are recovered by multiplying the marginal tax rates of all households by the same scalar.

In most of the tables in this section, we show the change in economic efficiency as measured by the sum over our 12 consumer classes of the present value of a stream of Hicksian equivalent variations. The figures show the welfare gain as a percentage of the present discounted value of consumption plus leisure in the base sequence of equilibria. The discounted value of future welfare is approximately $49 trillion. This is definitionally equal to the value of the total wealth (physical capital and human capital) of the economy.

We have calculated the welfare gain for a flat 5, 10, and 15 per cent VAT. Table 6.3 reports the results for a revenue-neutral, destination-based, consumption-type VAT, where revenue neutrality is achieved by scaling back the personal income tax in either an additive or multiplicative manner. For a given revenue requirement, a multiplicative adjustment changes the marginal tax rates of

Table 6.3 Efficiency gains from the substitution of a destination-based consumption-type flat VAT for some of the personal income tax revenue (equal yield), for a model with Stone–Geary commodity demands. (Note: figures are percentages of the total present value of welfare. Numbers in parentheses are in billions of 1973 dollars)

	Type of income tax scaling	
VAT rate (%)	Additive	Multiplicative
5	0.383%	0.596%
	($190.3)	($296.2)
10	0.719%	1.105%
	($357.4)	($549.2)
15	1.016%	1.544%
	($505.1)	($767.4)

high-rate households more than an additive adjustment. Thus, when tax increases are necessary for equal yield, additive replacement is more efficient. However, in these VAT simulations, where tax reductions are necessary for equal yield, multiplicative replacement is more efficient.

Several observations can be made regarding the numbers in table 6.3. First, they appear to be rather large, indicating that a switch to raising part of federal revenues from a flat consumption-type VAT could increase welfare considerably. The gain for a 10 per cent VAT with a multiplicative reduction of marginal tax rates is more than one per cent of the discounted value of future welfare or roughly $550 billion. It should be emphasized that this is a pure welfare gain, with the government spending the same amount of resources. It is somewhat larger than the gain we found for integrating the corporate and personal income tax systems and indexing capital gains for inflation. It also is about three-quarters of the gain that could be achieved by a total elimination of the personal income tax and a switch to a progressive consumption tax. Both of these benchmark results were reported on in Fullerton et al. (1983). Table 6.3 shows that the incremental gains from further increases in the rate of VAT are diminishing. The numbers also indicate that an additive adjustment for revenue neutrality is much less efficient than a multiplicative adjustment. The reason for this is that those whose labor supply decisions and inter-temporal consumption choices are most distorted by the income tax are the high-income, high-tax-rate households. The multiplicative adjustment reduces their tax rate more, and thus results in a larger efficiency gain.

In table 6.4, we show the distribution of the welfare effects among the various income classes, for two of the policy changes that were highlighted in table 6.3. It is clear that the aggregate welfare gains of table 6.3 are not shared equally by all groups. In fact, there is a fairly strong trade-off between equality and efficiency. Both with additive and multiplicative replacement, the gains from the consumption-type VAT are concentrated among the highest-income classes. The lowest-income classes are worse off under the new policy, and sometimes substantially worse off. The losses to the low-income groups are greatest under multiplicative replacement. This is because multiplicative replacement leads to much smaller decreases in their marginal income tax rates than does additive replacement.

Table 6.5 contains the overall welfare effects for a flat-rate income-type VAT. The gains are much smaller than the gains from

Table 6.4 Welfare effects of destination-based consumption-type VATs by consumer group

| | LES inner nest | |
Household income (in 1973 $)	10% flat VAT Additive replacement (%)	10% flat VAT Multiplicative replacement (%)
0–3	−0.618	−3.748
3–4	−0.319	−2.903
4–5	−0.116	−2.250
5–6	−0.014	−1.887
6–7	0.051	1.659
7–8	0.178	−1.203
8–10	0.318	−0.658
10–12	0.468	−0.047
12–15	0.540	0.275
15–20	0.779	1.248
20–25	0.947	1.957
25+	1.678	5.272

a consumption-type VAT; in fact, with additive replacement the gains barely exceed zero. This result is the consequence of two offsetting effects. The present income tax system is somewhat more efficient than a pure income tax (see Fullerton et al., 1983). This reflects the fact that the present income tax system (both in the real

Table 6.5 Efficiency gain for the substitution of a destination-based income-type flat VAT for some of the personal income tax revenue (equal yield). (Note: figures are percentages of the total present value of welfare. Numbers in parentheses are in billions of 1973 dollars)

| | LES inner nest | |
| | Type of income tax scaling | |
VAT rate (%)	Additive	Multiplicative
5	0.061% ($30.2)	0.281% ($139.7)
10	0.098% ($48.9)	0.503% ($250.1)
15	0.119% ($58.9)	0.680% ($338.1)

world and in the model) is somewhere between a consumption tax and an income tax, due to the ability to shelter certain forms of saving from the tax system. Roughly half of saving in 1973 utilized sheltered vehicles, primarily pension accumulation, the addition to life insurance reserves, and the acquisition of new residential housing. Switching towards an income-type VAT increases the inter-sectoral efficiency of the economy, but sacrifices some of the relative inter-temporal efficiency of the partial consumption tax nature of the present income tax. Depending on whether the personal tax adjustment takes the additive or multiplicative form, the efficiency consequences of the introduction of a revenue-neutral income-type VAT are either a very small or a modest efficiency gain. We interpret the results of tables 7.3 and 7.5 as indicating that a consumption-type VAT is the more desirable even though it involves the practical difficulty of distinguishing between consumption and investment goods.

Corresponding to the efficiency difference between a consumption- and income-type VAT is a very different allocation of resources. Perhaps the most important difference is that first-period saving is up 11.3 per cent with the 10 per cent consumption-type VAT with additive replacement, but down 2.5 per cent with the introduction of an income-type VAT.

In table 6.6, we show the distribution of the welfare effects among the various income classes, for the 10 per cent income-type VATs. The general pattern that we saw in table 6.4 is repeated here. The adoption of a VAT is a regressive change, regardless of whether multiplicative or additive replacement is used. The degree of regressivity is much greater under multiplicative replacement.

Table 6.7 compares the efficiency consequences of a VAT with the differentiated rates of table 6.2 (which are similar to the rate structures found in Europe) with that of a flat rate VAT of 6.52 per cent. Both taxes are of the consumption type and raise the same amount of first-period revenue. Table 6.7 suggests that rate differentiation reduces the efficiency gain offered by a consumption-type VAT by a significant amount. With either additive or multiplicative adjustments to preserve revenue neutrality, the efficiency gain is reduced by about $100 billion by the differentiation of the rates. This figure, like all the dollar figures in these tables, is in 1973 dollars. The welfare sacrifice caused by rate differentiation is eight per cent of 1973s GNP, and about 0.2 per cent of the present value of future welfare (including leisure).

The comparison of flat versus differentiated rates is continued in table 6.8, which displays the welfare change for each of our 12

Table 6.6 Welfare effects of destination-based income-type flat VATs by consumer group

| | LES inner nest | |
| | 10% flat VAT | 10% flat VAT |
Household income (in 1973 $)	Additive replacement (%)	Multiplicative replacement (%)
0–3	−1.279	−4.599
3–4	−1.040	−3.768
4–5	−0.825	−3.069
5–6	−0.711	−2.676
6–7	−0.622	−2.413
7–8	−0.486	−1.928
8–10	−0.324	−1.337
10–12	−0.154	−0.682
12–15	−0.035	−0.300
15–20	0.213	0.718
20–25	0.372	1.443
25+	1.009	4.744

consumer categories. Two things are immediately apparent. First, while a revenue-neutral substitution of a VAT for the personal income tax may be efficiency-improving, in three of the four cases it involves a regressive impact on the distribution of welfare (or income). Notice that the additive adjustment to the personal income tax concentrates more of the tax cut on the lower-income households and thus reduces the regressive nature of the VAT substitution

Table 6.7 Destination-based consumption-type VAT: efficiency gains for differentiated rates versus equal-yield flat-rate VAT. (Note: figures are percentages of the total present value of welfare. Numbers in parentheses are in billions of 1973 dollars)

| | LES inner nest | |
| | Type of income tax scaling | |
Type of VAT	Additive	Multiplicative
Differentiated rates	0.286% ($142.2)	0.558% ($277.2)
Flat rate (6.52%)	0.490% ($243.4)	0.759% ($377.3)

considerably. Table 6.8 also shows that rate differentiation does improve somewhat the welfare situation of the lower-income groups, but this improvement is achieved at the expense of the middle-income groups. Seven of our twelve income groups are worse off in an absolute sense with rate differentiation than without it. In some cases, the difference is considerable. For example, the present value of welfare is 0.39 per cent higher for those with 1973 incomes between $12,000 and $15,000 with a 6.52 per cent flat-rate VAT than it would be with the differentiated rates shown in table 6.2.

The results of table 6.8 lead us to three conclusions. First, rate differentiation is not a very efficient way in which to redistribute resources among households. The wealthy consume more of every commodity, although the consumption proportions do fall as income increases. It appears that adjustments to the personal income tax or even changes in the much-maligned means-tested transfer programs are more efficient ways of affecting the distribution of income or welfare. To some extent, this is simply another example of the principle that it is more efficient to use instruments that are more closely associated with the policy target. Affecting the income distribution by adjusting income-related transfers or taxes more directly

Table 6.8 Welfare effects of destination-based consumption-type VATs by consumer income class. (Note: the figures are percentages of the total present value of welfare)

Household income (in 1973 $)	Differentiated VAT Additive replacement (%)	Flat VAT Additive replacement (%)	Differentiated VAT Multiplicative replacement (%)	Flat VAT Multiplicative replacement (%)
0–3	0.009	−0.408	−2.007	−2.485
3–4	−0.016	−0.208	−1.745	−1.928
4–5	0.081	−0.072	−1.350	−1.496
5–6	0.083	−0.003	−1.174	−1.253
6–7	−0.052	0.041	−1.201	−1.101
7–8	−0.081	0.126	−1.010	−0.797
8–10	−0.028	0.219	−0.683	−0.431
10–12	−0.070	0.320	−0.414	−0.021
12–15	−0.020	0.368	−0.195	0.194
15–20	0.119	0.529	0.443	0.850
20–25	0.306	0.642	0.997	1.328
25	1.226	1.136	3.682	3.576

affects the income distribution than differentially taxing commodities whose consumption proportions are only weakly correlated with income.

Second, even though rate differentiation does reduce the regressive effects of the VAT somewhat, the VATs are generally regressive. Rate differentiation is not a sufficiently powerful tool to make an inherently regressive tax policy change into a progressive one. Third, the method of preserving revenue yield can be very important. If we compare the first and second columns of table 6.8, and then compare the first and third columns, it is clear that the choice between additive and multiplicative replacement is actually more important than the choice between a flat-rate structure and a differentiated one.

The major new model development associated with this paper is the incorporation of the linear expenditure system or Stone–Geary inner nest in the consumer utility functions. This closes off a portion of each consumer's income and reduces the overall degree of responsiveness of consumption choice, relative to the Cobb–Douglas formulation that has been used in earlier versions of this model. For purposes of comparison, we also include some results for the Cobb–Douglas formulation. In tables 6.9 and 6.10, we report on the aggregate welfare effects for a flat consumption-type VAT and a flat income-type VAT. Thus, these tables are comparable with tables 6.3 and 6.5. Once again, we see that a consumption-type

Table 6.9 Efficiency gain for the substitution of a destination-based consumption-type flat VAT for some of the personal income tax revenue (equal yield). (Note: figures are percentages of the total present value of welfare. Numbers in parentheses are in billions of 1973 dollars)

| | Cobb–Douglas inner nest | |
| | Type of income tax scaling | |
VAT rate (%)	Additive	Multiplicative
5	0.388%	0.605%
	($192.8)	($300.4)
10	0.729%	1.120%
	($362.2)	($556.3)
15	1.030%	1.562%
	($511.9)	($776.2)

Table 6.10 Efficiency gain for the substitution of a destination-based income-type flat VAT for some of the personal income tax revenue (equal yield). (Note: figures are percentages of the total present value of welfare. Numbers in parentheses are in billions of 1973 dollars)

| | Cobb–Douglas inner nest | |
| | Type of income tax scaling | |
VAT rate (%)	Additive	Multiplicative
5	0.075%	0.298%
	($37.2)	($148.0)
10	0.124%	0.531%
	($61.9)	($263.8)
15	0.154%	0.714%
	($76.8)	($354.7)

VAT is more efficient in the aggregate than an income-type VAT. Also, the earlier result on the greater efficiency of multiplicative scaling is confirmed in tables 6.9 and 6.10. In table 6.11, we report the aggregate welfare effects of the differentiated and flat consumption-type VATs. Thus, table 6.11 is comparable with table 6.7. The results in the Stone–Geary and Cobb–Douglas cases are qualitatively similar, but the efficiency disadvantage of rate differentiation is noticeably greater in the Cobb–Douglas case. This is not

Table 6.11 Destination-based consumption-type VAT: efficiency gains for differentiated rates versus an equal-yield flat-rate VAT. (Note: figures are percentages of the total present value of welfare. Numbers in parentheses are in billions of 1973 dollars)

| | Cobb–Douglas inner nest | |
| | Type of income tax scaling | |
Type of VAT	Additive	Multiplicative
Differentiated rates	0.011%	0.267%
	($5.4)	($132.6)
Flat rate (6.242%)	0.477%	0.740%
	($236.9)	($367.7)

surprising, since the Cobb–Douglas formulation is more elastic than the Stone-Geary one. Finally, in table 6.12, we present the distribution of welfare effects among the various income classes, for the differentiated and flat VATs. Table 6.12 is to be compared with table 6.8. The basic stories that emerge from table 6.8 and table 6.12 are fairly similar. If anything, our conclusions about the equity/efficiency trade-off and the inefficiency of rate differentiation are supported more strongly in the Cobb–Douglas case. Whereas the four poorest groups were better off under a differentiated VAT than with a flat VAT with the Stone–Geary model, now it is only the bottom two income groups that are better off under a differentiated VAT. Notice that in all cases we have the result that the VAT is regressive, even with differentiated rates and additive scaling.

Table 6.12 Welfare effects of destination-based consumption-type VATs by consumer group. (Note: the figures are percentages of the total present value of welfare)

Households classified by $thousand of 1973 gross income	Cobb–Douglas inner nest			
	Differentiated VAT Additive replacement (%)	Flat VAT Additive replacement (%)	Differentiated VAT Multiplicative replacement (%)	Flat VAT Multiplicative replacement (%)
0–3	−0.132	−0.405	−2.076	−2.422
3–4	−0.186	−0.208	−1.806	−1.896
4–5	−0.118	−0.073	−1.460	−1.472
5–6	−0.136	−0.006	−1.317	−1.239
6–7	−0.282	0.037	−1.358	−1.089
7–8	−0.324	0.121	−1.191	−0.788
8–10	−0.280	0.214	−0.891	−0.428
10–12	−0.336	0.313	−0.656	−0.025
12–15	−0.291	0.360	−0.452	0.188
15–20	−0.165	0.516	0.138	0.831
20–25	0.008	0.624	0.653	1.296
25 +	0.894	1.106	3.198	3.500

Conclusion

The message of this research to date is clear. The efficiency advantages of a VAT compared with other tax sources strongly favor a consumption basis for the tax. Also, achieving progressivity through rate differentiation is expensive in terms of efficiency. An important question raised by this research is the political feasibility of a flat VAT. Most of Europe has failed to maintain a flat rate, although Denmark, Norway, and Sweden have done relatively well in that regard. Both Australia and New Zealand are currently proposing the introduction of flat consumption-type VATs and are under some considerable political pressure to exempt certain items. Furthermore, no one has come up with a satisfactory way in which to tax financial services.

Finally, it may be appropriate to mention some other important issues that we have not discussed. To the extent that the VAT is used to replace a portion of the income tax, special problems of inter-generational equity arise. The imposition of a VAT would place an extra burden on the elderly, who must pay taxes on consumption that has already been taxed by the income and payroll tax. Similar problems exist for housing. If previously built houses are exempt from tax while new construction is subject to VAT, owners of existing houses receive windfall gains upon the imposition of the VAT. These problems of inter-generational equity are important under any change in the relative degree of taxation of consumption and saving, including the adoption of a consumption tax or a wage tax. For further discussion of these inter-generational issues, see Auerbach et al. (1983).

Another important issue is the treatment of the non-profit sector. The non-profit sector in the United States is much larger than in Europe. The tax treatment of this sector under a VAT is not clear. How should non-profit and for-profit hospitals be treated? If they are made exempt, how should other educational and training activities, such as secretarial and technical schools, be treated?

Determining the taxable income of financial institutions is complex. Services at such institutions are provided at little or no cost. In return, depositors and shareholders permit their funds to be used. To some degree the investment income is merely held by financial institutions acting as fiduciaries for depositors and shareholders. These types of complexities account for the exemption of financial institutions in the European VATs.

Despite these problems, the Europeans have successfully implemented VATs often with fewer problems than had originally been anticipated. Our research suggests that if the VAT is considered for the United States, efficiency will be substantially enhanced by implementing a consumption-type VAT with as flat a rate structure as possible.

References

Aaron, Henry J. (ed.) 1981: *The Value-Added Tax: Lessons from Europe.* Washington, DC: The Brookings Institution.

Auerbach, Alan J., Kotlikoff, Laurence J. and Skinner, Jonathan, 1983: The efficiency gains from dynamic tax reform. *International Economic Review*, 24, 81–100.

Ballard, Charles L., Fullerton, Don, Shoven, John B. and Whalley, John, 1985a: *A General Equilibrium Model for Tax Policy Evaluation.* Chicago: University of Chicago.

Ballard, Charles L., Shoven, John B. and Whalley, John, 1985b: General equilibrium computations of the marginal welfare costs of taxes in the United States. *The American Economic Review*, 75, 128–38.

Birnbaum, Jeffrey, 1985: Senate finance panel members begin talking about consumption tax to raise new revenue. *Wall Street Journal*, 26 June.

Cnossen, Sijbren, 1982: What rate structure for a value-added tax? *National Tax Journal*, 35, 205–14.

Dresch, Stephen P., An-loh Lin and Stout, David K. 1977: *Substituting a Value-Added Tax for the Corporate Income Tax: First Round Analysis*, Cambridge, Mass.: NBER–Ballenger.

Fullerton, Don, Shoven, John B. and Whalley, John, 1983: Replacing the U.S. income tax with a progressive consumption tax: a sequenced general equilibrium approach. *Journal of Public Economics*, 20, 3–23.

Goulder, Lawrence H., Shoven, John B. and Whalley, John. 1983: Domestic tax policy and the foreign sector: the importance of alternative foreign sector formulations to results from a general equilibrium tax analysis model. In M. Feldstein (ed.), *Behavioral Simulation Methods in Tax Policy Analysis.* Chicago: NBER–University of Chicago, 333–67.

Harberger, Arnold C. 1962: The incidence of the corporation income tax. *Journal of Political Economy*, 70, 215–40.

—— 1966: Efficiency effects of taxes on income from capital. In M. Kryzanick (ed.), *Effects of Corporation Income Tax*, Detroit: Wayne State University, 107–17.

Scott, Claudia and Davis, Howard, 1985: *The Gist of GST: A Briefing on the Goods and Services Tax.* Wellington, New Zealand: Victoria University Press for the Institute of Policy Studies.

7   The Wage–Productivity Hypothesis: its Economic Consequences and Policy Implications

JOSEPH E. STIGLITZ

It is a pleasure to contribute a paper to a volume honoring Al Harberger. Harberger's and my interests have overlapped in a number of areas, including the analysis of the effects of the corporation tax and the development of better (should I say 'correct') procedures for cost–benefit analysis, and the application of these procedures to less-developed countries (LDCs). Although not necessarily formal students of Harberger, all of us who have toiled in these fields are, in a sense, his students. I have had not only the benefit of learning from his written work, but also the further pleasure of endless hours spent discussing these issues with him.

I have chosen for this occasion to focus on some problems in cost–benefit analysis, in particular, the determination of the shadow wage in LDCs that arise when a worker's productivity depends on his wage. I explore both the causes of this wage–productivity nexus, and its consequences for a variety of policy issues, in addition to the determination of shadow wages.

Financial support from the National Science Foundation and the Hoover Institution is gratefully acknowledged. An earlier version of this paper was presented at the 1982 meetings of the American Economic Association, New York, 28–30 December. The author is indebted to Debra Ray for helpful comments. I have also greatly benefited from discussions with Raaj Sah. Our joint work (Sah and Stiglitz, 1985) generalizes and extends many of the results reported here.

Harberger has made important and lasting contributions in developing systematic procedures for the evaluation of projects in LDCs. His work is marked by the conviction that economists could make a contribution to LDCs, by ensuring that their scarce resources were wisely allocated. However, unlike some economists, who almost blindly took models designed for more developed economies and tried to apply them to LDCs, Harberger has shown a sensitivity to the special features of LDCs. This is evident, for instance, in his justly celebrated paper, 'On Measuring the Social Opportunity Cost of Labor'. (Harberger, 1971).

In that paper, Harberger noted that the number of unemployed individuals may be an endogenous variable; as a result, as the government hires one more worker, it may displace more than one worker from the rural sector: it is possible that the social opportunity cost of hiring one worker in the urban sector may exceed the rural wage.[1] This paper represents a further development of that basic idea.

However, while in Harberger's earlier work the urban wage was taken as given, here we treat the urban wage as endogenous. We seek to explain the determinants of the urban wage; this enables us to ascertain the effects of alternative government policies (such as wage subsidies or an increase in government employment) on the wage rate, and thus indirectly on the level of unemployment. Our results serve to strengthen Harberger's basic insights: the opportunity cost of labor will in general exceed the rural wage.[2]

This work was motivated by three well documented regularities in LDCs.

(i) The persistence of urban unemployment.

(ii) The persistence of wage differentials between the urban and rural sector, and of wage differentials across industries within the urban sector.

(iii) The persistence of differences in unemployment rates among different groups in the population (with changes in aggregate demand having markedly different effects on different groups).

Several explanations of the first phenomena have begun with the *assumption* of wage differentials. (See, for instance, the work of Todaro (1968, 1969) and Harris and Todaro (1970).) They (as well as Harberger in his 1971 paper) argue that in the presence of these wage differentials, workers will migrate to the point where the expected income in the urban sector (taking into account the expected length of unemployment) is equal to the wage in the rural sector.[3]

The actual intra- and inter-sector wage differentials are (in these papers) ascribed to institutional considerations. Institutional considerations are undoubtedly of importance; they may be particularly important in describing how (or more particularly, how fast) an economic system adapts to changes in the environment. However, leaving the matter at that provides an incomplete theory and an inadequate basis for policy prescriptions. One must explain why the economic forces, which normally work to eradicate wage differences, are, in these instances, inoperative. One must explain why, whatever those forces are that lead to wage differentials, they did not lead to still larger wage differentials.

Moreover, although institutions may adapt slowly, they do adapt. Thus, it would be unwise simply to assume that wage differentials would remain unchanged in the face of some government policy changes. Some economists have argued that if the government cannot lower urban wages, it should increase the prices urban workers have to pay, thus indirectly lowering their real wages. There is, in this, more naivete on the part of the economists than on the part of the urban workers: they are likely to respond to these increases in prices by a demand for an increase in their wages.

We argue that different policies have different consequences for equilibrium wages and unemployment. Policy conclusions derived from models that simply take the urban wage as exogenously given may, accordingly, be seriously misleading.

The theory of wage determination that we present here is able both to explain the persistence of wage differentials (both across types of individuals and types of jobs) and differentials in the unemployment rates across groups in the population. It is based on the hypothesis that the wage a firm pays has an important effect on the productivity of its labor force.

This simple observation, which we refer to as the wage–productivity hypothesis, has profound implications for the nature of market equilibrium and for the consequences of alternative government policies. It implies, in particular, that firms may not be wage takers – that they set their wage taking into account the effect that the wage has on the productivity of their labor force. There may be competitive equilibria in which demand does not equal supply: wages may not be cut, even in the face of an excess supply of labor; for to do so might lower the productivity of the labor force more than proportionately to the reduction in the wage, and hence lead to higher labor costs. The law of supply and demand is repealed! It also implies that, since the wage–productivity relationship may differ for different jobs, equilibrium may be characterized by (*ex ante*) identical workers receiving different wages. Even with identical firms, equilibrium may be characterized by a wage distribution with the higher wages paid by some firms being exactly offset by the higher productivity. If the wage–productivity curves characterizing different groups differ, there may be high rates of unemployment in some groups, while other groups are fully employed. Moreover, reductions in the demand for labor (associated, say, with business cycles) may have their impact concentrated on particular groups, those for whom the (maximal) ratio of productivity to wage is lowest. Cyclical reductions in demand may be accompanied by lay-offs rather than work-sharing (as predicted by most of the standard implicit contract theory).

This paper is divided into five sections. We start by reviewing the basic arguments for why wages affect productivity. We then discuss the implications of the dependence of productivity on wages for market equilibrium. Next we assess the efficiency of the market equilibrium. The presence of unemployment, of wages in excess of the market clearing level, does not, in itself, indicate that the economy is inefficient. In a planned economy, wages too might well be in excess of the market clearing level. We show, however, that there is no presumption that the competitive equilibrium is efficient; and in particular, that the level of unemployment that emerges in the market equilibrium, what macroeconomists might be tempted to refer to as the natural level of unemployment, has no optimality properties. In the penultimate section we then explore the policy implications, focusing in particular on the implications for tax policy and cost–benefit analysis. Finally we present some concluding remarks.

Why do Wages Affect Productivity?

There are a large number of reasons for which a firm may expect that an increase in the wage it pays may have a positive effect on the productivity of its labor force.

The Efficiency–Wage Hypothesis

This is the oldest explanation provided within the development literature (see, e.g., Leibenstein, 1957).[4] When workers are close to the subsistence level, then increases in their nutritional level and health care will lead to an increase in their productivity.[5] An increase in wages is generally believed to result in an increase in nutrition and hence in productivity. The relationship between the wage paid by the ith firm, w_i, and the productivity of its labor force, λ_i, is conventionally depicted as in figure 7.1, with an initial region in which increases in wages lead to more than proportionate increases in productivity. We write

$$\lambda_i = \lambda_i(w_i) \quad \lambda'>0 \quad \lambda_i''(w_i) \lesseqgtr 0 \text{ as } w_i \lesseqgtr \hat{w}_i . \tag{1}$$

The curve shows that, for low wages, increases in wages have a marked (and an increasing) effect on productivity; at high wages, however, diminishing returns set in: although increases in wages continue to increase productivity somewhat, the increment in productivity from each successive increase in wage becomes smaller and smaller. The shape of the curve is important for many of the results obtained below.

If the urban worker is sharing his or her wage with family members in the rural sector who receive a wage of w_r, then the productivity of an urban worker will depend not only on the firm's wage, w_i, but also on the rural wage, w_r:

$$\lambda_i = \lambda(w_i, w_r) \qquad \partial \lambda / \partial w_r < 0. \tag{2}$$

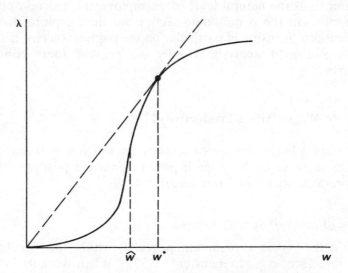

Figure 7.1 Wage–productivity relationship

Moreover, the magnitude of the increase in productivity from a given change in wages will be smaller than it would be if they did not share. As a consequence, firms may attempt to provide meals and health care to their workers, to ensure that a larger proportion of the wage is spent on productivity-enhancing expenditures. They may also subsidize other productivity-enhancing expenditures, e.g. through a company store. Thus, equation (2) can be generalized to $\lambda_i = \lambda_i(w_i, w_r, p)$ where p is the price vector. Firms may also hire members of the same family, to reduce the dissipation of the benefits of high wages from sharing. If the worker is sharing an income with family members who are unemployed or who are employed elsewhere in the urban sector, then productivity may be positive related to the amount of wages paid by other firms, $\bar{w}$,[6] and negatively related to the unemployment rate:

$$\lambda_i = \lambda_i(w_i, \bar{w}, w_r, U) \quad \partial\lambda_i/\partial w_i > 0$$

$$\partial\lambda_i/\partial\bar{w} < 0 \quad \partial\lambda_i/\partial w_r < 0 \quad \partial\lambda_i/\partial U > 0 . \quad (3)$$

An alternative explanation of the dependence of λ on the unemployment rate is that individuals go into debt during job search; they must repay these debts after obtaining employment, thus reducing the funds available for consumption.

In the limiting case where the interest rate is zero and where individuals engage in rent-seeking activity to the point where the lifetime consumption of the individual who obtains a high-wage job is the same as that of one who remains in a low-wage job (and does not search), then an increase in the wage increases expenditures on job search, but does not increase labor productivity.[7] However, this is an extreme case. If there is a positive interest rate, then even if lifetime expected utilities are equalized by rent-seeking expenditures, consumption during periods of employment will be higher in high-wage firms. Moreover, to the extent that this is an important problem, firms will be induced to recruit workers in ways that ameliorate these effects.

Labor Turnover

A second important way in which workers' behavior affects the productivity of firms is through labor turnover.[8] In most jobs, there are costs of hiring and training that are specific to the firm. As long as individuals do not pay these full costs at the moment they are hired (recouping them later in the form of higher wages), then the greater the quit rate, the greater the firm's expenditures on training and hiring costs. Increasing the wage rate will, in general, lead to a reduction in the quit rate, and hence to an increase in the profits of the firm.

The retention rate r (which equals one minus the quit rate) and hence the turnover costs, depend on the relationship between the given firm's wage and all other wages in the economy. Lower-wage individuals have a higher probability of finding a job at a higher wage, and thus of quitting. This is true whether there is costly search, or whether all individuals apply to all firms offering a higher wage than their present firm, and the firm simply randomly picks among the applicants. Moreover, the greater the unemployment rate, the less likely it is that the worker will find a better job. Thus, in this hypothesis

$$r = r(w_i, \bar{w}, w_r, U) \quad r_1 > 0 \quad r_2 < 0 \quad r_3 < 0 \quad r_4 > 0. \qquad (4)$$

The effect of higher quit rates is to decrease the 'net' productivity (net of turnover cost). Firms would not have to pay higher wages to reduce turnover costs if either (i) they could force workers to sign binding contracts; or (ii) workers paid for all of the training costs. Indentured servitude is, in most countries, illegal.

An an empirical matter, it appears that workers seldom pay the full turnover costs at the moment they are hired; and so long as workers are risk-averse and there is some chance that they will leave the firm (either because they are badly 'matched' with the firm or because of some exogenous reason that induces them to leave) the optimal contract between the firm and the worker will entail the firm bearing some of the risks associated with the costs of labor turnover (so turnover will be costly to the firm). (See Arnott and Stiglitz, 1985.) There are further reasons for workers not bearing the entire costs of training and hiring. Workers may have insufficient capital; and the costs of training and hiring may not be verifiable. Were the worker to have to pay the full training and hiring costs, there might be an incentive for firms to overstate these costs, and then to fire workers, making a profit out of the difference between the payments and the true training costs.

Incentive Effects[9]

It is, in general, costly to monitor workers. If there were no unemployment and if all firms paid the market clearing wage, then the threat of being fired would not lead individuals to reduce their shirking: they would know that they could quickly obtain another job. However, if firms pay wages in excess of those of other firms, or if there is unemployment (so that fired workers must spend a period in the unemployment pool before they again obtain a job) then workers have an incentive not to shirk; there is a real cost to being fired.[10]

This again gives rise to a productivity–wage relationship of the form (3), with

$$\frac{\partial \lambda}{\partial w_i} > 0 \quad \frac{\partial \lambda}{\partial w_j} < 0 \quad \frac{\partial \lambda}{\partial w_r} < 0 \quad \frac{\partial \lambda}{\partial U} > 0.$$

An increase in others' wages reduces productivity; an increase in unemployment increases productivity.

Morale Effects

It is sometimes postulated that an individual's behavior is affected by his views of how fairly he is being treated, or more generally, how he sees himself being treated in relationship to others. Thus, the wage relative to others' wages enters into the utility function, and consequently also enters into the effort supply function.[11]

Quality Effects[12]

Changes in the wage affect the mix of applicants for a job. If reservation wages are correlated with productivities on the job, then by offering a higher wage, a firm obtains, on average, a higher-quality labor force.[13] Again, in this hypothesis the productivity of the worker is a function of the wage paid by the given firm relative to the wages paid by all other firms.[14]

Recruitment Effects

It is costly for firms to recruit workers, particularly to find workers who are 'well matched' with the firm. Even if searching were costless, a firm paying a higher wage would have a larger applicant pool among which to choose workers, and this would enable it to recruit a more productive labor force.[15]

Implications of the Dependence of Productivity on Wages for Market Equilibrium

Regardless of the explanation, the dependence of productivity on wages has one critical consequence: firms may not lower wages in the presence of an excess supply of labor, for to lower the wage will lower the productivity of the labor force, and if its productivity is lowered enough, the profits of the firm will be reduced.

Introduction: the Basic Efficiency–Wage Model

This is seen most simply in the basic efficiency–wage model (equation (1)). We assume that output of the firm is a function of the effective labor supply[16]

$$Q = F(\lambda L) \tag{5}$$

where L is the number of workers. We call this technology the *multiplicative* technology. Then profits of the firm, π, are

$$\pi = Q - wL \tag{6}$$

(taking output as our numeraire, so w is the real wage); the firm maximizes this with respect to w and L to obtain

$$F'\lambda'L = L \tag{7a}$$

and

$$F'\lambda = w \tag{7b}$$

or, dividing (7a) by (7b),

$$\lambda' = \lambda/w \tag{8}$$

Equation (8) simply says that the firm chooses a wage to minimize its wage per efficiency unit

$$\min \{w/\lambda\} \tag{9}$$

depicted as the point of tangency of the line through the origin with the productivity curve. The solution to (8) is referred to as the efficiency wage, w^*. At the efficiency wage, the demand for labor, given by

$$L^d = F'^{-1}(w/\lambda)/\lambda \tag{10}$$

may be less than the supply; nonetheless firms will not be induced to lower their wages. A firm knows that an unemployed worker who offers to work for a wage less than w^* will have a lower productivity, a sufficiently lower productivity that its labor costs will be higher, and its profits lower.

This argument holds, with equal force, for any of the other explanations we have proffered for the dependence of productivity on wages. Thus, for instance, in the labor turnover model firms will not lower their wages, even in the face of an excess supply of labor, knowing that if they do so, they will face higher turnover costs, which may more than offset the direct savings from the lower wages.

Although all of the models can yield equilibrium unemployment, the different models do, however, differ in their welfare consequences and policy implications. We shall note some of these differences below.

A General Model

In this section, we analyse the equilibrium of a more general version of the wage–productivity model. We focus our attention on symmetric equilibria, in which all firms in the urban sector pay the same wage. Then the productivity curve facing the ith firm can be written as

$$\lambda = \lambda_i(w_i, \bar{w}, w_r, U). \tag{11}$$

when $\bar{w}$ is the wage paid by other firms in the urban sector. (In the symmetric equilibrium, $w_i = \bar{w}$.)

We employ a general production function of the form (where Q_i is the value of *net* output and L_i is the number of workers)

$$Q_i = Q_i(\lambda_i, L_i). \tag{12}$$

One special case of this is the labor turnover model, in which

$$Q_i = F_i(L_i) - T_i(\lambda_i)L_i \tag{13}$$

where λ_i now has the interpretation of the retention ratio, $T_i(\lambda)$ is the expected turnover cost; $T_{i'}(\lambda) < 0$, so $\partial Q_i/\partial\lambda > 0$.

Another special case is that discussed earlier, where the production function takes on the simple form

$$Q = F(\lambda L). \tag{5'}$$

In this version, a more productive worker is just a 'multiple' of a less productive worker. (In the more general case, a more productive worker may be capital-saving.)[17]

Profits are still represented by (6). Profit maximization requires that the real wage equal the value of the marginal product

$$\partial Q/\partial L_i = w_i \tag{14a}$$

and w_i being chosen so that

$$(\partial Q_i/\partial\lambda)(\partial\lambda_i/\partial w_i) = L_i . \tag{14b}$$

Note that for the labor turnover model, equation (14b) has a familiar interpretation. The total labor cost per unit time of a worker is

$$w_i + T^*_i (q+\rho) \tag{15}$$

where the T^*_i are the training costs (not paid by the worker), q the quit rate ($= 1-r$, the retention rate), and ρ the interest rate. Here ρT^*_i are the interest costs associated with the training expenditure, and qT^*_i are analogous to the depreciation costs on physical capital. Thus, turnover costs $T_i(\lambda)$ can be written as

$$T_i(\lambda) = T^*_i (q + \rho) \tag{15a}$$

so (14b) takes on the familiar form

$$-T^*_i(\partial q/\partial w_i) = 1 . \tag{15b}$$

The quit rate function facing any firm, taking the wages of other firms, the wage in the rural sector, and the unemployment rate as given is usually depicted as in figure 7.2; the solution to (15b) is represented by the tangency between the quit rate function, and the iso-cost curve (15). Thus, there exists an optimal wage for the

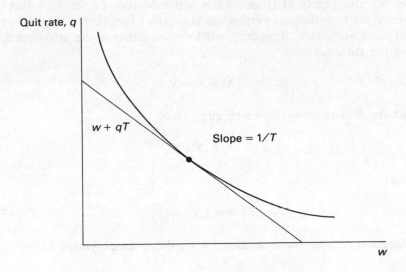

Figure 7.2 Labor costs are minimized with $-T_i^* \, \delta q/\delta w_i = 1$

firm, in excess of w_{min}, the minimum wage at which the firm can recruit workers.

The Generalized Efficiency–Wage Condition. Dividing (14b) by (14a) we obtain the generalized efficiency–wage condition

$$\frac{\partial \lambda}{\partial w_i} \frac{w_i}{\lambda_i} = \frac{\partial \ln Q_i / \partial \ln L_i}{\partial \ln Q / \partial \ln \lambda}. \qquad (16)$$

The elasticity of productivity with respect to wages should equal the ratio of the elasticity of output with respect to employment to the elasticity of output with respect to wages.

Urban-Sector Equilibrium. We assume a fixed number of identical competitive firms. It is easy to establish that the aggregate behavior of the sector is determined by functions of the form (14a) and (14b) or (16), where we substitute the aggregate production function for the firm's production function. From now on, L_u will denote the aggregate urban employment, $\bar{w}$ average urban wages, w_i the wage of a representative firm. Thus (14a) and (14b) can be thought of as determining the demand for labor and the wage rate as a function of N_u, the supply of labor to the urban sector. To see how this is done, we note that the rural wage is simply a function of the number of rural workers N_r; however, workers are either in the urban sector or the rural sector:

$$N_u + N_r = \bar{N}$$

where $\bar{N}$ is the total labor supply. Thus

$$N_r = \bar{N} - N_u$$

and

$$w_r = w_r(\bar{N} - N_u) . \tag{17}$$

Moreover, from the definition of U, the unemployment rate

$$1 - U = L_u/N_u \tag{18}$$

Substituting (17) and (18) into the productivity equation. we obtain

$$\lambda = \hat{\lambda}(w_i, \bar{w}, L_u, N_u) = \lambda(w_i, \bar{w}, w_r(\bar{N} - N_u)(1 - L_u/N_u)) . \tag{3'}$$

Substituting this into (16) we can solve for the equilibrium urban wage as a function of N_u and L_u:

$$\bar{w} = \phi(N_u, L_u) . \tag{19}$$

We can solve (14a) for the demand for labor by the ith firm as a function of $\bar{w}$, U, and w_r; and again using (17) and (18) we write L_u as a function of $\bar{w}$ and N_u:

$$L_u = L_u(\bar{w}, N_u) . \tag{20}$$

We can solve (19) and (20) simultaneously to obtain the demand for labor and the wage as functions of N_u:

$$L_u = L_u(N_u) \tag{21a}$$

$$\bar{w} = \bar{w}(N_u) . \tag{21b}$$

Note that, in general *the demand (L_u) for labor depends on the supply (N_u)*.

An increase in supply of labor increases unemployment, which increases productivity at any given wage, and hence increases demand if the elasticity of demand for labor is large, but may decrease demand if the elasticity is small.[18]

The effect of a change of N_u on $\bar{w}$ is more complicated, and is discussed below.

Migration. When the wage in the urban sector exceeds that in the rural sector, we need to have a theory to determine how labor allocates itself between the two sectors. We assume that the supply of laborers to the urban sector, N_u, is a function of the urban wage, $\bar{w}$, the unemployment rate, the number of urban jobs, L_u, and the rural wage:

$$N_u = H(\bar{w}, U, L_u, w_r). \tag{22}$$

We can simplify (20) using (19) and (18):

$$N_u = N_u(\bar{w}, L_u) \tag{23}$$

giving the supply of workers to the urban sector as a function of urban wages and employment.

The Harris–Todaro Model. A special case of our migration model (22) is the so-called Harris–Todaro migration hypothesis, in which migration continues until the expected urban wage equals the rural wage:

$$\bar{w}(1-U) = w_r.$$

Then (23) takes on the form

$$N_u = L_u w_r/\bar{w} \tag{23'}$$

and, using (17), equation (23) becomes

$$N_u = L_u w_r(N-N_u)/\bar{w}. \tag{23''}$$

Market Equilibrium.   Notice that in this model the supply of labor in the urban sector is a function of the demand, just as we noted earlier that the demand for labor is a function of the unemployment rate, and hence indirectly of supply. There is not the simple dichotomy between supply and demand that characterized simple equilibrium models. Moreover, while in traditional competitive supply and demand analysis, firms and workers treat the wage parametrically, now firms determine the wage. Thus, while traditional analysis depicts demand and supply as a function of the wage, here the wage is endogenous, and the demand can, accordingly, be thought of as simply a function of the supply (equation (21a)) and the supply simply as a function of demand. The derivation of the pseudo-supply curve is straightforward. Substituting (21b) into (23) we obtain

$$N_u = N_u(\bar{w}(N_u), L_u). \tag{24}$$

At a fixed wage, an increase in the demand for labor reduces unemployment, and so leads to an increase in the supply of labor. The same holds even if wages adjust, so long as the wage does not fall too much as a result of an increase in N_u.

The equilibrium, the intersection of the pseudo-supply curve (24) and the pseudo-demand curve (21a), is depicted in figure 7.3.

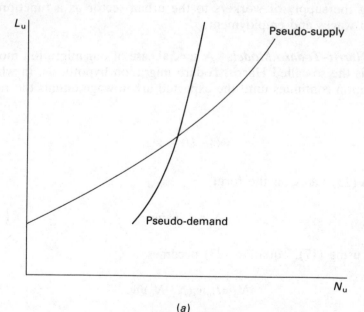

(a)

Figure 7.3(a)

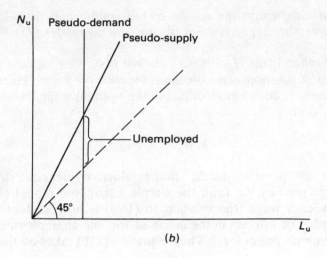

(b)

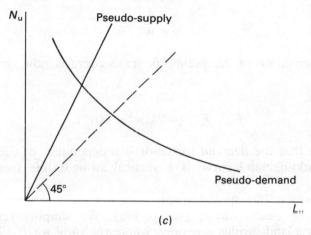

(c)

Figure 7.3(a) The demand for labor is a function of the supply, and the supply a function of demand. While supply normally increases with demand, demand may increase or decrease with supply. Here we depict the former case. (**b**) The Harris–Todaro migration model with the absolute-wage–efficiency model and a fixed rural wage. (**c**) The Harris–Todaro migration model with the relative-wage–efficiency model, a fixed rural wage, and low urban demand elasticity for labor

Some Special Cases

To gain insight into the nature of the equilibrium, it is useful to investigate three special cases of our general model (22).[19]

The Absolute-Wage Hypothesis.   In the first, we postulate that the production function takes on the multiplicative form. Then, as we noted earlier, equation (16), giving the optimal wage, takes on the simple form:

$$\lambda_i/w_i = \partial\lambda_i/\partial w_i. \tag{16'}$$

If we now postulate further that productivity depends simply on the wage paid by the firm, the simple nutritional model (1), then the efficiency wage (the solution to (16')) is independent of both the number of workers in the urban sector, the unemployment rate, and the employment level. Thus, equation (21b) takes on the simple form

$$\bar{w} = w^*. \tag{21b'}$$

The derivation of the pseudo-demand curve is now straightforward:

$$L_u = F'^{-1}(w^*/\lambda(w^*))/\lambda(w^*). \tag{21a'}$$

Notice that the demand for labor is independent of the supply: the pseudo-demand curve is a vertical straight line (see Figure 7.4(a)).

We focus on the special supply equation (22') corresponding to the Harris–Todaro Model (see p. 143). We simplify further by assuming a land-surplus economy, where the rural wage is independent of the number of individuals in the rural sector:

$$w_r = \bar{w}_r.$$

Then (22') takes on the particularly simple form

$$N_u = L_u \bar{w}_r/\bar{w} \tag{19''}$$

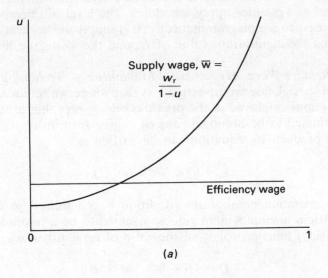

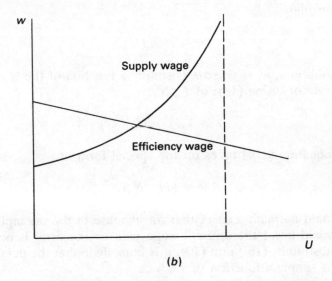

Figure 7.4 The supply wage gives that urban wage that generates the indicated level of unemployment (in these diagrams w_r is fixed, so $\bar{w}^s = w_r/(1-u)$). (a) The absolute-wage–efficiency wage hypothesis. (b) The relative-wage–efficiency wage hypothesis

(see figure 7.4(a)). There is a unique intersection of the pseudo-demand and pseudo-supply schedules. The level of unemployment is also easy to see diagrammatically: it is simply the vertical distance between the equilibrium value of L_u and the 45-degree line.

The Relative-Wage Hypothesis, Multiplicative Technology. The second special case we investigate is that where we retain all of the assumptions employed in the previous one, except that productivity is postulated to be homogeneous of degree zero in w_i, $\bar{w}$, and w_r.

The productivity equation can be written as

$$\tilde{\lambda}_i = \tilde{\lambda}_i(w_i/\bar{w}, w_r/\bar{w}, U).$$

The migration equilibrium condition is generalized so that the equilibrium unemployment rate is assumed to be a (monotonically decreasing) function solely of the ratio of rural–urban-wage ratio:

$$U = M(w_r/\bar{w}) \quad M' < 0 \tag{25}$$

or inverting

$$w_r/\bar{w} = m(U). \tag{25a}$$

In equilibrium, $w_i = \bar{w}$, so λ is simply a function of the unemployment rate or, using (18), of L_u/N_u:

$$\lambda_i = \tilde{\lambda}_i(1, m(U), U) \tag{16''}$$

Thus equation (21b) takes on the special form of

$$\bar{w} = \phi(L_u/N_u). \tag{19'}$$

We would normally expect that an increase in the unemployment rate would lower the optimal wage paid by the firm; hence $\phi' > 0$.[20] Substituting (16'') into (10), it is immediate that the demand for labor is simply a function of L_u/N_u:

$$L_u = F'^{-1}\{\phi(L_u/N_u)/\lambda[1,m(1-(L_u/N_u)), 1-(L_u/N_u)]\}/\lambda = z(U). \tag{21a''}$$

We would normally expect that an increase in the unemployment rate reduces the cost of an efficiency unit of labor; the effect of this on the demand for laborers would depend on the elasticity of the demand for labor. If, for instance, the elasticity of demand for labor is low, then the demand for workers actually decreases.

The equation describing the supply of labor is now, from (25a),

$$N_u = L_u/[1 - M(w_r/\bar{w})].$$

In the case of a fixed rural wage, we can write

$$N_u = L_u/[1 - M(\bar{w}_r/\phi(L_u/N_u))] \tag{24''}$$

Although (21a'') and (24'') thus describe the equilibrium for this model, it is easier to see the effects of various policies if we express both the 'supply wage' (the wage at which a given unemployment is generated by the market) and the demand wage (the wage set by firms) as functions of the unemployment rate. For simplicity, we focus on the case where w_r is fixed. Then

$$\bar{w} = \bar{w}_r/(1 - U) \quad \text{(migration equilibrium)}$$

and

$$\bar{w} = \tilde{\lambda}(1, m(U), U)/\tilde{\lambda}_1(1, m(U), U) \quad \text{(wage determination)}.$$

See figure 7.3(c). Notice that in this case, the unemployment rate and the wage are determined independently of the demand for labor. Rural employment is determined essentially as a residual:[21]

$$N_r = \bar{N} - N_u = N - \frac{L_u(U^*)}{1 + U^*}$$

The Relative-Wage Hypothesis: The Labor Turnover Model. The labor turnover model yields similar results. Labor turnover depends only on relative wages and the unemployment rate, but the efficiency wage condition takes on the form (15b), again yielding

$$\bar{w} = h(U).$$

The equation describing demand for labor is slightly different from (10). It takes on the form

$$F'(L) = w + T.$$

where, it will be recalled, T is the turnover cost per worker (given by (15″)).

Both T and w are functions of U, so, inverting, we obtain

$$L_u = F'^{-1}(h(U) + T(U)).$$

The demand for labor is again simply a function of the unemployment rate. The equilibrium is again depicted by a diagram, such as figure 7.4.

Efficiency of the Market Equilibrium

The fact that some workers are unemployed suggests that resources are not being used efficiently. However, assessing the efficiency of the market in the presence of the wage–productivity nexus is not an easy matter. We need to specify what the government's objectives are, as well as the set of available instruments. If, for instance, the government could control migration directly, then it could eliminate unemployment. It might, for instance, randomly assign some individuals to the high-paying urban jobs, but require all other individuals to remain in the rural sector. Such control of migration requires a level of repression that many LDCs find objectionable. Accordingly, the more relevant question may be, if the government could directly control the urban wage rate and the level of urban *employment* would it set these variables at levels different from those of competitive markets?

Alternatively, the government may not be able to control wages and employment directly; it may have to resort to wage subsidies or taxes. Again, we need to ask, if these are the only instruments available, would the government wish to impose such subsidies or taxes, and, if it did, at what rates?

In this section, we assume the government has direct control of $\bar{w}$ and L_u. We first assume that the government wishes to maximize national output, and then consider the more general objective of (constrained) Pareto-efficiency.

Maximization of National Output

We assume that the government is simply concerned with maximizing net national output.

Let Q_u and Q_r be output in the urban and rural sectors respectively; then the government[22] chooses $\bar{w}$ and L_u to maximize

$$\{Q_u[\hat{\lambda}(w,\bar{w},L_u,N_u(\bar{w},L_u)),\ L_u] + Q_r(N-N_u(\bar{w},L_u))\} \tag{26}$$

yielding the first-order conditions

$$L_u\frac{\partial Q_u}{\partial L_u} - L_uQ'_r\frac{dN_u}{dL_u} + \frac{\partial Q_u}{\partial\lambda}\left(\hat{\lambda}_3 L_u + \hat{\lambda}_4 N_u\frac{d\ln N_u}{d\ln L_u}\right) = 0 \tag{27a}$$

$$\frac{\partial Q_u}{\partial\lambda}\left(\hat{\lambda}_1 + \hat{\lambda}_2 + \hat{\lambda}_4\frac{dN_u}{dw}\right) + Q'_r\frac{dN_u}{dw} = 0. \tag{27b}$$

Rewriting,

$$\frac{\partial Q_u/\partial L_u - \bar{w}}{w} = \frac{Q'_r\,N_u}{w\,L_u}\frac{d\ln N_u}{d\ln L_u} - 1 - a\frac{d\ln Q_u}{d\ln L_u} \tag{28a}$$

$$\frac{\hat{\lambda}_1 w}{\lambda} = \frac{d\ln N_u/d\ln w}{d\ln N_u/d\ln L_u}\frac{(1+a)}{(1+b)}\frac{\partial\ln Q_u/\partial\ln L_u}{\partial\ln Q_u/\partial\ln\lambda_u} \tag{28b}$$

where

$$a = \frac{d\ln Q_u/\partial\ln\hat{\lambda}}{d\ln Q_u/\partial\ln L_u}\frac{Q_u}{wL_u}\frac{\partial\ln\hat{\lambda}}{\partial\ln L_u} + \frac{\partial\ln\hat{\lambda}}{\partial\ln N_u}\frac{\partial\ln N_u}{\partial\ln L_u}$$

$$b = \frac{\hat{\lambda}_2\bar{w}}{\lambda} + \frac{\partial\ln\hat{\lambda}}{\partial\ln N_u}\frac{\partial\ln N_u}{\partial\ln w} \tag{29}$$

Thus, the market is efficient only if (comparing (28a) and (28b) with (14) and (15))

$$Q_{r'}\frac{dN_u}{dL_u} = \bar{w}\left(1 + a\frac{d\ln Q_u}{d\ln L_u}\right) \tag{30a}$$

and

$$\frac{1+a}{1+b} = \frac{d\ln N_u/d\ln L_u}{d\ln N_u/d\ln w} \tag{30b}$$

To see what is entailed, we consider some special cases:

Labor Supply with Harris–Todaro Model.   Assume $w_r = Q_r'$, the rural wage equals the value of the marginal product of labor in the rural sector. If migration equilibrium entails equating the rural wage to the expected urban wage,

$$w_r = \bar{w}\,\frac{L_u}{N_u}$$

then the elasticity of urban labor supply with respect to the urban wage and employment are identical:

$$\frac{d \ln N_u}{d \ln w_u} = \frac{d \ln N_u}{d \ln L_u} \tag{31}$$

and

$$\frac{d \ln N_u}{d \ln L_u} = \frac{1}{1+\xi} \tag{32}$$

where

$$\xi = -\frac{Q_r'' N_r N_u}{Q_r' N_r}$$

$\xi = 0$ when the rural wage is independent of the number of workers in the rural sector.

Labor Supply with Risk Aversion.   If individuals are risk-averse, and set their expected utility in the urban sector equal to that in the rural, then, letting $v(0) = 0$, where $v(w)$ is the utility associated with wage w, with $v'' < 0$, as a result of risk aversion and

$$Ev = v(w)\,(1-U) + U\,v\,(0) = v\,(w)\,(1-U) = v(W_r),$$

$$\frac{d \ln N_u/d \ln \bar{w}}{d \ln N_u/d \ln L_u} = \frac{u'(\bar{w})\bar{w}}{u(\bar{w})} < 1, \quad \frac{d \ln N_u}{d \ln L_u} = \frac{1}{1+\xi}$$

Absolute-Wage–Efficiency Model: Harris–Todaro Migration.   In the absolute-wage–efficiency model described above, $a = b = 0$. Thus, for that model, with expected wages in the two sectors equalized, the market wage is set at its efficient level ((equation 28b) is satisfied) even though there is unemployment. Moreover if $a = 0$ and $\xi = 0$ (the wage in the rural sector does not change as workers migrate to the urban sector) urban employment in the market economy is set at its efficient level, for then (30a) becomes

$$w_r N_u = \bar{w} L_u$$

which is clearly satisfied. If $a = 0$ but $\xi > 0$, it is set too low.

Relative-Wage–Efficiency Model. Under the relative-wage–efficiency hypothesis, with a fixed rural wage, and the Harris–Todaro migration equilibrium condition, a is again zero, employment is at the right level, contingent on the wage being offered, but the wage may be either too large or too small, depending on whether a proportionate increase in the employment rate has a greater or lesser effect on productivity than a proportionate increase in the average urban wage.

Under the relative-wage–efficiency hypothesis, and the Harris–Todaro migration equilibrium condition, but with a variable rural wage, $a < 0$. On the other hand, under those circumstances

$$\frac{Q'_r}{\bar{w}} \frac{dN_u}{dL_u} < 1. \tag{31}$$

Hence, from (28a), it is clear that employment, conditional on the wage, may be either too large or too small (since the above expression does not depend on the properties of the productivity function but clearly a does, the right-hand side of (28a) may be either positive or negative).

Similarly, from (28b), it is clear that the wage may be either too high or too low. While

$$\frac{d \ln L_u / d \ln \bar{w}}{d \ln N_u / d \ln L_u} \tag{32}$$

will be less than unity if individuals are risk averse, the sign of b depends on the sensitivity of productivity to changes in the average urban wage relative to its sensitivity to the rural wage rate and the level of unemployment.

Pareto-efficiency

The fact that the competitive allocation does not maximize net national output does not imply that the market economy is not Pareto-efficient. Pareto-efficiency may be most easily examined in the context of the case where the rural wage is fixed and, hence (under the Harris–Todaro hypothesis), so is the welfare of workers. Pareto-efficiency then requires the maximization of profits in the urban sector, i.e.

$$\max \{Q_u - wL_u\} \tag{33}$$

so

$$\partial Q_u/\partial L_u - w = (\partial Q_u/\partial \lambda)\left[\partial \hat{\lambda}/\partial L_u + (\partial \hat{\lambda}/N_u)(\partial N_u/\partial L_u)\right] \tag{34}$$

$$(\partial Q/\partial \lambda)\hat{\lambda}_1 - L_u = -(\partial Q_u/\partial \lambda)\left[\hat{\lambda}_2 + (\partial \hat{\lambda}/\partial N_u)(\partial N_u/\partial w)\right]. \tag{35}$$

Contrasting (34) and (35) with (15) and (16), it is clear that the market will essentially never be Pareto-efficient unless $\hat{\lambda}_2 = \hat{\lambda}_3 = \hat{\lambda}_4 = 0$. Further distortions obtain in the case of variable w_r.

Sources of Market Failure

There are several sources of market failure in this economy. First, firms fail to take into account the effect of their wage and employment policy on the productivity of workers at other firms, both directly and indirectly through their effect on the unemployment rate and rural wages. (These productivity externalities[23] would arise regardless of the explanation of the wage–productivity relationship.) Some of these externalities are positive, some are negative. Policies that lead to a reduced unemployment rate are likely to reduce productivity (e.g. as a result of incentive effects). Increases in productivity as a consequence of a higher-quality applicant pool are at the expense of the quality of those working at other firms, except to the extent that the wage/employment policy has resulted in a better matching of workers with firms (on the basis of comparative advantage).

As a result, in this class of models the wage does not measure the correct opportunity cost of labor. For instance, if the reason for which productivity increases with the wage is that reservation wages are correlated with productivity, then the applicant pool consists of all of those whose productivity in the rural sector is less than the wage offered by the firm; in that case, the wage clearly exceeds the opportunity cost of a randomly selected applicant.

If by hiring an additional worker, more than one worker migrates from the rural sector (to seek employment in the urban sector) the loss in output exceeds the rural wage. Later, we present an example where the loss in output equals the urban wage.

Throughout this section we have assumed that the government cannot affect migration indirectly through subsidies to the rural sector. As we show later, such subsidies are, in general, desirable (although it will not be in the interest of any firm to provide such a subsidy).

Policy

Indirect Intervention

The government can attempt to use taxes and subsidies to effect the constrained optimum. Since there were two variables that the government controlled, it requires at least two instruments to attain the constrained optimum. In particular, if we impose *ad valorem* and specific wage subsidies at the rates τ and t, the firm

$$\max \{Q_u - [w(1-\tau) + t]L_u\} \tag{36}$$

and so sets

$$\partial Q_u/\partial L_u = w(1-\tau)+t \tag{37}$$

$$(\partial Q_u/\partial \lambda)(\partial \lambda/\partial w_i) = (1-\tau)L_u. \tag{38}$$

If t and τ are set appropriately, so that

$$\frac{t - \tau w}{w} = \frac{Q_r' N_u}{w L_u} \frac{d \ln N_u}{d \ln L_u} - 1 - a \frac{d \ln Q_u}{d \ln L_u} \tag{39}$$

$$(1-\tau)L_u = \frac{\partial Q_u}{\partial \lambda}\left(\hat{\lambda}_2 + \lambda_4 \frac{dN_u}{dw}\right) - Q_r' \frac{dN_u}{dw} \tag{40}$$

then the market solution will be a constrained optimum.

Note that a pure *ad valorem* subsidy leaves unchanged the equation for the optimal wage (dividing (38) by (37)) but does increase the level of employment. Thus, in the pure wage–efficiency model, where the market wage was optimal, the government will only employ an *ad valorem* wage susbidy. A specific wage subsidy will increase the wage paid: it will be partly shifted backwards towards workers (see figure 7.5).

If the wage subsidy is shifted backwards towards workers, it will result in an increase in the unemployment rate, as depicted in figure 7.6. In contrast, in the pure efficiency–wage model, where an *ad valorem* wage subsidy leaves the market wage unaffected, the unemployment *rate* is unchanged, if the rural wage is fixed (under the Harris–Todaro migration hypothesis) but because the number of employed workers increases, the number of unemployed people increases. On the other hand, if the rural wage is not fixed, the out-migration from the rural sector raises the rural wage, and this reduces the level of unemployment. The consequences of this are described more fully below.

Additional Taxes.   Although by assumption the government cannot directly control migration, it may be able to affect the level of migration (and the associated unemployment) by providing subsidies

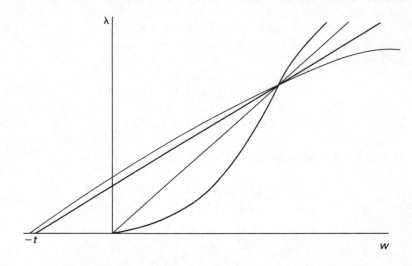

Figure 7.5 An *ad valorem* wage subsidy leaves the wage unchanged, but increases employment. A specific wage subsidy increases the wage paid

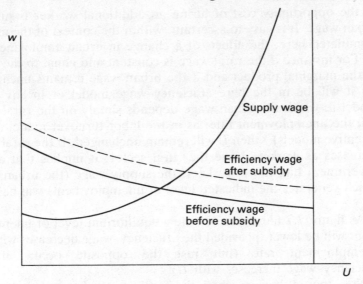

Figure 7.6 A specific wage subsidy increases unemployment rates

to the rural sector, financed, for instance, by a tax on profits in the urban sector. In the pure efficiency–wage model, such subsidies unambiguously increase national output and lower unemployment. In models where productivity in the urban sector is affected by the rural wage, such a policy has a positive effect on rural output and a negative effect on urban output. The optimal rural subsidy entails a balancing of these two effects.

Shadow Prices. The models formulated in this paper have very different implications for shadow pricing from those of the standard model. First the opportunity cost of having an additional worker in the urban sector depends critically on the effect this has on the unemployment rate. If the government's hiring of an additional worker left unemployment unchanged, it would imply an induced migration of $1/(1-U)$ workers, and hence a loss in output in the rural sector of $w_r/(1-U)$, if w_r is the marginal product of labor. Under the hypothesis that expected income in the urban sector equals the rural wage

$$w_r = \bar{w} \, L_u/N_u = \bar{w}(1-U)$$

so the opportunity cost of hiring an additional worker is just the urban wage. It is easy to ascertain, within the context of the models formulated here, the effects of a change in urban employment on U. For instance if the rural wage is constant and equal to the value of the marginal product and if the urban wage remains unchanged (as it will be in the pure efficiency–wage model or in any other model in which the urban wage depends simply on the rural wage and the unemployment rate, as in the labor turnover model or the incentive models)[24] then U will remain unchanged. If the rural wage increases as workers leave the rural sector, it implies that as the government hire more workers, the supply wage (the urban wage which generates the indicated level of unemployment) will be higher.[25]

As figure 7.7 illustrates, the new equilibrium level of unemployment will be lower, provided the efficiency–wage decreases with the unemployment rate (but just the opposite occurs if the efficiency–wage increases with U).

Note too, in the case where the rural wage is fixed, that changing the level of urban employment has no effect on aggregate workers' consumption; hence if all profits are invested, investment is maximized by maximizing net national output. Regardless of the relative weight associated with investment, the shadow price on labor is the

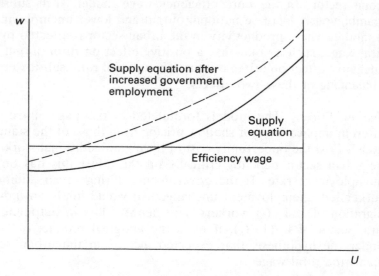

Figure 7.7   Government employment reduces unemployment rates, and hence the shadow wage is less than the urban wage

urban wage. (These results are in marked contrast to those from the earlier studies, such as Sen (1968), which ignored the endogeneity of migration and of urban-wage determination.)

If the rural wage increases as individuals leave the rural sector, then at a fixed urban wage, the unemployment rate will be reduced, and hence the opportunity cost of labor is less than the urban wage (but still greater than the rural wage). The reduction in the unemployment rate may lead to an increase in urban wage, but presumably by an amount that is less than proportionate to the rise in the rural wage.

Disequilibrium versus Equilibrium Models and Wage Dispersion

In all of the models presented here, we have assumed that the wage is determined endogenously. There is another important class of models in which wages are set arbitrarily (say by custom, unions, or government fiat). Such models do not provide a basis for inferring what will happen as a result of a change in, say, taxes, and thus provide an inadequate basis for the analysis of policy. Since the pure efficiency–wage model is one in which the wage does not depend on the level of hiring in the sector, unemployment, public employment, wages paid by other firms, or *ad valorem* subsidies, the analysis of the rigid-wage model corresponds (for these policy variables) to that special case of our general model. On the other hand, our model predicts that even in the pure efficiency–wage model, a specific wage subsidy will have an effect on wages paid in the urban sector.

In the disequilibrium models, the observed productivity differences between different sectors (or different firms within a given sector) may be viewed as being caused by differences in the exogenously given wages. In our more general equilibrium formulation, there may exist differences amongst the wages paid by different firms; labor turnover may be more important to some firms than to others; physical health may be more important in some occupations than in others; in such cases, wages may be higher. Even more interesting, however, is the possibility that identical firms (identical jobs) may pay different wages; the differences in wages being perfectly offset by differences in productivity. Equilibrium may be characterized by wage dispersion, even amongst otherwise identical firms. In these models, there is no single direction of causation:

productivity is higher because wages are higher, and wages are higher because productivity is higher.

This chapter has considered only some of the important facets of the wage–productivity nexus and its implications for development policy. It has not considered, for instance, important consequences for education policy (whether education is for screening or human capital formation) and investment policy (including the allocation of capital between the urban and rural sectors). These are questions that we hope to explore elsewhere.

Notes

1 I had independently and simultaneously reached very similar conclusions. See Stiglitz (1969), parts of which were subsequently published as Stiglitz (1974b, 1982b).
2 We simplify by assuming all workers are unskilled (although we also consider the consequences of different ability levels). For a discussion of cost–benefit analysis with different educational levels, see Stiglitz (1977) and Fields (1972).
3 It is straightforward to include in the analysis attitudes towards non-pecuniary benefits and costs of living in the urban or rural sector; risk aversion; and costs of transportation and job seeking. The basic Harris–Todaro model entails a hiring hall, where all workers are hired on a daily basis. More realistically, job seekers face a period of unemployment, after which they either succeed in obtaining a job or return to the rural sector. The general model presented here is consistent with this formulation as well. See also Stiglitz (1974b) and Fields (1975).
4 Some of the analytic implications have been explored by Mirrlees (1975), Stiglitz (1976b), and Dasgupta and Ray (1986).
5 Recently Bliss and Stern (1978) have examined the empirical validity of this hypothesis.
6 $\tilde{w}$ is the vector of wages paid by other firms. Since we focus on symmetric equilibria, all components of $\tilde{w}$ are identical.
7 Assuming, that is, that productivity depends on lifetime consumption, or, if it depends on current consumption, at a zero interest rate, that individuals smooth their consumption evenly throughout their lives.
8 In the context of developed countries, this hypothesis has been explored by Salop (1973), Stiglitz (1985), Schlicht (1978) and Hall (1975) among others. In the context of less-developed countries, see Stiglitz (1974b).
9 The incentive effect of paying high wages, within the context of developed countries, has been analysed by Shapiro and Stiglitz (1984), Calvo (1979), and Calvo and Phelps (1977).
10 A full analysis of this motive for paying higher wages again requires an

investigation into alternative methods of providing incentives. One such method is to provide a bond, which the individuals forfeit if they shirk. The difficulties with this are similar to those discussed above. Alternatively, the firm could threaten to lower the wage of any individual caught shirking, but lowering the wage simply increases the likelihood that the individual will shirk in subsequent periods, and hence is not an effective incentive device. (See Shapiro and Stiglitz, 1984.)

11 Like the previous explanation, this requires that it be costly to monitor the actual level of effort put out by the individual. For a discussion of evidence for this effect in the psychological literature, see Akerlof (1984). For an earlier discussion of these morale effects, see Stiglitz (1973, 1974a).

12 In the context of developed countries, this model has been explored by Stiglitz (1976a), Weiss (1980), and Nalebuff and Stiglitz (1982). For LDCs see Stiglitz (1982a).

13 The assumptions that firms can imperfectly observe the inputs of individuals (as in the previous two explanations), and that they can imperfectly screen individuals prior to hiring them are critical. Moreover, we also require that individuals are not able to guarantee their performance (either for one of the reasons presented above, or because individuals are risk-averse, and imperfectly informed concerning their skills relative to the job).

14 When workers are heterogeneous, there is not, in general, a single rural wage; what turns out to be relevant for most of the analysis is the wage of the marginal migrant. When labor is heterogeneous, this is what w_r will denote.

15 In models with costly search, it may take some time before a firm is successful in filling a vacancy. The expected length of time is dependent on the wages the firm pays. The effect of this is analogous to that of a direct increase in productivity resulting from a wage increase.

16 Where there is no risk of confusion, we drop the subscript i denoting the ith firm.

17 To use the vocabulary of traditional growth theory, in the formulation $(5')$, increases in labor productivity are 'Harrod neutral' or 'labor-augmenting'. A more general formulation would have

$$Q=F(\alpha(\lambda)K,\beta(\lambda)L).$$

Thus, if $\beta' = 0$, increases in productivity are purely capital-augmenting.

18 It is apparent with elastic demands that there will be a unique equilibrium. With inelastic demands, it is difficult to rule out multiple equilibria.

19 We emphasize that this is still not the most general model. We have, in particular, ignored the dependence of productivity on relative prices. The omission of this would be particularly serious in the analysis of a closed-

economy model, where the relative price of agricultural and industrial goods affects industrial productivity. See Sah and Stiglitz (1985).

20 This is, however, not necessarily the case. Under the assumption that productivity is homogeneous of degree zero in w_i, $\bar{w}$, and w_r, the first-order condition for the optimal wage can be written as

$$\frac{\partial \bar{\lambda}}{\partial(w_i/\bar{w})} \; \frac{w_i}{\bar{w}} = \lambda_i \, .$$

The effect of a change in U on the equilibrium level of w thus depends on the sign of

$$\frac{\partial \bar{\lambda}_i}{\partial m} m' + \frac{\partial \bar{\lambda}_i}{\partial U} - \frac{\partial^2 \bar{\lambda}_i}{\partial(w_i/\bar{w})\partial m} m' - \frac{\partial^2 \bar{\lambda}_i}{\partial(w_i/\bar{w})\partial U}.$$

21 In the more general case, where w_r is a function of N_r, the pseudo-supply function takes on the form

$$\bar{w}(1-U) = w_r(N_r) = w_r(\bar{N}-N_u) = w_r\left[\bar{N} - \frac{L_u(U)}{1-U}\right]$$

22 We ignore efficiency–wage considerations in the rural sector.

23 Some of the externalities appear to be pecuniary externalities, which in traditional economic theory do not interfere with the productive efficiency of the economy. However, the result that pecuniary externalities do not matter is special, and does not hold in the class of models with which we are concerned here, and more generally, as Greenwald and Stiglitz (1986) show, in any economy in which there is imperfect information and/or an incomplete set of markets.

24 However, in the efficiency–quality model, the mix of applicants applying to jobs in the urban sector changes as urban employment changes, and this may lead to a change in the urban wage.

25 Equilibrium requires

$$\bar{w} = w_r(N-N_u]/(1-U) - w_r\left(N - \frac{L_u}{1-U}\right)/(1-U)$$

where, letting L_g denote government employment,

$$L_u - F'^{-1} \bar{w}/\bar{\lambda}(1,m(U),U) + L_g$$

in the relative-wage model, and

$$L_u = F'^{-1} \bar{w}/\lambda(\bar{w}) + L_g$$

in the absolute-wage model.

References

Akerlof, George A. 1984: Gift exchange and efficiency wage theory: four views. *American Economic Review Proceedings*.

Arnott, R. and Stiglitz, J. E. 1985: Labor turnover, wage structures, and moral hazard, the inefficiency of competitive markets. *Journal of Labor Economics*, September.

Bliss, C. and Stern, N. 1978: Productivity, wages and nutrition. *Journal of Development Economics*, 5, 331–98.

Calvo, Guillermo 1979: Quasi-Walrasian theories of unemployment. *American Economic Review*, 69, 102–7.

Calvo, Guillermo and Phelps, E. S. 1977: Appendix: employment contingent wage contracts. In Karl Brunner and Allan H. Meltzer (eds), *Stabilization of the Domestic and International Economy*, 5, Carnegie–Rochester Conference Series on Public Policy. *Journal of Monetary Economics Supplement*, 160–8.

Dasgupta, P. and Ray, D. 1986: An economic theory of malnutrition.

Fields, G. 1972: Private and social returns to education in less developed countries. *Eastern Africa Economic Review*.

—— 1975: Rural–urban migration, urban unemployment and underemployment, and job-search activity in LDCs. *Journal of Development Economics*, 165–87.

Greenwald, Bruce and Stiglitz, J. E. 1985: Externalities in economies with imperfect information and incomplete markets. *Quarterly Journal of Economics*, CI, 229–64.

Hall, Robert 1975: The rigidity of wages and the persistence of unemployment: *Brookings Papers on Economic Activity*, 2, 301–35.

Harberger, A. 1971: On measuring the social opportunity cost of labor. *International Labour Review*, 103.

Harris, J. E. and Todaro, M. 1970: Migration, unemployment and development: a two-sector analysis. *American Economic Review*, 60, 126–42.

Leibenstein, H. 1957: *Economic Backwardness and Economic Growth*. New York: Wiley.

Mirrlees, J. 1975: A pure theory of underdeveloped economies. In L. A. Reynolds (ed.), *Agriculture in Development Theory*, New Haven: Yale University.

Nalebuff, B. and Stiglitz, J. E. 1982: Quality and prices. *Econometric Research Program Research Memorandum* no. 297, May.

Sah, R. K. and Stiglitz, J. E. 1985: The social cost of labor and project evaluation: a general approach. *Journal of Public Economics*, 28, 135–63.

Salop, S. C. 1973: Wage differentials in a dynamic theory of the firm. *Journal of Economic Theory*, 6, 321–44.

Schlicht, Ekkehart 1978: Labour turnover, wage structure and natural unemployment. *Zeitschrift für die Gesamte Staatswissenschaft*, 134, 337–46.

Sen, A. K. 1968: *Choice of Techniques*, Oxford: Basil Blackwell.

Shapiro, C. and Stiglitz, J. E. 1984: Equilibrium unemployment as a worker discipline device. *American Economic Review*, 74, 433–44.

Stiglitz, J. E. 1969: Alternative theories of the determination of wages and employment on LDCs. University of Nairobi, Institute for Development Studies, mimeo.

—— 1973: Approaches to the economics of discrimination. *American Economic Review*, 62, 287–95.

—— 1974a: Theories of discrimination and economic policy. In von Furstenberg (ed.), *Patterns of Racial Discrimination*, Lexington, Lexington Publishing Company, 5–26.

—— 1974b: Alternative theories of wage determination and unemployment in L.D.C.s: the labor turnover model. *Quarterly Journal of Economics*, 88, 194–227.

—— 1976a: Prices and queues as screening devices in competitive markets. *IMMSS Technical Report* no. 212, August, Stanford University.

—— 1976b: The efficiency wage hypothesis, surplus labor and the distribution of income in L.D.C.s. *Oxford Economic Papers*, 28, 185–207.

—— 1977: Some further remarks on cost–benefit analysis. In H. Schwartz and R. Berney (eds), *Social and Economic Dimensions of Project Evaluation*, IDB, (proceedings of the symposium on cost–benefit analysis, IDB, Washington, March 1973), 253–82.

—— 1982a: Alternative theories of wage determination and unemployment: the efficiency wage model. In M. Gersovitz et al. (eds), *The Theory and Practice of Development*, London: George Allen and Unwin.

—— 1982b: The structure of labor markets in L.D.C.s. In R. Sabot (ed.) *Migration and the Labor Market in Developing Countries*, Boulder: Westview.

—— 1985: Equilibrium wage distributions. *Economic Journal*, 95. (Earlier versions appeared as a *Cowles Foundation Discussion Paper* (1972) and as an *IMSSS Technical Report* (1974).)

—— 1986: Theories of wage rigidity. NBER Working Paper.

Stiglitz, J. E. and Weiss, A. 1983: Incentive effects of terminations: applications to the credit and labor markets. *American Economic Review*, 73, 912–27.

Todaro, M. 1968: An analysis of industrialization, employment and unemployment in less developed countries. *Yale Economic Essays*, 8, 331–402.

—— 1969: A model of labor migration and urban unemployment in less developed countries. *American Economic Review*, 59, 38–48.

Weiss, A. 1980: Job queues and layoffs in labor markets with flexible wages. *Journal of Political Economy*, 88, 526–38.

Yellen, J. 1984: Efficiency wage models of unemployment. *American Economic Review*.

8 Commercial Policy for Panama in the 1980s

LARRY A. SJAASTAD

Introduction

During the past decade, the dynamism that characterized the Panamanian economy since the early 1960s has faded. The rate of growth of gross domestic product (GDP) has fallen sharply, and unemployment is high and rising. The traditional sectors of the economy (agriculture and industry) have vegetated with average growth rates of value added even below that of the economy as a whole. The leading sectors have been those associated with services – banking, the Zona Libre de Colón, and activities associated with the Panama Canal.

The study reported here, which is part of a larger research effort to define the causes and cures of the Panamanian economic stagnation, examines the contribution of international trade in the Panamanian economy and, more specifically, the role of commercial policy in shaping that contribution. The study is analytical rather than descriptive, and seeks to define an optimal foreign trade policy for Panama at its current stage of development.

This report is divided into five parts. The first, 'Protection and Trade in Panama', discusses the distinguishing features of the Panamanian economy insofar as they relate to international trade. The second section, 'The Trade and Relative Prices Model', develops

Prepared for the Ministerio de Planificación y Política Económica in connection with the economic policy studies program financed by AID/Panama. The author wishes to thank John Panzer for valuable aid in the preparation of this report, and Kenneth Clements and Daniel Wisecarver for useful comments on an earlier version.

the formal analytical apparatus, and the third section, 'The Optimum Tariff', defines alternative means by which Panama can best exploit her geographic position. The fourth section, 'Empirical Evidence', presents the findings of the statistical investigation. The final section, 'Policy Implications', sums up the findings and relates them to other parts of the study program, particularly the fiscal issues. It goes without saying that one of the major contributions of a more rational commercial policy in Panama would be enhancement of import-tariff revenues.

Protection and Trade in Panama

As is shown in table 8.1, over 40 percent of Panama's expenditure is currently devoted to imported goods and services, and nearly 40 percent of her GDP is derived from exports of goods and services. These ratios are high by international standards, even taking into account the fact that the Panamanian economy is tiny – smaller than that of Luxembourg, when measured in terms of GDP. Panama's international trade is particularly highly developed once we recognize that the ratio of value added to value of exports is extremely high; apart from exports of petroleum products, which are no longer important quantitatively, the import content of Panamanian exports is very low indeed. It is particularly noteworthy in this context to recognize that about three-quarters of Panama's exports are service exports, where the ratio of value added to value of exports is literally 100 percent. While some countries have higher ratios of trade to GDP than does Panama, it is generally true in those countries that much of their exports consist of domestically processed imports.

Moreover, Panama's foreign trade has grown, relative to GDP, despite the import-substitution policies of the 1960s and 1970s. Those policies have been singularly unsuccessful in developing the industrial sector of Panama, as is evident from table 8.2. Measured in constant dollars, value added in the industrial sector has increased, relative to GDP, from a mere 10.5 percent in 1961 (prior to the import-substitution drive) to 14.2 percent in 1981. In current dollars, that ratio has actually declined (owing to changes in relative prices). Employment in the industrial sector exhibits no trend whatsoever. Moreover, exports of industrial goods are nil, apart from a small amount of petroleum products; virtually all exports of goods with significant value added come from the agricultural and fishery sectors. In short, the strong performance of foreign trade together

Table 8.1   Panamanian foreign trade 1960–1981

	Trade volume[a]				
	Exports[b]		Imports[b]		Service Exports[c]
	Value	% GDP	Value	% GDP	Total exports (%)
1960	127.3	30.6	149.1	35.9	83.3
1961	143.1	31.2	164.7	35.9	83.5
1962	164.4	33.0	177.9	35.7	77.8
1963	171.7	31.7	187.6	34.6	75.5
1964	186.4	32.8	195.5	34.4	71.2
1965	203.7	32.6	218.4	35.0	69.8
1966	236.3	32.0	247.9	33.6	70.3
1967	270.0	33.7	276.5	34.6	71.4
1968	298.9	34.7	290.9	30.8	71.1
1969	322.0	34.1	338.1	32.3	69.1
1970	354.4	33.9	389.0	33.6	71.9
1971	389.4	33.7	434.5	33.5	73.0
1972	423.7	32.7	487.6	33.1	73.7
1973	466.8	31.7	529.6	28.9	74.1
1974	558.9	30.5	725.4	37.5	72.5
1975	625.1	32.3	764.2	38.1	67.0
1976	675.9	33.7	808.1	37.2	71.9
1977	762.6	35.1	834.4	34.0	72.9
1978	850.9	34.6	964.7	39.3	75.0
1979	960.0	33.8	1206.5	42.5	73.8
1980	1333.7	39.3	1464.2	43.1	77.4
1981	1417.4	38.1	1557.6	41.9	80.4

[a]   In millions of current dollars.
[b]   *Source: Cuentas Nacionales, Contraloría General de la República.* From total exports and imports of goods and services we have subtracted the value of imports that are exported.
[c]   *Source: Cuentas Nacionales and Anuario de Comercio Exterior, Contraloría General de la República.* Derived from the FOB value of goods exports (from Anuario de Comercio Exterior) and the total value of exports, of goods and services (from Cuentas Nacionales).

with the weak showing of the industrial sector over the past two and a half decades strongly support the hypothesis that protection in Panama is very modest. This conclusion is reinforced by the observation that, as of 1980, total tariff collections amounted to a mere six percent of total value of imports; as very few import duties are prohibitive, the average tariff rate on goods subject to duty (that is, excluding approximately 35 percent of imports that are specifically exonerated by law) must be of the order of 10 percent. This figure, of course, does not include internal taxes, such as the gasoline tax, which are equivalent to import tariffs in the Panamanian case.

Turning to the trade barriers themselves, tariffs are indeed low (by regional standards), the majority of them being 20 percent or less in *ad valorem* terms (or *ad valorem* equivalents of specific duties). Quota protection has been quite different; the bulk of the quotas are so small that they are equivalent to prohibitive tariffs. Nevertheless, the precise *protective* content of the quotas is very difficult to ascertain, as the quotas are often defined on a very narrow base. For example, resolution no. 460 of 1974 established an annual import quota of one dozen 'camisas de vestir, sport, de trabajo y otras camisas de un valor FOB menor de B/.65.89 la docena.' While an annual quota of 12 shirts is a virtual prohibition, the fact that slightly more expensive shirts can be imported free of quantitative restriction clearly robs this quota of much of its protective content. Moreover, replacement of such quotas with tariffs will have little if any effect on either protection or import-substitution activity.

In other areas, quota protection is eroded by either a failure to enforce the quota administratively or by the existence of special trading arrangements such as the 'common list' with Costa Rica. The main conclusion in this context is that quota protection has been far less effective than one might believe merely on the basis of the number and size of quotas. With some notable exceptions (e.g., certain food products), Panama has retained a high degree of openness.[1] Of the 343 quotas in effect at the end of 1982, only 14 were introduced prior to 1961, and these covered mainly dairy and tomato products – hardly sources of industrialization. During the 1960s, quota protection in the food industry expanded and that protection was also extended to certain hardware items, mainly light construction materials. The quota system was applied to the clothing and shoe industry during the 1970s, but again it is apparent from table 8.2 that there was no great response from the manufacturing sector. While the quota system of Panama has certainly generated some industrial activities that otherwise would not exist, one cannot escape the conclusion that Panama's import-substitution policy has been extraordinarily mild in comparison with that of other countries of Latin America.

Table 8.2 Size and structure of the industrial sector: Panama

	Value of production[a]		Value added[a]		Employment[b]			Growth rates[c]	
	$ 1000s	% of GDP	$ 1000s	% of GDP	Blue collar[c]	Other[d]	Percentage of total	GDP[f]	Industrial sector
1961	102.2	22.0	49.1	10.6	9544	2574	12.7	10.7	15.6
1962	113.1	22.4	50.5	10.0	10,068	2575	12.5	8.2	19.5
1963	116.4	29.8	60.5	10.8	10,362	2837	12.4	8.5	13.7
1964	183.4	30.5	71.9	12.0	11,306	2922	13.1	4.4	5.7
1965	204.0	30.9	78.7	11.9	12,007	3051	12.8	9.2	8.4
1966	229.2	31.3	89.5	12.1	13,272	3367	13.1	7.7	9.1
1967	264.1	33.0	99.6	12.4	14,712	3879	13.5	8.5	12.2
1968	287.1	33.3	109.1	12.7	15,480	4143	13.4	7.1	9.7
1969	314.0	33.2	114.9	12.2	16,272	4341	13.5	8.3	9.3
1970	356.5	34.1	146.7	14.0	17,528	4653	12.9	6.9	6.7
1971	437.7	37.8	163.3	14.1	20,594	5071	13.5	8.8	8.5
1972	483.2	37.2	173.9	13.4	20,841	5417	13.0	6.3	6.2
1973	579.1	39.3	213.0	14.5	21,917	5938	13.1	6.6	4.2
1974	861.3	46.9	257.6	14.1	21,325	5857	12.0	2.5	-4.4
1975	975.5	50.5	272.1	14.1	21,081	6077	11.7	0.6	-0.01

1976	942.3	47.0	267.8	13.4	20,548	6120	11.6	0.0	−12.0
1977	950.7	45.7	293.2	13.5	21,188	6080	12.0	4.6	0.0
1978	957.8	40.6	300.2	12.2	22,205	6225	13.2	6.5	5.7
1979	1225.4	44.9	374.4	13.2	23,551	6397	11.2	6.9	14.9
1980	n/a	n/a	n/a	n/a	n/a	n/a	n/a	5.0	3.9
1981	1655.8		527.6	14.2	26,679	7547	10.0	3.6	−2.3
Annual average rate of real growth (%)	9.7		6.7		5.1	5.2		6.2	6.2

a Average rate of real growth was calculated deflating nominal terms by GDP deflator.

b Employment data for c and d are from Industrial Sector Survey and do not represent total employment of the sector. Percentage of total employment is from Encuesta de Hogares and is based on an estimation of total employment of the sector and the economy.

c Defined as 'Operarios y obreros'.

d Includes owner-operators, family workers, non-paid workers, administrative staff, and technicians.

e In constant Balboas.

f Based on *Panamá en Cifras*, 1960 dollars.

Source: Industrial Survey, Contraloría General de la República. (The survey base was expanded in 1965 to cover industries with five or more workers. Previously it covered industries with ten or more workers.)

Panama's Service Trade

A key feature of Panamanian foreign trade is the degree to which export earnings are derived from services; historically, the ratio of services to total exports is approximately two-thirds (see table 8.1). Very few countries have this pattern of exports trade, a pattern that derives in large part from Panama's unique geographical position. The characteristics of the former canal zone, the development of the Zona Libre de Colón, the great expansion of international banking in Panama, and tourism have all contributed to service exports. Those exports are highly labor intensive, and the fact that they account for nearly a quarter of Panama's GDP indicates that approximately one half of the wage bill of Panama is paid directly by foreigners.

The dominant position of service exports in total foreign exchange earnings has several very important implications for Panama. First, trade liberalization is unlikely to have a significant impact on the industrial development of Panama; second, the overall level of protection – difficult as it may be to measure – has probably not been excessive.[2]

Turning to the first point, it is now widely held that protection can be counter-productive to the development of a country's industrial sector, and hence that trade liberalization might well be a vehicle for industrial development. It is commonly understood that protection reduces the *volume* of foreign trade and with it the scope for industry-based exports. Trade liberalization, by increasing that trade, enhances the possibility for development of export-oriented industrial activities.

For most purposes, the effects of protection can be summarized in terms of its impact on internal relative prices. Tariffs and export subsidies both increase the internal prices of the goods to which they apply, whereas export taxes and import subsidies reduce those prices. To deal with these relative price effects, we distinguish among three broad classes of goods: (1) importables, or those goods actually imported under the existing commercial policy regime; (2) exportables; and (3) those goods which are prevented by natural or artificial protection from being traded internationally. The latter will be referred to as home goods.

The key difference between home goods and tradeables (i.e., exportables and importables) lies in the nature of market equilibrium. Internal prices of tradeables are determined by external prices together with the exchange rate, import duties, export taxes, and subsidies. Roughly speaking, domestic *prices* of tradeables are determined by conditions of *international* supply and demand whereas the *quantities* produced and consumed are determined by *domestic* supply and demand conditions. In contrast, both prices *and* quantities of home goods are determined by *domestic* supply and demand. Equilibrium in the home goods market requires prices for those goods that equate supply with demand, whereas equilibrium in the market for tradeables is consistent with either excess demand or excess supply. Excess demand for (supply of) tradeables is reflected in a deficit (surplus) in the trade account of the balance of payments rather than in upward (downward) pressure on the price of tradeables.

Although prices of home goods are determined by domestic demand and supply, those prices can be influenced by commercial policy. A tariff, for example, raises the prices of importables relative to exportables and, in the first instance, relative to home goods as well. This increase in domestic prices of importables induces shifts in demand away from those goods and towards both exportables and home goods; at the same time, producers will find it more advantageous to supply import-competing goods. Accordingly, resources are drained from both the home and exportables sectors toward import-competing activities, thereby reducing the supply of both sets of goods. The reduced supply of and increased demand for home goods drives up their prices until the excess demand has been eliminated. Thus a tariff not only increases internal prices of importables relative to exportables and home goods, but also those of home goods relative to exports. Thus, a tariff reduces the real income of exporters much as does an explicit export tax.

The key issue, then, is the *incidence* of import duties and export taxes or subsidies. A uniform import duty of, say 10 percent, clearly raises the domestic prices of importables *relative* to exportables by 10 percent; in addition, it will raise prices of home goods. We might assume for example, that the latter prices increase by 6 percent (export prices being constant), with the result that domestic prices of importables have risen by only 3.8 percent relative to home goods, and domestic prices of exports have *fallen* by 5.7 percent relative to home goods. The same pattern of change in relative prices would obtain had we imposed an import duty of only 3.8 percent *and* an explicit export tax of 5.7 percent. Alternatively, we would have the same relative prices with *no* import duty, but with an export tax. Obviously, an infinite number of combinations of import duties and export taxes can produce the same relative prices.

Although the tariff in the above example is nominally paid by importers, the resulting change in relative prices is such that about 60 percent of the tariff burden is borne by producers of exportables, the other 40 percent being a subsidy for import-competing firms. 60 percent of the tariff is perceived by exporters as a reduction in their purchasing power (*vis-à-vis* home goods) whereas the command over home goods of income generated in the import-competing sector has risen by only 40 percent of the tariff.

As home goods are mainly labor-intensive services, the price of those goods is very closely related to wages. Given this similarity between wages and the price of home goods and the importance of wages in production costs, it is natural to measure the net effect of protection on any particular sector by comparing the change in the price of its output with the change in wages. A sector enjoys positive net (or 'true') protection when commercial policy increases its output price by more than wages; when wages rise by more than the output price, the sector is disprotected.

In some circumstances, the burden of a tariff falls entirely on exporters. For example, a high degree of substitutability between home goods and importables implies that the price of home goods, *relative* to importables, cannot change (or can change only by very little); consequently, a uniform import duty would increase prices of *both* importables and home goods relative to exportables by the full amount of the duty, causing 100 percent of that duty to fall on exporters in the form of reduced purchasing power over home goods and importables. Alternatively, if home goods and exportables were close substitutes, the internal price of importables would rise relative to *both* home goods and exportables by the amount of the import duty and hence that duty is equivalent, in terms of incidence, to a pure subsidy for import-competing firms.

In general, the incidence of a tariff can be decomposed into an implicit subsidy for import-competing firms and a tax on the producers of exportables. Similarly, an export subsidy, by increasing domestic prices of both exportables and home goods relative to importables, is only in part a subsidy to exporters; it is also an implicit tax on producers of importables. Finally, an export tax can be viewed as a combination of an implicit subsidy to producers of importables and an explicit tax on exporters, the latter being less than the nominal tax rate. Any combination of tariffs, export subsidies, and export taxes can, in principle, be similarly decomposed.[3]

How Panama Differs

The Panamanian situation is quite different from that of the typical country described in the foregoing pages. In Panama, the distinction between home and internationally traded goods is not appropriate owing to the key importance of service exports; Panama is a heavy exporter of what would be classified as non-traded (home) goods in most countries. In short, many so-called 'home' goods are tradeable in Panama. Thus the classification for Panama must be along the lines of goods that are importable, goods that are exportable, service exports, and domestically consumed services. The key point is that the two service activities are close substitutes owing to the high degree of potential labor mobility between the two sectors. These observations have two important implications for a study of commercial policy in Panama.

First, owing largely to extraneous factors, the service export sector of Panama has been highly dynamic, thereby limiting the arousal of intense protectionistic pressures by permitting the maintenance of an extraordinarily high volume of import trade even in the absence of an export-oriented industrial sector. Indeed, the very dynamism of service exports has 'crowded-out' industrial development in Panama. This is, of course, a variant of the 'Dutch' disease that has been widely observed in countries suddenly coming into possession of new and lucrative export industries, usually through discovery of natural resource endowments such as oil or gas. As a direct consequence of the dynamism of services, the industrial sector's share of national value added (in current Balboas) declined from 15.3 percent in 1965 to 10.5 percent in 1979, a decline that occurred despite a significant increase in protection during the 1970s.

The essential point is that any country's ability to export is constrained, in the final analysis, by its *willingness to import*. Restrictions on imports are identical in their effects to restrictions on exports; in either case a variety of subtle substitution effects are at work that maintain a relationship between imports and exports that is dictated by the determinants of expenditure relative to income. Thus there is no way in which Panamanian *commercial* policy can induce a larger export trade without simultaneously permitting a commensurate increase in imports. Trade liberalization stimulates exports precisely by opening the way for imports, thereby creating a latent trade deficit that is avoided by internal relative price changes (the main effect being a decline in real wages in the export sector).

In the Panamanian case, the restrictive effect of existing trade barriers is, as has been pointed out, quite minor; the corollary is that reduction or elimination of those barriers will induce an expansion of industrial exports only to the extent of a marginal strengthening of import demand. In a country that already expends 40 percent of its income on imports, even a country as tiny as Panama, the scope for further expansion of imports is obviously limited.

The future, of course, may be different from the past. It is clearly possible that growth of service exports will decline, thereby paving the way for an expansion in non-traditional (industrial) exports. Moreover, there is the distinct possibility that foreign supplies of capital to finance the bloated and deficit-ridden public sector of Panama will, in the face of one of the largest *per capita* external debts in the world, dry up, thereby forcing a genuine fiscal austerity that would be quickly reflected in a trade surplus. As a trade surplus implies either fewer imports or larger exports, the industrial sector is likely to benefit. The important point, however, is that neither of these developments is contingent upon, or even related to, trade liberalization.

A second implication is that, while rationalization of existing trade barriers might be highly desirable on its own merits, it is not at all clear that a reduction in the overall level of Panamanian protection is beneficial. Even after the conversion of the quota system into tariffs, there is a high variability in effective tariff rates, a variability that is magnified when translated into effective protection. The overall degree of protection, however, is quite low, owing in part to the fact that import duties on many of the goods subject to higher-than-average tariff rates are exonerated. In 1980, for example, tariff exonerations amounted to $67.21 million, whereas actual tariff collections were only $48.15 million, or 3.3 percent of the CIF (Cost, Insurance and Freight) value of Panamanian imports. Indeed, there might well be a case for increasing the overall degree of protection.

In Panama, as in other countries, trade restrictions increase wages relative to the price of exportables (as was argued earlier). As a substantial proportion of Panamanian labor services are exported directly, an increase in those wages implies an increase in Panamanian income. In short, protection is the means by which Panama can exploit her monopoly power in the market for her service exports. This point needs to be developed at length.

It is quite readily apparent that Panama does not possess any appreciable power in world markets for goods; relative to the volume of world trade, Panama imports and exports but minute quantities of goods, none of which are highly specific to either Panamanian consumption or production. The only possible exception that might come to mind is bananas, and even there Panama's share is so small (and decreasing) that her market power is undoubtedly very limited. With respect to exports of services, however, the situation is different. No other country is in the same position to supply services directly to activities in the former Canal Zone, no other country has the geographic location and corresponding transport facility that give the Zona Libre de Colón its natural, special advantages, and no other country in Latin America has the monetary system that is so crucial to Panama's role as a regional banking center. It is precisely these factors that cause Panamanian service exports to loom so large in total exports and enable Panama to gain from what is locally referred to as her 'geographic position'. However, to maximize the benefits of that position, Panama must artificially restrict the delivery of those services so as to drive up their price (i.e., Panamanian wages). In short, Panama has a monopoly position to be exploited for her own benefit.

How to be a Monopolist

There are at least three manners in which Panama can exploit whatever monopoly position she enjoys in the service export trade. The alternatives differ not only in terms of their effectiveness, but also in the degree of convenience and aesthetic quality. The most direct alternative is a flat tax on service exports, that is, a special tax on wages earned from service exports. Such a tax is attractive in that it is clean and direct; its disadvantages lie in the difficulty of identifying and isolating employments dedicated to service exports, and political difficulty associated with imposing a tax that has the appearance of discriminating against labor. In some sectors, such as retail and wholesale trade, banking, and tourism, it might well be impossible to disentangle those services that are sold to foreigners and those that are consumed at home. While these difficulties might be surmountable, they are of sufficient force to merit consideration of alternatives.

One alternative, and one that is equivalent to a direct tax on wages earned in the service export trade, is to tax all imports and subsidize all exports of goods *at the same rate*. Such a tax would induce an increase in nominal wages in Panama, thereby accomplishing the same effect as an export tax on services: relative to external prices of imports and exports of goods, Panamanian wages would be increased.

Suppose, for example, that it were desirable to increase Panamanian wages paid by foreign consumers of service exports by 10 percent, and that it turned out that this would be accomplished by imposing a 15 percent tax on service exports (if that were feasible).[4] The result would be that wages received *net of tax* by Panamanian workers would decline by 5 percent, prices of all tradeable goods remaining constant. Under the alternative tax subsidy scheme, then, it would also be necessary to reduce wages received by Panamanian workers by 5 percent relative to prices of traded goods to achieve the same set of relative prices. This could be accomplished by a uniform 15 percent import duty coupled with a 15 percent export subsidy on exports of goods; in the face of a 15 percent increase in the price of all goods, Panamanian workers would demand a 15 percent increase in their wages as well; that is, the *supply price* of labor would go up by exactly the same amount as it would after the imposition of the 15 percent export tax on services.[5] Given the assumption that the service export tax of 15 percent generated a net increase in the gross-of-tax wage rate, the import duty/export subsidy would generate exactly the same result in terms of relative prices as would the service export tax – the only difference being that nominal prices and wages would be higher under the former scheme than with the latter. This result is, of course, nothing more than an example of the Lerner symmetry theorem which demonstrates that a tax on one export is identical in its real effects to a subsidy on all other exports coupled with a tax at the same rate on all imports.

This second method of exploiting Panama's monopoly power (i.e., geographic position) is also fraught with difficulty. Although the export subsidy for goods in this context is not a true subsidy, in the sense that it merely offsets the effect in that sector of the across-the-board import duty, the rules of the existing international trade regime make no such distinction. In short, this scheme would run counter to the rules of the General Agreement on Trade and Tariffs (GATT) and would probably trigger countervailing duties in countries such as the US, thereby defeating its purpose. While both the export duty on services and the import-duty/export-subsidy for goods arrangements are 'first-best', neither appears to be feasible in practice. Only some 'second-best' alternative appears to be available.

Various second-best possibilities exist. One arrangement would be an across-the-board tax on labor income; this is second best because such a tax fails to discriminate between labor employed in activities in which Panama possesses monopoly power and those in which she does not and/or where the output is consumed domestically. As such a tax would have the effect of increasing the (gross-of-tax) supply price of labor, it would permit exploitation of monopoly power, but at the cost of introducing distortions in other segments of the Panamanian labor market. Such a tax is also excessively 'transparent' in that its discrimination against labor would be entirely too evident to make it politically feasible.[6] Whether or not it would be superior to other second-best arrangements on other grounds has not been investigated.

Another second-best scheme consists of an across-the-board tax on all imports, with no subsidy for exports of goods. Such a tax permits exploitation of monopoly power in the external services market by driving up the supply price of labor (in response to the higher cost of importables), but at the cost of increasing the real wage as seen by the goods export sector and hence effectively introducing a distortion in that sector.[7] The main advantages of this arrangement lie in its simplicity, lack of transparency, and political acceptability (given the general political bias in favor of protection and against undue taxation of wage income).

In what follows, we will formally examine the propositions discussed in the foregoing pages, and then turn to an empirical analysis. The thrust of the latter will be to determine whether or not the data support the proposition that Panama has market power in the services market, and then to estimate the optimal trade restrictions to take advantage of that power.

The Trade and Relative Prices Model

We begin with a formal model that determines the volume of trade and the structure of internal relative prices. The basic distinction is between tradeable and non-tradeable (home) goods, with tradeable goods subdivided into importables and exportables. Initially the model is defined in a general manner in which services are non-tradeables; subsequently we adapt the model to fit the Panamanian case. The basic model is taken from Sjaastad (1980).

The General Model

Import demand, or the excess demand for importables, is taken to depend upon the two relative prices in the system (p_1, p_2), the level of aggregate real production (y), and aggregate real expenditure (y^e). That demand function is assumed to be linear in logarithms, and the logarithm of a variable will be denoted by upper-case character (e.g., $M = \ln m$, where m is a quantum index of imports). We specify the import demand function in deterministic form as

$$M = \alpha + \beta P_1 + \gamma P_2 + \psi Z \qquad (1)$$

where Z is a (column) vector of all non-price variables including income (Y) and expenditure (Y^e), and ψ is a (row) vector of the relevant parameters. The export supply (i.e., excess supply of exportables) function is similarly specified:

$$X = \alpha' + \beta' P_1 + \gamma' P_2 + \psi' Z. \qquad (2)$$

Only three nominal prices exist in the model: the internal price of importables (p_m), the internal price of exportables (p_x), and the price of non-traded goods (p_h). With only three nominal prices, there can be only two relative prices, which will be arbitrarily defined as p_1 and p_2. The coefficients of P_1 and P_2 in equations (1) and (2) will depend upon the specification of p_1 and p_2, to be given later.

The implicit coefficients of Y^e and Y in equation (1) are expected to be positive and negative, respectively; at least part of an increase in aggregate expenditure will be on importables, increasing the excess demand for those goods. Likewise, part of any increase in aggregate output is likely to take the form of import-competing goods, thereby decreasing the excess demand for those goods. Note, however, that these coefficients are not to be treated as expenditure and output elasticities for importables, respectively, as M refers not to the *demand* for importables but rather the *excess* demand for those goods (i.e., imports).

Similarly, the implicit coefficients of Y^e and Y in equation (2) are expected to be negative and positive, respectively. Again, for the reason given above, they are not to be treated as the elasticities of supply of exportables with respect to aggregate production and the demand for those goods with respect to expenditure.

We shall define P_1 as $\ln(p_m/p_x) = P_m - P_x$ and P_2 as $\ln(p_h/p_x)$ $= P_h - P_x$. Consequently, the relevant substitution effects (partial derivatives of the system) together with their expected signs are as follows:

$$\partial M/\partial P_m = \beta \leq 0 \quad \partial M/\partial P_h = \gamma \geq 0$$
$$\partial M/\partial P_x = -\beta - \gamma \geq 0 \quad \text{which implies } |\beta| \geq \gamma$$
$$\partial X/\partial P_x = -\beta' - \gamma' \geq 0 \quad \partial X/\partial P_h = \gamma' \leq 0$$
$$\partial X/\partial P_m = \beta' \leq 0.$$

Subtracting (2) from (1) and rearranging, we obtain

$$P_2 = \text{constant} + [(\beta'-\beta)/(\gamma-\gamma')]P_1 + [(\psi'-\psi)/(\gamma-\gamma')]Z \quad (3)$$
$$+ [1/(\gamma-\gamma')](M-X).$$

If the substitution parameters have the expected signs indicated above, and if the integrability condition is met, the coefficient of P_1 (which we shall subsequently designate as ω) in equation (3) will be a non-negative fraction.[8] However, even if the integrability condition is not met, it has been demonstrated by Sjaastad (1980) that the absence of complementarity is sufficient to confine that coefficient to the zero-unity interval.

Equation (3) indicates the impact of protection on internal relative prices. Protection obviously increases the price of importables (p_m) relative to exportables (p_x), and hence P_1 in equation (3), but that protection also increases the price of non-traded goods relative to exportables, as the coefficient of P_1 is positive. The mechanism is a complex set of substitution effects in both demand and supply.

Equation (3) is central to estimating the *incidence* of protection discussed earlier. For example, consider the consequence of, say, a 20 percent uniform tariff.[9] The *change* in $P_2 = P_h - P_x$ is $(\beta'-\beta)/(\gamma-\gamma') \equiv \omega$ times the increase in P_1, which is approximately 0.20. If ω were to be 0.60, the equilibrium price of home goods would rise by about 12 percent relative to that of exportables. Clearly the same *relative* price structure could have been obtained by imposing a uniform tariff of approximately 8 percent together with an explicit and uniform export tax of approximately 12 percent.[10] In this sense, a tariff clearly constitutes an implicit tax on exportables, and the full effect of a tariff is better appreciated by what are defined as 'true' tariffs and 'true' subsidies.

'True' tariffs and 'true' export subsidies are defined as the hypothetical set of nominal tariffs and subsidies that would replicate the relative price structure induced by the actual tariffs and subsidies. In addition, true tariffs and subsidies, if imposed, would leave the home goods market equilibrium undisturbed. Consider the simple case of a uniform import duty at a rate t. We define the true tariff as the resultant change in the internal price of importables relative to home goods. Taking that relative price to be unity under free trade, we have

$$\tau \equiv \Delta(p_m/p_h) = [(1+t)/(1+\omega t)] - 1 = (1-\omega)t/(1+\omega t) \qquad (4)$$

where ω is the coefficient of P_1 in equation (3). The true export subsidy is similarly defined as the change in the internal price of exportables relative to home goods:

$$\sigma \equiv \Delta(p_x/p_h) = 1/(1+\omega t) - 1 = -\omega t/(1+\omega t) < 0 \qquad (5)$$

These are the 'true' tariff and subsidy counterparts of a tariff whose rate is t in the sense that τ and σ generate the same relative price structure as does the actual tariff.[11] They make explicit the fact that only part of the tariff is a true subsidy to producers of import-competing goods (and a tax on the consumers of importables), while the remainder is an implicit tax on producers of exportables (and an implicit subsidy to the consumers of those goods).

The general expressions for (4) and (5), in the presence of both the uniform import tariff t and an export subsidy at a rate s are readily shown to be

$$\tau = (1-\omega)(t-s)/[1+s+\omega(t-s)] \qquad (6)$$

$$\sigma = \omega(s-t)/[1+s+\omega(t-s)]. \qquad (7)$$

Clearly, whenever $t > s$, $\tau > 0$ and $\sigma < 0$.

The true distortion in the tradeable goods market is obviously $\tau-\sigma$. By taking the ratio of σ to $\tau-\sigma$, we see that ω is the fraction of that distortion that is an implicit tax on exporters:

$$\omega = -\sigma/(\tau-\sigma) \qquad (8)$$

and similarly, $(1-\omega)$ is the fraction of the distortion that constitutes true protection.[12]

It is straightforward to estimate equation (3) on the basis of time series data on relative prices and the other relevant variables; this estimation has been made for a number of countries, and the results are presented in table 8.3. The estimates indicate that between 50 and 60 percent of nominal protection in Argentina, Chile and Uruguay is shifted onto exporters. For Australia, Brazil and El Salvador, the proportion rises to 70 percent, and to over 90 percent in the case of Colombia. Bearing in mind the differences in structures of these economies, and in the levels of protection, there is surprising uniformity in the proportion of protection that is shifted onto the export sector.

We turn now to the effect of protection on the *volume* of international trade. As the relative price variable P_2 is endogenous in the system, it is convenient to eliminate it from equations (1) and (2). To do that, we substitute equation (3) into (1) and (2) to obtain

$$M = \text{constant} + A_1 P_1 + A_2 Z + A_3 (M-X) \tag{9}$$

$$X = \text{constant} + B_1 P_1 + B_2 Z + B_3 (M-X) \tag{10}$$

where

$$A_1 = (\beta'\gamma - \beta\gamma')/(\gamma - \gamma') \quad A_2 = (\gamma\psi' - \gamma'\psi)/(\gamma - \gamma')$$
$$A_3 = \gamma/(\gamma - \gamma') \quad B_1 = A_1 \quad B_2 = A_2$$
$$B_3 = A_3 - 1.$$

Table 8.3 Estimates of the percentage of protection paid for by exporters in seven countries. (The primary source of the results for Australia, Chile and Uruguay is Sjaastad and Clements (1981); for Argentina, Sjaastad (1980); for El Salvador, Díaz (1980); for Brazil, Fendt (1981); and for Colombia, García (1981).)

Country	Period	Percentage of protection paid for by exporters (ω)
Chile	July 1959 – December 1970	55
Uruguay	January 1966 – October 1979	53
Argentina	1935 – 1979	57
El Salvador	1st quarter 1962 – 4th quarter 1977	70
Australia	March 1950 – June 1980	70
Brazil	1950 – 1978	70
Colombia	January 1970 – December 1978	95
Mean		66

Note that for the sake of expositional simplicity, we have treated the two vectors ψ and ψ' as scalars. It is clear, however, that all variables contained in the (column) vector Z enter into equations (9) and (10) in a linear fashion.

It is obvious that equations (9) and (10) are not independent, as their respective coefficients are either identical or are characterized by linear cross-equation constraints. Moreover, ordinary least-squares estimation of either equation automatically imposes the cross-equation constraints; indeed, the transformation of equations (1) and (2) into (9) and (10) has the effect of lending least-squares estimates of equations (9) and (10) the same properties as 'seemingly unrelated regression' estimates of equations (1) and (2). Moreover, it is demonstrated in Sjaastad (1980) that least-squares estimates of the residuals of equation (9) are identical with those of equation (10). Thus it is a matter of indifference, then, whether one estimates an import demand function – equation (9) – or an export supply function – equation (10). In the final analysis, all that can be estimated, at this level of aggregation, is a trade function – either equation (9) or (10) – and the relative price equation (3). Note further that the coefficient estimates for either (9) or (10) *cannot* be treated as price or income elasticities of demand; they merely indicate the impact upon the volume of trade of distortions (or changes in the terms of trade) and changes in income and expenditure. At such a high level of aggregation, it is logically impossible to estimate the underlying elasticities without using *a priori* information.

The model developed above, while applicable to most countries as it stands, requires some modification to be used for Panama. The reason is that, in Panama, service exports are a very important part of total exports. If the price variable p_x were to include the price of services (essentially the wage rate in the service sector), that variable would be endogenous, whereas the only endogenous price variable in the model as it stands is p_h – the price of home goods (again, essentially the wage rate). Put another way, the price of home goods in Panama (p_h) is determined by the interaction of the domestic and external markets for Panamanian services.

This problem can be made evident in the context of equation (3). If p_x reflects only the prices of goods exports and if, departing from free trade, Panama were to impose a, say, 10 percent uniform tariff on all imports *and* a 10 percent export subsidy on all exports of *goods*, p_m and p_x would rise in the same proportion (10 percent), leaving P_1 of equation (3) unchanged. Holding the other variables on the right-hand side of equation (3) constant, this implies that P_2 – the dependent variable – would also be unchanged, implying that p_h would also rise by 10 percent. Normally, this would be the correct result. Imposition of a 10 percent uniform tariff and uniform export subsidy is tantamount to a devaluation of 10 percent, and it is well known that, in the final analysis, a 10 percent devaluation increases *all* prices, including wages, by 10 percent.[13] However, this is not what we would anticipate in the Panamanian case; as we have argued earlier, wages in Panama would rise by less than 10 percent in these circumstances. The reason is that the export subsidy does not apply to service exports, and hence wages earned in that activity. Consequently, equations (3), (9) and (10) do not capture the essence of Panamanian reality, and some modification is required.

The Panama Model: Incidence of Protection

The solution to the problem described above is to revise equation (3) – and hence equations (9) and (10) – to reflect the dominant role of service exports in Panama. The way to do this is to recognize that the equilibrium level of wages in Panama is reached when the supply of Panamanian service exports equals the external demand for those exports. The supply of those service exports will be taken to depend upon (among other things that will not be specified) the real wage in Panama, and the external demand to depend upon their relative price as seen by the foreign consumers. The following notation will be used:

$$P_{1g} = \ln(p_m/p_{xg}) = P_m - P_{xg}$$
$$P_{2g} = \ln(p_h/p_{xg}) = P_h - P_{xg} \simeq W - P_{xg}$$

where p_{xg} is a price index for exports of *goods only*, and W is the (logarithm of the) nominal wage rate in the service sector of Panama. Assuming internal labor mobility sufficient to equalize wages across sectors in Panama, P_{2g} is the (logarithm of the) real wage rate in the goods export sector, and $P_{2g} - P_{1g} = W - P_m$ is the (logarithm of the) real wage rate in the import-competing sector.

We specify the supply of service exports as

$$x_s^S = S[(W-P), Z^0] \quad S_1 = \partial S/\partial(W-P) > 0 \tag{11}$$

where x_s^S is to be thought of as a quantum index of service exports, and Z^0 is a vector of all other relevant variables. P is the logarithm of the domestic price level as seen by employees in the service vector, which we define as a geometric weighted average of individual prices:

$$P \equiv aP_m + bP_{xg} + (1-a-b)P_h = W + a(P_m-W) + b(P_{xg} - W).$$

Thus $W-P$ can be written as

$$W-P = (a+b)P_{2g} - aP_{1g}. \tag{12}$$

The external demand for Panamanian services is taken to be

$$x_s^D = D[(W-P^*), Z^*] \quad D_1 = \partial D/\partial (W-P^*) < 0 \tag{13}$$

where x_s^D is a quantum index of that demand, P^* the logarithm of the relevant external price level, and Z^* a vector of all other relevant (external) variables. The index P^*, of course, consists of the external prices of Panamanian exports (P_{xg}^*) and those of the rest-of-the-world tradeables, (P_R^*); again using a geometric weighted average, we define P^* as

$$P^* \equiv cP_R^* + (1-c)P_{xg}^*.$$

Given her traditionally open trade regime, Panama's imports include the vast majority of the world's tradeables, so it is a reasonable approximation to take $P_R^* = P_m^*$, where the asterisk refers to external (i.e., pre-tariff) values. Furthermore, as there are no export tariffs or other barriers (except for a few agricultural products), we take $P_{xg}^* = P_{xg}$. Accordingly, $W-P^*$ can be written as

$$W-P^* = P_{2g} - cP_{3g} \tag{14}$$

where

$$P_{3g} \equiv P_m^* - P_{xg}^* = P_m^* - P_{xg}.$$

Substituting equations (12) and (14) into (11) and (13), respectively, differentiating the latter totally, and setting $dx_s^S = dx_s^D$, we obtain

$$dP_{2g} = \omega(dP_{1g}) + \delta(dP_{3g}) + (D_2/\Delta) dZ^* - (S_2/\Delta) dZ^0, \tag{15}$$

where $\omega = aS_1/\Delta > 0$, $\delta = -cD_1/\Delta > 0$, $D_2 = \partial D/\partial Z^*$, $S_2 = \partial S/\partial Z^0$, and $\Delta = (a+b)S_1 - D_1 > 0$.

Equation (15) is the relevant version of equation (3) for Panama, and it indicates the relationship between the nominal wage in Panama and internal as well as external relative price structure. As in equation (3), the coefficient ω measures the effect of protection on nominal Panamanian wages.

The coefficients of equations (15) are themselves functions of the degree to which Panama has monopoly power in the market for her service exports. If Panama faces a perfectly elastic demand for those exports, then $-D_1 \to \infty$, which in turn implies that $\omega \to 0$ and $\delta \to c$. Given that Panamanian imports are highly heterogenous and the fact that her exports of goods are highly concentrated in a few commodities (bananas, sugar, coffee, shrimp, etc.), one suspects that P_m^* dominates P^*, with the implication that the weight c is very close to unity. Estimates of ω nd δ that are significantly positive and less than unity, respectively, will be taken as evidence that Panama does indeed possess monopoly power in the service export market. Estimates of equation (15) are presented in a subsequent section.

The above derivation can be used to demonstrate the effect of the 'first-best' commercial policy on Panamanian wage rates. Recalling that such a policy requires a uniform tariff on imports coupled with a uniform subsidy (at the same rate) on exports of goods, we have

$$p_{xg} = p_{xg}^*(1+t)$$

where t is the uniform tariff/subsidy rate, and hence

$$P_{m} \simeq P_{m}^* + t$$

with the result that

$$W - P^* \simeq P_{2g} - cP_{3g} + t. \tag{14'}$$

As a result, equation (15) becomes

$$dP_{2g} = \omega\, dP_{1g} + \delta\, dP_{3g} + (D_1/\Delta)t \tag{15'}$$

in which the terms involving Z^* and Z^0 have been neglected.

Noting that the coefficient of t in equation (15') is a negative fraction, we see that an increment to the common tariff/subsidy rate will leave P_{1g} and P_{3g} unaffected, but will *reduce* $P_{2g} = W - P_{xg}$ by some fraction of the increment in t. Thus the nominal wage will increase somewhat, indicating an increase in the real Panamanian wage from the viewpoint of external consumers of Panamanian service exports. This is precisely the manner in which an explicit service export tax would exploit Panama's monopoly position in that market. Note, however, that the real internal wage would fall, as W declines relative to both P_m and P_{xg}.

The Panama Model: Protection and the Volume of Trade

The trade model described in equations (1) and (2) above has a somewhat different reduced form in the Panamanian case owing to the fact that the wage rate – the price of service exports – enters into both relative prices, P_1 and P_2. While the influence of protection on the wage rate is given directly by equation (15), its influence on the volume of trade has to be traced through its effects on both P_1 and P_2 of equations (1) and (2).

As commercial policy in Panama has its most direct effect on P_1, we shall approach the reduction of the trade model by eliminating P_2 from equations (1) and (2).

In addition to the definitions of P_1, P_2, P_{1g}, P_{2g} and P_{3g}, we shall introduce a new definition of P_x:

$$P_x \equiv eW + (1-e)P_{xg}$$

where e is the share of service exports in total export receipts. By direct substitution, we can obtain

$$P_2 = (1-e)P_{2g} \tag{16}$$

$$P_1 = P_{1g} - eP_{2g}. \tag{17}$$

Given that P_{1g} and P_{2g} are related through the 'omega' equation (15), we can now write P_2 in terms of P_1 and P_{3g}. Neglecting dZ^* and dZ, we can obtain the following expression for equation (17) by substituting (15) into (17) and simplifying:

$$dP_1 = (1/\omega - e)\, dP_{2g} - (\delta/\omega)\, dP_{3g}. \tag{17'}$$

Using (16) to eliminate dP_{2g} from (17'), we finally obtain

$$dP_2 = [\omega(1-e)/(1-\omega e)]\, dP_1 + [\delta(1-e)/(1-\omega e)]\, dP_{3g} \quad (16')$$

which can then be used to eliminate P_2 from the differential form of equations (1) and (2):

$$dM = A_m\, dP_1 + B_m\, dP_{3g} + \psi\, dZ \tag{1'}$$

$$dX = A_x\, dP_1 + B_x\, dP_{3g} + \psi'\, dZ \tag{2'}$$

where

$$A_m = [\beta(1-\omega e) + \gamma\omega(1-e)]/(1-\omega e)$$

$$B_m = \gamma\delta(1-e)/(1-\omega e)$$

$$A_x = [\beta'(1-\omega e) + \gamma'\omega(1-e)]/(1-\omega e)$$

$$B_x = \gamma'\delta(1-e)/(1-\omega e).$$

Rather than estimate equations (1') and/or (2') directly, it is preferable to develop forms similar to equations (9) and (10), the estimates of which have the superior properties already pointed out. By subtracting equation (2') from (1'), solving the result for dP_{3g}, and substituting that expression back into (1'), we obtain

$$\begin{aligned}
dM = {}& [(A_xB_m - A_mB_x)/(B_m-B_x)]\, dP_1 \\
&+ [(B_m\psi' - B_m\psi)/(B_m-B_x)]\, dZ \\
&+ [(B_m/(B_m - B_x))]\, (dM - dX)
\end{aligned}$$

A similar expression can be obtained for dX.

It is readily established that A_m, A_x and B_x are negative and that B_m is positive; this establishes that the numerator of the coefficient of dP_1 in equation (9') is negative. Moreover, from the definitions of B_m and B_x, it is readily seen that the sign of B_m-B_x is the same as that of $\gamma-\gamma'$, which is unambiguously positive. As expected, the volume of imports varies inversely with P_1, and hence is reduced by protection. Finally, it can be shown with sufficient effort that the coefficients of equation (9') are identical, in terms of the basic parameters of equations (1) and (2), with those of equation (9). That is

$$(A_xB_m-A_mB_x)/(B_m-B_x) = A_1 = (\beta'\gamma-\beta\gamma')/(\gamma-\gamma')$$

etc. Thus the estimation is simple and straightforward for the Panamanian case, and the results have the same interpretation as for any other country.

One difference must be kept in mind, however, and that is the effect of protection on the volume of trade. In those cases where P_x is exogenous (the country being a price taker), the elasticity of trade with respect to protection is simply the coefficient of dP_1 in equation (9'). However in the Panamanian case,

$$P_1 = P_m-P_x = P_m - eW - (1-e)P_{xg}.$$

As a consequence

$$dP_1/dt = dP_m/dt - e(dW/dP_m)\,dP_m/dt.$$

Taking $dP_m/dt = 1$, and $dW/dP_m=\omega$ (from equation (15)), we have

$$dP_1/dt = 1 - e\omega$$

rather than unity, as would be the case for a country that is a price taker in the export market. The final result – the effect of protection on the volume of trade – is

$$dM/dt = A_1(1 - e\omega). \qquad (18)$$

The Optimum Tariff

In this section we derive a precise statement of the 'optimum' tariff for Panama, optimum in the sense that it maximizes available gains from exploitation of Panama's monopoly position in the international services market. We consider two cases, the 'first-best' solution, which involves a tax on service exports, and a 'second-best' arrangement, in which monopoly power is exploited by an across-the-board import duty.

Export Tax on Services

This case is depicted in figure 8.1. The curve labelled S is the supply of Panamanian services available for export, and the curve labelled D is the external demand for those services.[14] Under free trade, the equilibrium position is at the intersection of S and D, with the Panamanian wage rate of $\bar{w}$ and a quantity of service exports equal to $\bar{x}$ (the s subscript being suppressed for convenience). In this case, no monopoly power is being exploited, and the problem is to find the rate of taxation that will maximize the benefits to Panama from her service exports.

To do that, let us arbitrarily fix a tax on service exports such that the gross-of-tax cost of services to foreigners is w_0^*; as a result the internal Panamanian wage declines to w_0, and the volume of service exports falls to x_0. The export tax is defined by $w_0 = (1-t)w_0^*$, where t is the tax rate and w^* indicates the external 'price' of services. Now consider incrementing that tax by a small amount, so that w^* increases, w decreases, and x declines as indicated by broken lines in figure 8.1.

As a consequence, the rectangle labelled A becomes a loss to foreigners but a gain of tax revenue to the government as a result of the tax increase. The hatched rectangle labelled B is a loss of tax revenue to the government, and is gained by no one. The

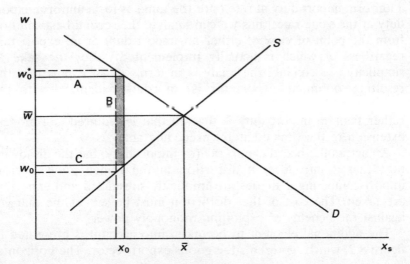

Figure 8.1 The first-best solution

rectangle labelled C is also a gain in tax revenue to the government, but as it comes at the expense of income to Panamanian workers, the net gain to Panama associated with area C is zero. The net gain to Panama is the sum of the areas A and B. The point of the experiment is to continue incrementing the tax rate until the net incremental gain is zero so as to exploit the monopoly position fully.

The area A is equal to $x \Delta w^*$, and B is obviously $tw^* \Delta x$, where Δ now indicates the change in a variable. Thus we set

$$x \Delta w^* + tw^* \Delta x = 0$$

and solve for t:

$$t = -(x/w^*) \Delta w^*/\Delta x = -1\eta$$

where η is the elasticity of external demand for services. This is, of course, a familiar result.

If, as was argued earlier, it is not feasible to tax Panamanian service exports no employ any other first-best arrangement, we must consider a second best; that is, tax all imports at a flat rate, which we will also designate as t.

The Second-Best Solution

By the Lerner symmetry theorem, we know that the real effects of a uniform import duty at rate t are the same as for a uniform export duty at the same rate; thus we can analyse the second-best solution from the point of view of either an import duty or an export tax, regardless of which is actually implemented.[15] For the sake of simplicity, we conduct the analysis in terms of an export tax; the resulting 'optimum' export tax is, of course, identical with the 'optimum' import tax. The advantage of imagining an export tax rather than an import duty is that all that is required is a modest extension of the (immediately) preceding analysis.

An across-the-board export tax (or import duty) has the disadvantage that it introduces a distortion in the traded *goods* sector; import-competing activities are implicitly subsidized and exporters are taxed. The cost of that distortion must be set, at the margin, against the benefits of exploiting monopoly power.

The additional element to be taken into account is presented in figure 8.2, which represents the goods export sector. The horizontal

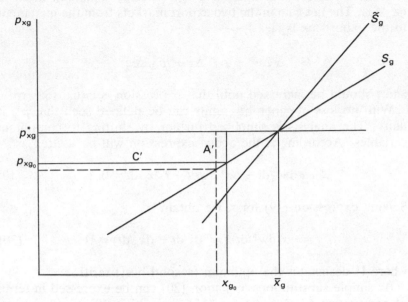

Figure 8.2   The second-best solution

line labelled p^*_{xg} is the external demand for goods exports, and the curve labelled $\tilde{S}_g$ is the supply of those goods at a given wage rate. The less steep curve labelled S_g is the supply of those goods taking into account the fact that introduction of a general export tax (on services as well as goods) will reduce the wage rate and hence the costs as seen by exporters.

Under free trade, a volume $\bar{x}_g$ of goods would be exported at a price to producers of p^*_{xg}. Let us now imagine that we have an export tax that reduces the price to exporters to $P_{xg_0} = (1-t)p^*_{xg}$, and the quantity exported to x_{g_0}. Let us now consider incrementing that tax slightly; as a consequence, the government loses tax revenue in an amount indicated by the rectangle A'; the government gains revenue by an amount indicated by the rectangle C', but as that gain comes at the expense of Panamanian exporters, the net gain to Panama with respect to the area C' is zero. The consequence is a net *loss* of revenue equal to the rectangle A'; this loss has to be set against the gain of rectangle A in figure 8.1 and the loss of rectangle B in the same figure.

The rectangle A' in figure 8.2 is obviously equal, in area, to $tp_{xg}^* \Delta x_g$. The net gain in the two export markets from the increment to the export tax is clearly

$$x \Delta w^* + tw^* \Delta x + tp_{xg}^* \Delta x_g$$

and t should be increased until that expression is equal to zero.

With no loss of generality, units can be defined such that p_{xg}^* is unity. The analysis is simplified further by shifting to continuous variables. Accordingly, the above expression will be written as

$$x \, dw^*/dt + tw^* \, dx/dt + t \, dx_g/dt = 0. \tag{19}$$

Solving expression (19) for t, we obtain

$$t = -x(dw^*/dt)/(w^* \, dx/dt + dx_g/dt) \equiv \Pi \tag{20}$$

where Π designates the optimum (second-best) tariff.

By simple substitutions, equation (20) can be expressed in terms of parameters from equations (15) and either (9) or (9′). First, define r as total revenue from exports:

$$r = w^*x + p_{xg}^* x_g = w^*x + x_g.$$

Now the change in total revenue in response to an increment in the tariff rate is

$$dr/dt = w^* \, dx/dt + x \, dw^*/dt + dx_g/dt$$

which permits us to write the denominator of equation (20) as

$$w^* \, dx/dt + dx_g/dt = dr/dt - x \, dw^*/dt.$$

Defining $W^* = \ln w^*$ and $R = \ln r$, and introducing the immediately preceding expression into the denominator of equation (20), we obtain

$$\Pi = -(dW^*/dt)/[(r/w^*x) \, dR/dt - dw^*/dt].$$

Note that if we interpret Π as a uniform import duty, there is no distinction between W and W^* (i.e., before- and after-tax wage rate). Furthermore, changing the import duty rate will have no effect on P_{xg}, P^*_{xg}, or P^*_m in equation (15); the only effect will be on P_m. Consequently, in the context of equation (15), $dW^*/dt = dW/dt = dW/dP_m = dP_2/dP_{1g} = \omega$.[16]

In addition, note that in equation (9) the coefficient of A_1 (which is the same as that of P_1 in equation (9′)) is the elasticity of the quantum of imports with respect to P_1; consequently, holding P_{xg}, P^*_{xg}, and P^*_m constant as we vary the rate of the import duty, we have $dM/dt = (dM/dP_1) \, dP_1/dt$ which, from equations (9) and (18), is equal to $A_1(1-e\omega)$.

Given P^*_m, however, the elasticity of expenditure (net of import duty) on imports with respect to the import duty itself (t), is the same as the elasticity of the quantum of imports with respect to that duty. Denoting that expenditure as r' and setting $R' = \ln r'$, it follows that $dR'/dt = dM/dt = A_1(1-e\omega)$. Finally, given that commercial policy has no predictable effect on the difference between R and R' (that difference being determined by the relationship between income (y) and expenditure (y^c)), it follows that $dR/dt = dR'/dt$.[17] Noting that, by definition, $e = w^*x/r$, we can write the optimum (second-best) import duty as

$$\Pi = \omega/[\omega - A_1(1-e\omega)/e]. \tag{21}$$

In the Panamanian case, the coefficient $1/e$ is approximately 1.35 at the current time.

Finally, it is possible to estimate the elasticity of external demand for Panamanian service exports, η. Under the first-best solution, the term $\Pi \, dx_g/dt$ of equation (19) drops out, and we have

$$\Pi' = -x(dw^*/dt)/(w^* \, dx/dt) = -(dW^*/dt)/(dX/dt) \tag{22}$$

as the optimum tariff. Let us now define

$$\theta \equiv d[\ln(w^*x/r)]dt$$

as the response of the share of service exports in total exports to a change in the tariff rate. From the definition of θ, we have

$$\theta = dW/dt + dX/dt - dR/dt.$$

Hence

$$dX/dt = \theta - dW^*/dt + dR/dt$$
$$= \theta - \omega + A_1(1-e\omega).$$

Consequently,

$$\Pi' = -\omega/[A_1(1-e\omega) + \theta - \omega] = 1/\eta$$

and

$$\eta = [A_1(1-e\omega) + \theta - \omega]/\omega.$$

Empirical Evidence

In this section we present the empirical evidence based on estimates of the trade equation (9), the incidence equation (15), and the composition of exports equation. Time series data for the 1958–81 period were employed exclusively; data on all variables are presented in the appendix.

The precise definitions of the raw variables are to be found in the appendix. The wage series, w, refers to the private sector only (the public sector was excluded as the rate of growth of the wage rate in that sector was much lower, perhaps reflecting a change in composition) and is based upon social security data. Domestic prices of imports are drawn from the wholesale price index (WPI). PM2 refers to the imports subsection of the WPI, PM3 to that subsection with petroleum prices included, PM4 to a combination of parts of the import subsection with the prices of import-competing goods in the industrial subsection of the WPI, and PM5 is PM4 augmented by petroleum prices. The goods exports price index, PX_g, was constructed on the basis of export prices and quantities for Panama's principal exports of goods. Detail concerning the construction of that index, as well as the raw data concerning prices of the goods that enter into that index, are presented in the statistical appendix.

The overall export price index, PX, is a Divisia index of PX_g and w, in which the percentage change in the export index from year to year is a weighted average of the percentage change in the goods export price and nominal wages. The weights are e_t and $(1-e_t)$, where e_t is the share of service exports in total exports during year t. That is

$$\Delta PX = e_t\Delta w_t + (1 - e_t)\Delta PX_t^*$$

where PX, W and PX_g are taken to be the natural logarithms of the actual series.

External prices of tradeables, PM* and PX*, are obtained from the unit-value data on imports and exports as published by the IMF *International Financial Statistics* (IFS). Basic trade data are obtained from the *Anuario de Comercio Exterior*.

The quantum indexes of imports and exports are based on the basic trade data and the IFS unit values. A problem arises because of exports of petroleum products, which were very substantial during several years. These exports consist of imported crude petroleum plus a relatively small amount of value added in the refinery plus transport. To eliminate the effect of these petroleum exports, the value of both imports and exports was reduced in each year by the physical volume of exports of petroleum products (measured in gallons) times the average gallon price of crude petroleum imports. Thus the import data do not contain any imports of crude petroleum that were subsequently exported in the form of finished products, and the export series contains only the Panamanian value added in those products. The values of imports and exports were then converted to quantum indexes by deflating them by the IFS unit values of imports and exports, respectively.

The variable z in equation (9') involves a linear combination of output (y) and expenditure (y^c). Expenditure was eliminated from that variable by the following approximation: when the home goods market is in equilibrium, it follows that

$$y^c = y + (m' + x')$$

where m' and x' are the values of imports and exports in Balboas but at *external* (i.e., pre-tariff) prices. Thus $(m' - x')$ is the trade balance in domestic currency. Letting capital letters be natural logarithms of lower-case letters, we have

$$\begin{aligned} Y^c &= \ln(y + m' - x') \\ &= Y + \ln[1 + (m' - x')/y] \\ &\simeq Y + (m' - x')/y \simeq Y' + \text{BT}. \end{aligned}$$

That is, the BT variable is defined as the trade balance measured as a fraction of GDP. The variables Y and BT were then entered in the regressions in a linear fashion.

The main results of the study are summarized in tables 8.4 and 8.5. The definitions of the variables in those tables are as follows (all variables in natural logarithms):

$$P^a_{1g} = PM2 - PX_g$$
$$P^b_{1g} = PM3 - PX_g$$
$$P^c_{1g} = PM4 - PX_g$$
$$P^d_{1g} = PM5 - PX_g$$
$$P_{2g} = W - PX_g$$
$$P_3 = PM^* - PX^*$$
$$P^a_1 = PM2 - PX$$
$$P^b_1 = PM3 - PX$$
$$P^c_1 = PM4 - PX$$
$$P^d_1 = PM5 - PX$$
$$Y = \ln \text{ of GDP}$$

BT = trade balance as defined above

M = ln of quantum index of imports, as defined above

X = ln of quantum index of exports, as defined above

$$MX = M - X.$$

The results on the incidence equation, which estimate ω and δ in equation (18), are extremely strong. Depending upon the method of estimation (ordinary least-squares – OLS – or Cochrane–Orcutt – CORC), the estimates of ω range from 0.38 to 0.57, the average being almost exactly 0.50. The t-ratios are very high, and the overall fit is excellent. Despite very high serial correlation in the OLS estimates, the CORC versions produce surprisingly similar results.

The estimates of δ (coefficient of P_3 in table 8.4) are also very good. The range is from 0.35 to 0.56, the average being about 0.45 for the CORC estimates. The t-ratios are high, clearly sufficient to reject the hypothesis that the true value of δ is near unity. The evidence from these estimates is powerful in its support of the proposition that Panama does have a monopoly position in the market for service exports.[18] These estimates indicate that a, say, 10 percent uniform import (or export) tariff would increase Panamanian (private-sector) wages by about 5 percent, thereby increasing measured national income by about 1.3 percent.[19]

The Trade Equation

Table 8.5 contains the empirical results for the trade equations (9) and (9'). the BT variable was consistently and grossly insignificant statistically, and hence was dropped from the regression. The MX variable was at best marginally significant in some regressions, with a coefficient of about one quarter; as it is of no significance to our analysis, the results on that variable are not reported in table 8.5.

Table 8.4 Estimates of incidence equation (15).† 1966–81 annual data.
(*t*-ratios are given in parentheses)

	P_{1g}^a	P_{1g}^b	P_{1g}^c	P_{1g}^d	P_3	R^2	ρ	DW
OLS	0.54	—	—	—	0.43	0.84	0.51	0.96
	(8.36)				(3.17)			
CORC	0.57	—	—	—	0.35	0.79	—	—
	(6.45)				(2.60)			
OLS	—	0.46	—	—	0.56	0.83	0.50	0.98
		(8.05)			(3.84)			
CORC	—	0.48	—	—	0.50	0.77	—	—
		(6.16)			(3.43)			
OLS	—	—	0.47	—	0.45	0.82	0.53	0.91
			(7.63)		(3.05)			
CORC	—	—	0.51	—	0.37	0.76	—	—
			(5.87)		(2.60)			
OLS	—	—	—	0.42	0.56	0.81	0.52	0.93
				(7.49)	(3.60)			
CORC	—	—	—	0.44	0.50	0.75	—	—
				(5.71)	(3.27)			
CORC	0.57	—	—	—	—	0.66	—	—
	(5.07)							
CORC	—	0.42	—	—	—	0.53	—	—
		(3.86)						
CORC	—	—	0.50	—	—	0.61	—	—
			(4.55)					
CORC	—	—	—	0.38	—	0.51	—	—
				(3.67)				

† See the appendix for exact definitions.

The results of the estimation of the trade equation strongly support the model. Most of the estimates of the price elasticity of trade are highly significant and all are negative. The effect of income on the volume of trade is virtually one of proportionality – the elasticity of the volume of trade with respect to GDP is unity in Panama. The coefficient of the price elasticity, when internal relative prices are used (i.e., P_1^a through P_1^d), ranges from -0.33 to 0.59; the smaller values correspond to P_1^b and P_1^d which incorporate the price of crude petroleum in the price index for imports. As a consequence, those variables have a larger variance and hence a smaller coefficient. As petroleum exports do not enter into the export price

Table 8.5   Estimates of trade equation (9). (Estimates for the 1966–81 period, annual data; absolute value of t-ratios in parentheses. MX variable present but not significant; BT variable deleted as it was always grossly insignificant)

	P_1^a	P_1^b	P_1^c	P_1^d	Y	R^2	ρ	DW
OLS	−0.59				1.03	0.98	0.13	1.72
	(2.73)				(13.73)			
CORC	−0.55				1.02	0.98	0.13	—
	(2.31)				(12.43)		(0.51)	
OLS	—	−0.40			1.05	0.98	0.08	1.80
		(2.25)			(10.85)			
CORC	—	−0.36			1.04	0.97	0.08	—
		(1.92)			(9.95)		(0.33)	
OLS	—	—	−0.50		1.07	0.98	0.09	1.79
			(2.78)		(12.51)			
CORC	—	—	−0.47		1.06	0.98	0.09	—
			(2.42)		(11.41)		(0.37)	
OLS	—	—	—	−0.35	1.06	0.98	0.08	1.82
				(2.29)	(10.63)			
CORC	—	—	—	−0.33	1.05	0.97	0.08	—
				(1.98)	(9.76)		(0.31)	
OLS†	−0.74	—	—	—	1.04	0.98	0.25	1.47
	(2.62)				(13.11)			
CORC†	−0.64	—	—	—	1.01	0.97	0.25	—
	(2.10)				(11.91)		(1.02)	

† Price variable is PM* − PX rather than P_1^a.

index of any of the price variables, the importance of petroleum is likely to be overstated in P_1^b and P_1^d; consequently, greater significance should be attached to the results using P_1^a and P_1^c. The regressions with those price variables indicate that the volume of trade has an elasticity of approximately −0.5 with respect to the internal price of importables relative to exportables.

The final two regressions utilize a different relative price variable, that variable being the (logarithm of the) ratio of the external price of importables (PM*, defined as the IFS index of unit values of imports) to the internal price of exportables, P_x. The Cochrane–Orcutt estimate of the price elasticity using that variable is −0.64, well within the confidence interval for the estimates of the price elasticity using other variables. On the whole, the results suggest that the parameter A_1 of equation (9) lies in the range of

−0.45 to −0.65. We shall, for what follows, assume a value of −0.55 for A_1.

As was noted in equation (18), the effect of protection over the volume of trade is given by $A_1(1-e\omega)$. Using 0.50 as the value of ω and 0.80 for e (the value as of 1983), we have

$$dM/dt = -(0.55)[1 - (0.80)(0.50)]$$
$$= -0.33.$$

Increasing the overall level of protection by 10 points would result in a decline in the volume of trade by about 3.3 percent.[20]

The Optimum Tariff

Taking a value of 0.50 for ω, 0.33 for $A_1(1-e\omega)$ and using the current ratio of service to total exports of about 0.80, the second-best optimum tariff (equation (21)) is estimated to be 55 percent. There is a very strong caveat to be taken into account, however. This estimate of the optimum tariff does not take into account the social costs of smuggling that would be induced by such a high tariff. Smuggling is very much like 'diversion' in the context of regional integration, in that it involves the conversion of tariff revenue (essentially an internal transfer) into real resource costs. As smuggling is an activity with absolute freedom of entry, there is no presumption that smugglers would earn significant rents, and hence their earnings – the difference between the CIF and the internal price of the smuggled item – would be approximately equal to the loss in tariff revenue, and would reflect the loss in output in activities from which they are drawn. The income earned by smugglers, then, is pure social cost, with very little social return. In effect, smuggling involves a second distortion in the system, one that was not taken into account in the formal analysis.[21] An increase in the tariff rate would increase the magnitude of smuggling, thereby incurring a social cost far in excess of the social value of the activity. One can be very certain that if it were possible to take the costs of smuggling into account, one would arrive at a significantly lower optimum tariff for Panama, particularly in view of the excellent opportunities afforded that activity by the peculiar characteristics of Panama. We return to this topic in the next and final section.

Finally, we are able to estimate the elasticity of the external demand for Panamanian service exports. The final equation that was estimated was the following:

$$\ln(w^*x/r) = \text{constant} + \frac{0.26P_1^a}{(2.48)} \quad R_2 = 0.31$$

which provides an estimate of θ. Combining this with our other estimates, the indicated elasticity is -1.14.

Policy Implications

The main idea that emerges from the foregoing analysis is that there is a strong case for a uniform tariff in Panama, but it must be clearly understood that this is *not* a case for protection. Exploiting monopoly power is one thing, the idea of trying to promote domestic industry and employment via commercial policy is quite another. Indeed, attempting to do the two simultaneously is quite obviously self-defeating.

The results of the analysis in this paper indicate that restraints on trade in Panama, no matter what form they might take, have the effect of increasing Panamanian wages. As has been pointed out, that increase in wages has exactly the same effect as would a tax on exports. To attempt to promote industrial development and employment via protection is self-defeating; whatever jobs might be created in the protected import-competing sector are sacrificed in the export-oriented sector. The evidence supporting this proposition is overwhelming in Panama, as in a growing number of other countries.

The argument for a tariff in Panama, then, is on quite different grounds from those for protection. The case for a tariff in Panama is pure and simple: exploit monopoly power in the world market for Panamanian services.

As has been argued, a tariff is a second-best means of exploiting that monopoly position. Were it feasible to tax the earnings of service exporters directly, that would be a superior alternative. Indeed, it is not at all clear that monopoly power is uniform in the services export sector, but the data simply do not permit any discriminated analysis. Given the level of available information, the best that one can do is recommend an across-the-board tariff.

As was indicated in the preceding section, our best estimate of the level of the across-the-board tariff is 55 percent, but this is before taking the contraband issue into account. Past experience (e.g., the 1972 fiscal 'reform') indicates that smuggling emerges with great ease in Panama; apart from the philosophical issue involved in setting a government policy that promotes law avoidance, the economic issue is clear – smuggling is an activity with a very low ratio of social benefit to social cost (not withstanding the fact that the ratio of private benefit to private cost may exceed unity). Consideration of the smuggling issue clearly reduces the optimum tariff. On these grounds alone, it would appear foolhardy to re- commend a uniform tariff above the 20 to 25 percent range.

It is recognized that a proposal for a uniform tariff will meet with great opposition. Neither business people nor consumers can understand the logic of taxing the importation of items not produced domestically. The reason for that view is that everyone thinks of a tariff as a means of protection; as has been pointed out earlier, protection for some groups comes at the expense of disprotection for others: there is no free lunch.

The great advantage of a uniform tariff – one striking capital goods, raw materials, etc., as well as final consumer goods – is that *effective* protection will also be uniform and equal to the rate of nominal protection. In general, there is no basis whatsoever on economic grounds to favor one activity over another; the fact that certain parts of the industrial sector of Panama have been pampered in no way justifies an extension of that practice. Moreover, once an exception is made to the uniform-tariff principle, other exceptions will arise as surely as night follows day. Once exceptions are admit- ted, it is nearly impossible to determine the exact consequences in terms of effective protection. It goes without saying that the public sector, particularly public-sector enterprises, must be subject to the same treatment as is given the private sector in terms of commercial policy.

It must be further recognized that an across-the-board tariff at a rate of, say, 25 percent is an indirect tax on labor. Consideration must be given, in the grand design of fiscal policy, to tax offsets for labor. The intention of the uniform tariff is not to impoverish Panamanian labor, but rather to raise the cost of that labor to foreigners.

Fiscal Implications

Let us now consider the fiscal effects of establishing a *minimum* import duty of 25 percent. Estimates will be made on the basis of the 1980 volume of trade, as that is the last year for which sufficient information is available for this purpose.

Note that the estimates that follow do not correspond to a *uniform* import duty of 25 percent. Certain imports are currently taxed at a rate substantially in excess of 25 percent, whereas others are not taxed at all. In addition, the entire public sector is exonerated from import taxes, and the items subject to that exoneration tend, in most cases, to have very high import duties. Indeed, it almost appears as if the exonerations are matched to the more highly taxed items to ensure a state monopoly on importation of a wide variety of goods. For example, powdered milk imports are taxed at a rate in excess of 150 percent, but importation of powdered milk by the state marketing institution is exonerated. Obviously this is equivalent to giving that institution an exclusive import licence.

In deriving our estimates of the fiscal consequences of a minimum import duty of 25 percent, we shall assume the following features:

1. All duties currently in excess of 25 percent remain except for on those imports currently exonerated with importation monopolized by state institutions. In the latter case, it is assumed that all *exonerations will be eliminated* except for those of the central government and diplomats, and existing contracts with the private sector.
2. Crude petroleum will continue to be imported duty-free, as import-duty equivalents are already in place in the form of the gasoline tax, etc.
3. Bilateral agreements on 'common lists' will continue to be honored.

One estimate of the effect of the 25 percent minimum import duty is based on 25 percent of the non-exonerated import base, and hence is an underestimate of the increase in tax revenues, as it does not take into account actual revenues arising from the excess of some duties over 25 percent. That estimate is obtained as follows, using data supplied by the Ministerio de Hacienda for 1980. All figures are in millions of dollars.

1980 Imports of goods:	$1288.88
Less:	
Bilateral agreements	41.35
Diplomatic corps	5.11
Private sector contracts	241.45
Central government	17.73
Crude petroleum	386.88
Taxable imports:	$ 596.36

If taxable imports all paid 25 percent import duty, collections would be $149.09 million, in comparison with actual global tax collections on foreign trade of $78.4 million in 1980. The increase, $70.69 million, amounts to 2.1 percent of 1980 GDP (in current dollars). Given the increase in both nominal GDP and trade since 1980 of approximately one-third, the reform in question would generate at least an additional $95 million of fiscal revenue during 1984. As indicated, this is a lower limit, as the actual average import duty would in fact be in excess of 25 percent if a minimum duty of 25 percent were imposed.

An alternative computation is based on actual tariff collections, and estimates of what those collections would amount to if the rate were increased to 25 percent. The following tabulation summarizes the results:

Import category	Import base ($m)	to revenue ($m)
Free importation	65.138	16.285
Autonomous inst.	120.950	30.237
Mixed companies	7.560	1.890
Special laws	17.089	4.272
5% duties (to 25%)^{25}	55.455	11.091
10% duties (to 25%)^{25}	98.389	14.758
15% duties (to 25%)^{25}	31.603	3.160
20% duties (to 25%)^{25}	56.649	2.832
Total		84.535

The value of imports subject to 5, 10, 15, and 20 percent tariffs had to be estimated. For that purpose we used as a proxy for the share of the value of goods subject to the above tariffs, relative to total goods imports, the share of the *number* of goods subject to 5, 10, 15 and 20 percent tariffs relative to the total number of goods classified under diverse tariffs. We then proceeded to multiply that share by the hypothetical total import tax base calculated in the former procedure, thus obtaining an estimated value of imports subject to tariffs under 25 percent. This estimation was only applied to goods subject to *ad valorem* tariffs; all goods subject to specific import tariffs whose *ad valorem* tariff equivalent is lower than 25 percent would also be subject to higher tariffs under the new proposed scheme, thus allowing for the possibility of even higher tax collections on imports.

Under this calculation, 1980 revenues would increase by $84.535 million, or 2.5 percent of 1980 GDP. As of 1984, the increase would be approximately $112 million.

Neither of the above calculations takes account of the fact that the volume of trade would contract slightly as a consequence of the increase in tariff rates. Based on our estimate of the elasticity of the response of trade to protection of −0.33, and assuming that tariff rates are, on the average, increased by about 18 points in moving to a minimum duty of 25 percent, the decline in imports would be of the order of 6 percent. In view of that, it seems reasonable to expect that the reform suggested above would generate, as of 1984, approximately $100 million in additional revenue for the central government.

Appendix

PM2   Corresponds to the imported-goods subset of the wholesale price index (WPI). The price data are obtained by a survey of the wholesale prices charged by importers.
Source: Contraloría General de la República.

PM3   Was obtained by constructing a weighted average of the imported goods subset of the WPI index (PM2) and the oil and oil-related-products price index (P_{oil}) from the industrial subset of the WPI.

$$PM3 = 0.864 \; PM2 + 0.136 \; P_{oil}.$$

The weights are from the WPI renormalized such that they sum to 1.0.
Source: Contraloría General de la República.

PM4   Also based on the WPI, this is an alternative to PM2 in that it tries to capture the effect of prohibitive tariffs and quotas on the internal price of importables by surveying prices of import-substituting industries. For that matter, PM4 is a weighted average of groups in the import sector as well as the industrial sector of the WPI.

Import Component of the WPI:
Non-edible materials except industrial oil   (NEM): 0.01
Chemical products   (CP): 0.12
Manufactured articles classified by material   (MACBM): 0.28
Machinery and transport materials   (MTM): 0.29

Industrial Component of the WPI:

Food products	(FP):	0.13
Beverages and tobacco	(BAT):	0.03
Miscellaneous manufactured articles	(MMA):	0.14
		1.00

The weights correspond to those that each group has in the import classification of the renormalized WPI. The price indices of the various components are in table 8.A5.
Source: Contraloría General de la República.

PM5   A weighted average of PM4 and the oil and oil-related-products price index from the industrial subset of the WPI.

$$\text{PM5} = 0.864\ \text{PM4} + 0.136\ P_{oil}.$$

The weights are from the WPI renormalized such that they sum to 1.0.
Source: Contraloría General de la República.

PM*   Captures the international price of imports and corresponds to Panama's unit value of imports index.
Source: International Financial Statistics Supplement on Trade Statistics. Supplement Service no. 4, 1982.

W   A private sector wage index compiled for each year's month of August.
Source: Contraloría General de la República.

PX$_g$ Built as a weighted average of Panama's major goods exports. Since there is no direct source from which to obtain these prices, we proceeded to calculate the unit value per kilogram for sugar, coffee, shrimp and fishmeal and the unit value per bunch for bananas. In order to do so we obtained each year's total FOB value of exports and kilograms or bunches exported for each good. To build the index, we then normalized each unit-value series with the 1970 unit value of each good. We have assumed that these goods are homogeneous across time. The goods and their weights are:

Sugar	: 0.170
Banana	: 0.426
Coffee	: 0.061
Shrimp	: 0.292
Fishmeal	: 0.051
	1.000

The weights correspond to each good's share in the 1979 total of goods exports, renormalized such that they sum to 1.0. The unit values of these goods prior to normalization are in table 8.A4.
Source: Contraloría General de la República.

PX   Captures the price path of Panama's total exports. It is based on two series of prices: PX* which represents the price of goods exports and w representing the price of service exports. It is a Divisia index in which the percentage change of the export price index is a weighted average of the percentage change of PX* and w. The weights are variable and correspond to each year's share of service exports in total exports (e_t) and the share of goods exports in total exports ($1 - e_t$); these shares were obtained from the total values of exports and imports of both goods and services including petroleum as they appear in *Cuentas Nacionales*. For a given year base = 100 the index is constructed with this relation:

$$\frac{\Delta PX_t}{PX} = (e_t) \frac{\Delta w_t}{w} + (1 - e_t) \frac{\Delta PX_t^*}{PX^*}$$

PX*   Corresponds to Panama's external price of exports.
Source: International Financial Statistics Supplement on Trade Statistics. Supplement Service no. 4, 1982.

M   A quantum index of imports, built as the value of imports of goods and services net of crude oil imports that are exported in the form of oil derivatives (IMPORT), deflated by PM* the external price of Panama's imports. The total value of imports was obtained directly from Cuentas Nacionales while the amount of crude oil imports that are re-exported had to be estimated. From the *Anuario de Comercio Exterior* we obtained the average price of crude imports and the average price as well as value of derivative exports to the Canal Zone and countries. From *Balanza de Pagos* we obtained the value of exports to ships and airplanes. The value of total derivative exports is the sum of the sales to the Canal Zone, countries, ships, and airplanes which, divided by the average price of derivative exports from Commercio Exterior, gives an approximation of the amount of gallons valued at the price of crude oil imports, and yields an approximation of the value of crude re-exported.

Source: Contraloría General de la República. International
Financial Statistics Supplement Series no. 4, 1982.

X   A quantum index of exports, built as the value of goods and
services exports from *Cuentas Nacionales* net of crude oil
exports (EXPORT), deflated by PX, the overall price of exports
index.
Source: Contraloría General de la República. International
Financial Statistics Supplement Series no. 4, 1982.

Y   Real income corresponds to real GDP expressed in millions
of 1960 Balboas.
Source: Contraloría General de la República.

BT   Balance of trade as defined here corresponds to the difference of imports and exports of goods and services (BOP)
deflated by each year's nominal GDP (YNOMINAL). For the
period 1966–79 we used the capital account surplus from the
Balance of Payments to represent the difference of imports
and exports while for the years 1980–1 we used the current
account deficit. The current account deficit does not include
actual imports such as smuggled goods or 'secret imports';
that is the reason to use the capital account surplus as a
better approximation of what the actual current account
deficit is. For 1980–1 the behaviour of the capital account
shows a deficit and therefore we took the current account
deficit of those years to be a better representation of the
difference between imports and exports. The nominal GDP
series used is based on the 'old' (base 1960) national account
methodology.
Source: Contraloría General de la República.

For the purpose of presentation of the data all indexes have base
1970 = 100. Raw data in the construction of M, X, PX and BT are in
tables 8.A2 and 8.A3.

Table 8.A1 Price indices for imports (1970 base)

	PM2	PM3	PM4	PM5	PM*
1966	91.067	92.054	91.186	92.170	89.2
1967	92.541	93.359	92.659	93.473	90.9
1968	93.842	94.511	94.053	94.705	92.2
1969	95.577	96.071	95.687	96.174	94.6
1970	100.000	100.000	100.000	100.000	100.0
1971	105.464	106.072	106.931	107.376	103.2
1972	112.576	113.820	115.896	116.770	106.6
1973	125.672	126.650	130.474	130.907	124.1
1974	161.839	174.888	167.831	180.338	158.4
1975	182.134	195.688	191.512	204.138	177.3
1976	192.715	208.153	206.358	220.396	183.1
1977	210.755	229.713	225.413	242.894	189.7
1978	222.290	240.351	238.028	254.476	202.8
1979	238.855	270.191	260.903	290.051	230.8
1980	270.165	324.344	296.194	347.991	262.2
1981	307.459	368.285	333.996	392.458	286.3

Table 8.A2 Price indices for exports (1970 base)

	W	PXg	PX	PX*
1966	82.79	86.855	87.37	99.77
1967	86.85	92.345	90.60	100.55
1968	91.48	99.581	95.77	106.96
1969	94.86	98.483	96.25	99.68
1970	100.00	100.00	100.00	100.00
1971	102.59	97.870	101.90	100.00
1972	101.24	104.164	102.71	106.92
1973	106.26	115.031	110.52	123.11
1974	129.49	145.696	145.89	195.31
1975	136.09	165.357	155.07	212.58
1976	148.22	140.931	164.84	211.67
1977	158.26	130.911	172.43	208.92
1978	162.26	127.160	173.63	199.01
1979	175.01	138.760	196.90	264.67
1980	189.56	173.791	227.03	359.17
1981	201.01	177.377	242.47	395.98

Table 8.A3 Trade volume and income data

	M	X	Y[a]	BT
1966	71.44	76.31	664.1	−0.0341
1967	78.19	84.08	720.9	−0.0378
1968	81.10	88.06	771.2	−0.0275
1969	91.87	94.40	836.2	−0.0664
1970	100.00	100.00	894.5	−0.0948
1971	108.22	107.83	972.6	−0.1185
1972	117.58	116.39	1033.8	−0.1197
1973	109.62	119.17	1101.2	−0.1467
1974	117.72	108.09	1130.1	−0.1847
1975	110.80	113.74	1137.2	−0.1367
1976	113.45	115.68	1133.6	−0.1536
1977	113.07	124.79	1185.3	−0.1042
1978	122.28	138.26	1262.2	−0.0732
1979	134.38	137.57	1351.2	−0.2523
1980	143.44	165.76	1417.6	−0.0950
1981	139.85	164.94	1469.3	−0.1685

[a] In millions of 1960 dollars.

Table 8.A4 Export price data*

Year	Sugar	Banana	Coffee	Shrimp	Fishmeal
1966	0.133	2.49	0.950	1.967	0.136
1967	0.135	2.78	0.846	1.816	0.124
1968	0.142	3.04	0.791	2.030	0.106
1969	0.149	2.88	0.855	2.208	0.135
1970	0.155	2.90	1.093	2.014	0.170
1971	0.156	2.74	0.869	2.402	0.168
1972	0.166	2.74	1.020	3.240	0.195
1973	0.192	2.76	1.170	3.790	0.399
1974	0.471	2.68	1.470	3.580	0.333
1975	0.612	2.72	1.440	4.290	0.239
1976	0.317	2.66	1.770	6.540	0.289
1977	0.191	2.74	3.990	5.940	0.343
1978	0.171	2.59	3.600	6.310	0.401
1979	0.193	2.64	3.440	8.180	0.348
1980	0.504	2.76	3.240	7.090	0.359
1981	0.545	2.73	2.650	7.190	0.369

* Raw unit values, in dollars per kg or bunch, not yet normalized by their own 1970 unit value.

Table 8.A5 Price indices for import components of wholesale price index

Year	NEM	CP	MACBM	MTM	FP	BAT	MMA	P^{oil}
1966	104.2	103.1	104.1	105.0	105.2	106.2	99.2	94.4
1967	112.4	104.2	104.6	108.7	105.7	105.8	100.6	94.4
1968	120.5	104.8	106.6	110.0	109.2	105.3	101.0	94.4
1969	128.9	108.0	108.0	112.0	112.1	105.3	101.3	94.6
1970	133.3	110.3	115.9	118.9	112.5	110.0	102.6	94.7
1971	141.7	114.8	121.2	131.0	121.1	112.0	110.4	104.9
1972	150.8	120.9	124.5	145.8	139.0	137.7	118.0	116.9
1973	172.8	128.4	144.1	163.8	163.8	130.6	130.5	127.1
1974	216.5	173.3	196.2	206.9	198.3	161.0	160.5	261.2
1975	240.8	207.4	224.4	231.5	239.0	169.2	175.1	284.6
1976	251.1	210.8	235.2	255.2	279.6	169.8	183.6	310.2
1977	311.7	211.6	254.6	297.6	278.3	189.6	203.8	356.4
1978	318.8	220.4	266.3	320.2	299.8	192.4	207.5	359.9
1979	329.8	239.6	279.8	346.2	361.6	195.4	237.3	485.4
1980	391.4	275.5	320.2	395.8	378.9	222.3	283.6	704.0
1981	463.7	311.2	352.9	473.9	395.4	239.5	308.9	794.3

Table 8.A6 Value of trade and income data

	Import[a]	Export[a]	$(1-e_t)$	BOP*	YNOMINAL*
1966	247.9	236.3	0.297	−25.2	737.8
1967	276.5	270.0	0.286	−30.3	800.2
1968	290.9	298.9	0.289	−23.7	860.7
1969	338.1	322.0	0.309	−62.8	945.0
1970	389.0	354.4	0.281	−99.2	1045.7
1971	434.5	389.4	0.270	−137.1	1156.4
1972	487.6	423.7	0.263	−155.4	1297.4
1973	529.2	466.8	0.259	−216.1	1472.3
1974	725.4	558.9	0.275	−338.9	1834.2
1975	764.2	625.1	0.330	−264.3	1933.2
1976	808.1	675.9	0.281	−307.9	2004.2
1977	834.4	762.6	0.271	−226.3	2170.3
1978	964.7	850.9	0.250	−180.0	2457.5
1979	1206.5	960.0	0.262	−716.2	2838.9
1980	1464.2	1333.7	0.226	−322.2	3390.8
1981	1557.6	1417.4	0.196	−627.0	3720.2

[a] Millions of dollars.

Notes

1 This conclusion is shared by the World Bank group studying effective protection in Panama. See Alberto Bension, '*La Protección Efectiva en Algunas Industrias de la República de Panamá*', Center for Development Technology, Inc., May 1984.

2 The effect of the recent conversion of quotas into tariffs on the overall level of protection is not clear. Roughly speaking, the tariffs that replace the quotas are designed to grant 100 percent *effective* protection (i.e., to permit value added in Panama to exceed value added in the same activity in exporting countries by 100 percent). While this appears to be very high, the same factors that undermined the protection offered by the quotas are relevant to the new tariffs. For example, a high tariff on very inexpensive men's shirts offers little protection to the domestic shirt industry if slightly more expensive shirts can be imported at a much lower tariff.

3 A tariff is a combination of a subsidy to import-competing firms and tax on exporters in terms of *incidence*, but this decomposition is not relevant for other contexts. A direct subsidy to import-competing firms, for example, is less damaging than a tariff, as a subsidy would distort production but not consumption choices.

4 This example assumes that the supply of labor to the service export sector is not completely elastic, so part of the export tax is borne by labor. Given the large fraction of Panamanian labor engaged in the production of service exports, this assumption is certainly reasonable. Note that the income lost by labor due to the export tax could be returned to them via other adjustments in the fiscal system.

5 The rates of the import duty and export tax under the second alternative would have to be slightly higher (17.6 percent) than the 15 percent service export tax. The reason for this is that the latter tax strikes the gross wages whereas the import duty and export subsidy to goods are based on the CIF and FOB (free on board) prices, which are net of tax and subsidy, respectively. This refinement is ignored in the presentation of the example in the text.

6 Note that all schemes, first- or second-best, will be detrimental to the interests of labor as they will tend to reduce the real wage. The export tax on services would clearly reduce the nominal (net-of-tax) and hence the real wage. The import duty coupled with a tax on exports of goods would also reduce the wage relative to domestic prices of goods. The across-the-board tax on labor has the same effect, the only easily discernible difference being that the reduction in the (after-tax) real wage is much more visible.

7 That an import duty discriminates against exporters is readily evident by appeal once again to the Lerner symmetry theorem, which shows

that a uniform import duty is equivalent to a uniform export *tax*, both at the same rate. As either increases the internal price of importables *relative* to exportables, the final effects must be the same.

8 The integrability condition is $\beta'-\beta = \gamma$. Hence $\omega = (\beta'-\beta)/(\gamma-\gamma') = \gamma/(\gamma-\gamma')$. In the absence of complementarity $\gamma > 0$ and $\gamma' \leqslant 0$, so the coefficient of P_1 clearly lies between zero and unity.

9 A uniform tariff is used only to simplify the example, but the analysis applies to *any* set of trade restrictions, including non-uniform tariffs, quotas, and the like. In the latter cases, the variables t and s that appear in subsequent formulae are to be interpreted as the *uniform tariff and subsidy equivalents*; equivalents in the sense that, if imposed, they would restrict the volume of imports and exports, respectively, by the same amounts as do the actual trade barriers. For a definition of those uniform equivalents, see Sjaastad (1980).

10 More precisely, a 20 percent uniform import duty with a value of ω equal to 0.60 results in $\Delta P_2 = 0.182$ and $\Delta P_1 = 0.109$; therefore the rise in p_b/p_x is 11.5 percent. Taking all pre-tariff prices to be unity, the new set of relative prices is $p_m/p_h = 1.2/1.115 = 1.076$, and $p_x/p_h = 1/1.115 = 0.897$. Hence a uniform tariff of 7.6 percent coupled with a uniform export duty of 11.3 percent would result in the same set of relative prices as would the 20 percent uniform tariff with neither subsidies nor taxes on exports.

11 Note that τ and σ can be made product-specific; e.g., we can re-define equations (6) and (7) to refer to the ith importable and jth exportable:

$$\tau_i = \Delta(p_m/p_h = (1+t_i)/(1+\omega t)-1 = (t_i-\omega t)/(1+\omega t)$$

and

$$\sigma_j = \Delta(p_x/p_h) = (1+s_j)/(1+\omega t)-1 = (s_j-\omega t)/(1+\omega t).$$

12 In the above, all prices refer to products rather than value added, suggesting that one might refer to τ as 'true' nominal protection. To handle the case of 'true' effective protection, we begin with the usual formula for measuring the effective protection afforded the ith process (or completion of the ith product):

$$t_i^c = (t_i - \sum_j a_{ij}t_j)/(1 - \sum_j a_{ij})$$

where t_i is the nominal tariff on import of the ith good, a_{ij} is the share, in the exporting country, of the jth tradeable input in the production cost of the ith product, and t_i^c is the effective protection for the ith product; i.e., the excess of domestic value added in the completion of the product over 'world' value added.

By substituting τ_i for the t_i, we obtain

$$(\tau_i - \sum_j a_{ij}\tau_j)/(1 - \sum_j a_{ij})$$

$$= (t_i - \omega t - \sum_j a_{ij}(t_j - \omega t))/[(1 + \omega t)(1 - \sum_j a_{ij})]$$

$$= (t_i^c - \omega t)/(1 + \omega t)$$

$$= \tau_i^c$$

where τ_i^c is the 'true' effective protection for the ith process. Note that the distinction between 'true' effective and effective protection is exactly analogous with that between 'true' and nominal protection.

13 This proposition is nothing more, of course, than the celebrated homogeneity postulate. It holds only when the economy departs from full equilibrium, which has already been assumed in deriving equation (3).

14 Figure 8.1 is highly simplified for expositional simplicity. Along the curve labelled D, both P^* and Z^* of equation (16) are being held constant. Along the curve labelled S, we are also holding P and Z of equation (14) constant; the latter would require adjustments in other taxes as w is an element entering into P. The results are in no way affected by these simplifying assumptions.

15 The Lerner theorem holds identically only at balanced trade; otherwise net fiscal effects must be taken into account. These are ignored in the analysis.

16 Recall that $P_1 = P_m - P_x$, $P_2 = W - P_x$, and $P_3 = P_m^* - P_x^*$.

17 Recall that B_1 of equation (10) is equal to A_1 of equation (9).

18 As we pointed out earlier, if Panama had no monopoly power, the value of ω would be zero and that of δ near unity.

19 Service exports are currently about 75 percent of total exports, and total exports are about 35 percent of GDP; therefore service exports are a bit over one quarter of GDP. A 5 percent increase in the 'price' of those exports would increase GDP by about 1.3 percent.

20 This value is very similar to an estimate of the same model using Chilean data.

21 It would be quite straightforward to incorporate smuggling into the formal analysis, but virtually impossible to make empirical estimates in view of the lack of data inherent to smuggling itself.

References

Barrios, Javier 1984: *El Sistema de Cuotas en Panamá: Descripción, Evolución y Efectividad*. Panama: Ministerio de Planificación y Política Económica.

Bension, Alberto 1984: *La Protección Efectiva en Algunas Industrias de la República de Panamá*. Center for Development Technology (New York).

Días, D. B. 1980: *The Effects of Commercial Policy in El Salvador: An Estimate of the True Tariff and the True Subsidy*. Institut Universitaire de Hautes Etudes Internationales, unpublished thesis, Geneva.

Dornbusch, R. 1974: Tariffs and non-traded goods. *Journal of International Economics*, 4, 177–85.

Fendt, Roberto, Jr 1981: Brazilian trade liberalization: a reassessment. In L. A. Sjaastad (ed.), *The Free Trade Movement in Latin America*, London: Macmillan Press for the Trade Policy Research Center.

García, J. 1981: *The Effects of Exchange Rates and Commercial Policy on Agricultural Incentives in Colombia: 1953–1978*. Washington: International Food Policy Research Institute.

Jones, R. W. 1974: Trade with non-traded goods: the anatomy of interconnected markets: *Economica*.

Sjaastad, L. A. 1980: Commercial policy, 'true tariffs' and relative prices. In J. Black and B. Hindley (eds), *Current Issues in Commercial Policy and Diplomacy*, London: Macmillan Press for the Trade Policy Research Center.

9 Costs and Consequences of the New Protectionism. The Case of Canada's Clothing Sector

GLENN P. JENKINS

Introduction

Over the past two decades, Canadian commercial policy has been schizophrenic in its approach to the protection of import-substituting industries. On the one hand, the use of tariffs as import policy instruments has declined for a wide range of manufactured products.[1] In general, this trend can be expected to continue. At the same time, however, a few specific sectors have not only continued to receive high tariff protection, but have also received support from quotas designed to control the competition from imports. These sectors include primary textiles, knitting, clothing, and footwear. Without this assistance, these industries would have been forced to undergo major restructuring.

The encouragement of Margaret Biggs to undertake this project and her support throughout have been greatly appreciated. Similarly, the assistance of Professors T. T. Hsueh of the Chinese University, Hong Kong, and C. C. Chen of Taiwan University in obtaining information on the clothing trade in Hong Kong and Taiwan has been greatly appreciated. Very helpful comments and suggestions were received from Antal Deutsch, Graham Glenday, Chun-Yan Kuo, John Evans, Dale Orr and Michael Roemer. Special thanks go to all those members of the clothing industries in Canada, Hong Kong, and Taiwan who gave considerable time in discussing the operations of their industry. Financial support for this research was provided by the North–South Institute and the World Bank.

The Canadian government has given several reasons for its highly protectionist policy in these sectors. They have ranged from the prospect of a significant decline in employment in specific regions and the pursuit by other developed countries of similar policies to avoidance of the costs of industrial adjustment. However, the chief rationale has been employment.

What has been ignored in the discussion of protection versus adjustment is the cost of the former, especially relative to the latter. It is clear that any policy of industrial adjustment will produce costs, both social and private, for the owners of the factors of production utilized by the declining firms. These adjustment costs, although generally only temporary, are still very real. Only recently has some empirical information become available on the nature and size of the costs of adjustment in Canada.[2] It appears that the estimates of both the private and economic costs of labor adjustment are quite modest, although severe for a small segment of the affected labor market. It therefore becomes highly relevant to compare these costs with the economic and private costs of the protectionist policies that have stifled industrial adjustment. If the economic costs of maintaining protection are larger than those of adjustment, then protection will make the economy as a whole worse off. At the same time, if adjustment assistance policies were in force that fully compensated the individuals who incurred the adjustment costs, the elimination of protection could leave everyone in the economy better off.

To date, most of the research on the cost of protection in Canada has focused on the impact of the tariff policy (Helleiner, 1975; Boadway and Treddenick, 1978; Dauphin, 1978; Pinchin, 1979; Hazledine, 1978; Auer and Mills, 1978; Wonnacott and Wonnacott, 1967, 1980). This paper takes another approach: it analyses the impact of the present tariff and bilateral quantitative restrictions for clothing on the welfare of consumers and producers specifically, the resource cost of this policy for Canada as a whole, and the implications of these policies for the future development of the clothing sector. This sector was chosen because it is a relatively important industry in Canada and illustrates clearly how protection has generated both economic waste and a perverse restructuring of the industry.

Overview of Protection Policies for Textiles and Clothing

Throughout the history of the textile and clothing sectors in Canada, an important determinant of their financial viability has been tariff protection from imports. During World War II, tariffs facilitated the expansion of these sectors, following which came a period of considerable modernization and diversification. By the late 1950s, however, imports of textiles produced in developing countries (starting with Japan) began to force a retrenchment in certain commodity lines, despite the heavy tariff protection.

The government responded to this competition by negotiating a number of 'voluntary' export restraints with various importing countries, beginning with Japan in 1960. Then, in 1970, it formulated a Canadian Textile Policy which attempted to encourage product specialization while at the same time maintaining quotas on imports of goods particularly vulnerable to competition.

From 1970 to 1977, voluntary export restraints were also applied to several clothing items. The restraints were not, however, particularly successful at restraining trade – from 1975 to 1976, imports of knitted and clothing items increased by over 43 percent (Canada, Department of Industry, Trade, and Commerce, 1979). This growth can be attributed to three factors: first, there was considerable excess supply in the exporting countries because of the US and European bilateral quotas: second, the Canadian dollar was significantly overvalued; and third, exporters and importers anticipated that future quotas would be based on current performance and reacted accordingly.

These expectations were correct. In late 1976, the government imposed a global import quota system on a number of clothing items, thus breaking the export restraint agreements. The new system applied to all countries exporting clothing and affected imports in 1977 and 1978. However, because of the large inventories of goods carried over from 1976, the new quantitative restrictions did not truly become effective until 1978. Under the new system, the federal government gave Canadian importers licences to import, with the freedom to find the manufacturers in the exporting countries able to offer the most favourable terms.

This system of quotas had two fundamental drawbacks for the federal government. First, the allocation of the quota licences to importers soon took on political dimensions, with the provincial governments agitating on behalf of their importers. Second, the system lumped the US and other European producers in with low-cost producers such as Hong Kong, Taiwan, and the Republic of Korea (South Korea). As a result, the higher-cost producers, particularly the US ones, feared they would lose their market shares and initiated a vigorous political response.

In June 1978, the government announced it was going to abolish the global quota system in favour of a system of bilateral agreements between Canada and the most important of the low-cost exporting countries. Initially it signed agreements with the seven largest exporting countries but, by early 1980, the number had expanded to fourteen. No quotas were levied on clothing imported from the United States and other high-cost European producers. (For a more extensive treatment of the history of protection in these sectors, see Biggs, 1980.)

These agreements set the maximum quantity of an item that could be exported from a textile- or clothing-producing country to Canada. The coverage of items varied widely across countries, ranging from Hong Kong, where a variety of goods, classified into 30 broad categories of textiles and clothing, were placed under quantitative control, to Sri Lanka, where only two classes of goods (shirts with tailored collars and jackets) were specified (the details are contained in Memoranda of Understanding between the Government of Canada and the Hong Kong and Sri Lanka Governments Related to the Export from Hong Kong and Sri Lanka of Textile Products to Canada, issued in 1979). In general, the level of the quota for any item was to be equal to 90 percent of the 1975 level of shipments from the exporting country to Canada. The remaining 10 percent was to be withheld to allow for flexibility, in particular to accommodate countries that were new entrants into the market.[3]

The key element in the operation of this system of bilateral quotas was that it gave the exporting country administrative control over who obtained the licence to sell to Canadian importers. Canadian importers were no longer able to seek the lowest-cost supplier; instead, they had to go to a manufacturer who either had received a licence from its government or was able to purchase a licence from another supplier. Licences for items where the demand was expected to be greater than the number specified by the quota ceiling quickly gained a market value: importers indirectly bid against each other for the quota, or exporters anticipated the probable degree of scarcity over the year and set a price for the quota amongst themselves.

Superficially, it may appear that the only difference between the global quota system, in which the importing country administered the licences issued to its importers, and the bilateral quota system was that the former allotted the scarcity premiums attached to the import licences to the importers, while the latter gave the windfall income to the exporters. However, as will be shown later, the bilateral quantitative controls also led to behaviour that inflicted greater costs on both the economy and consumers in Canada.

Canada's move from global to bilateral quotas did not affect the system of tariffs applying to the goods. However, in conjunction with the imposition of the global quota in 1977, the base for estimating the tariff liability (i.e., the value for duty) was increased $33\frac{1}{3}$ percent on clothing imports from Taiwan, and 15 percent on similar imports from South Korea. By January 1979, the effective increase in the tariff rate had changed to 25 percent for Taiwan, although it remained 15 percent for South Korea. Furthermore, an adjustment factor of 25 percent was imposed on the value for duty on imports from Hong Kong for the first time.

In addition to the system of bilateral quotas and tariffs, the then Office of Special Import Policy of Canada's Department of Industry, Trade, and Commerce also initiated, or threatened to initiate, unilateral actions to prohibit the import of garments that were manufactured in countries not covered by a bilateral agreement or garments that were not under quota in a country that had signed an agreement. However, the Canadian courts ruled that the Office of Special Import Policy had to be more restrained in its actions.[4] Still, the magnitude of the losses by importers who had goods blocked at the Canadian border was sufficient to prevent them from seriously attempting to obtain new supplies from countries that had not been traditional suppliers. As a result, the importers had to increase their demand for items from the traditional exporting countries, hence bidding up the value of the quotas and the amount Canadians paid for imported garments.

Bilateral Quotas on Garments: Administration and Impact on Industrial Structure

Before attempting to estimate the private and economic costs to Canada of its protectionist package, it is useful to examine the way in which the bilateral quotas and their administration have altered the incentives facing producers and consumers, and their likely responses. Because sales from Hong Kong, Taiwan, and South Korea have accounted for more than 70 percent of Canada's total imports of garments from low-cost countries, this study focuses on the activities in these markets when analysing likely outcomes.

In all three countries, the bilateral agreements have over about 95 percent of the value of the exports of garments to Canada. The export licences have been issued by a special branch of the ministry of trade in each of these countries and allocated to producers or exporters on the basis of past performance. In Taiwan the export licences have been issued only to current or previous manufacturers, while in Hong Kong they have gone to both manufacturers and trading companies that historically had been exporting commodities to Canada. The governments also held back some of the quota, to be issued throughout the year to those exporters that were short of quotas and met certain qualifications.[5]

Hong Kong has gone the farthest in treating the quota as a commodity: there has been active buying and selling, through brokers, of quotas that are either temporary (one year) or permanent (for the remainder of the agreement). A manufacturer or exporter that did not get a sufficient quota has been free to purchase it from another. Under most conditions, the quotas could then be filled under the buyer's name, without any reference to the licensee initially assigned the quota. The rules for the sale of quotas have been very generous: as long as the original licensee itself used over 50 percent of its quota allocation in a given year, it would not suffer any reduction in allocation the following year. Even when this restriction was violated, the penalties were not severe, with any future loss in quotas distributed across all of the licensee's quota holdings (both low and high value).

In Taiwan, the quotas have been administered by the Taiwan Textile Federation, a body set up by the government but largely controlled by the textile and clothing industries. This organization has allocated the quotas based on companies' past performance, with a holdback of 10–15 percent which has been issued as a 'free' quota either to new entrants or to firms short of quota. It has been possible to buy or sell export permits on a permanent or temporary basis under the supervision of the federation. A significant portion of the actual trading of quotas in Taiwan has been carried out by brokers. However, the final export of an item has had to be made under the name of the original quota holder.

To encourage full utilization of the quotas, the Taiwan Textile Federation has been taking back any quota not used in a given year and reassigning it to others the following year. Therefore, if a firm does not fully utilize its assigned quota for one year, it not only loses the current value of the export licence, but also the value of the licence for the remaining years of the agreement.

The assignment of 'free' quotas and the reassignment of quotas have been carried out on the basis of the FOB (export) price, computed at the time of export. A manufacturer short of quota for any item has been able to take a potential order to the Taiwan Textile Federation when the additional export licences were being distributed. The licences have then been assigned on the basis of the FOB prices stated on the orders for goods within each quota category, with the exporters with the highest prices per unit receiving priority.

As the FOB price and the quality of the garment are positively correlated, this system has provided a powerful inducement to restructure production into higher-quality lines within the clothing categories. Thus, Taiwan has used the assignment of garment quotas very deliberately as a tool to get exporters to restructure upward in the market in order to increase the value added of the sector. This policy has been largely successful: all the manufacturers interviewed in Taiwan indicated that they had restructured the quality of their exports to Canada upward and planned to do so further. In addition, the Taiwan Textile Federation has employed a cadre of designers to improve the design of textiles and to assist its members.

In South Korea, the market for export licences for clothing has not been as open as in Hong Kong or Taiwan. However, there has been an active, informal market among the large trading companies for buying and selling quotas. Because of the amount of collusion among the companies, and given that they collectively have had exclusive rights to sell certain clothing items to Canada, it appears that there has been strong potential for their behaving as a monopoly.

The garment quotas Canada has negotiated through the bilateral agreements are defined according to somewhat broad types of garments, such as winter outerwear garments (men's, boys', women's, girls', children's and infants') or shirts with tailored collars (men's and boys'). There have been no restrictions as to quality or price range. For example, boys' shirts selling for $25 a dozen use up the same amount of quota as top-quality men's shirts selling for $50 a dozen. Therefore, excess demand for the quotas for any item will create an incentive to move to the higher-valued items, since normally the absolute amount of the trade margin is larger on garments of higher value.

To illustrate further how quantity quotas tend to shift trade toward higher-quality items, consider the following situation. Two importers, A and B, buy from two exporters, X and Y. Assume that before the quotas, there was C$1 million in trade between A and X, with A purchasing low-quality men's shirts from X at $25 a dozen. Similarly, B and Y were completing $1 million of business, but in expensive men's shirts – at $50 a dozen. Now assume that a quota system is imposed, under which the two producers get a large enough quota to produce their previous volume, but other producers are cut back. Suppose, too, that the equilibrium market value of the export licence is $10 a dozen. If this cost is passed through to the consumers, it will increase the price of the low-quality shirts to $35 a dozen, a rise of 40 percent, while increasing the price of the expensive mens' shirts to $60 a dozen, or 20 percent. From the consumers' point of view, the price of high-quality shirts relative to that of low-quality shirts has fallen from 2/1 to 1.7/1. Therefore, they will tend to shift their purchases from the low- to the high-quality items.

Producers will also have an incentive to shift to the production of higher-quality items. The export licences will limit any expansion of business in terms of quantity, but not in terms of the total value of sales. Moreover, it is more reasonable to think of a producer's profit margin as being related to a fraction of sales rather than the number of units sold. Hence, if the demand for low- and high-quality shirts is growing at about the same rate, producer X can expand the value of sales and profits by producing fewer low-quality shirts and more high-quality ones. Based on previous sales of $1 million, the producer's quota will be 40,000 dozen shirts. By switching to the production of only high-quality shirts, but maintaining the same quantity, sales could be increased to $2 million. If the profit margin were 10 percent of sales net of the quota charges, then switching from low- to high-quality items could increase the profits from $100,000 to $200,000.

The reason that producers are able to make this switch profitably is that the quota will cause an excess of consumer demand in the consumer country for both qualities of items if the prices reflect the foreign producers' costs plus normal profits. However, the excess demand for the high-quality items should grow relatively more rapidly because the quota charge will have caused a smaller proportional increase in the price of these items than in that of the low-quality goods. Hence, both consumers and foreign producers will have an incentive to move toward consumption and production of the high-quality goods. (For an excellent theoretical discussion of the effect of quotas on the quality of imported goods, see Falvey, 1979.)

Where does that leave importers and domestic producers? To analyse this issue, it is useful to look at the market for clothing and the production technology in the industry. Two aspects are important. First, with respect to production, many producers can switch from production of lower- to higher-quality items almost overnight if there is a market. In general, the constraints on switching product lines at the manufacturing stage involve problems of communication rather than production technology. As a result, it is not unusual for a clothing producer to manufacture different product lines in successive years. However, time is a more critical factor with high-quality items than with low-quality ones; location and communications may therefore make it more difficult for producers in some countries to upgrade quickly.

By contrast, the marketing of clothing of the same species but different qualities may require very different skills. The retailer and the importer determine the fashion and design of what a foreign producer makes. Instructing producers and marketing lower-quality clothes for discount houses as opposed to higher-quality items for boutiques requires very different training, skills and knowledge. As a result, importers typically specialize in different segments of the market – each may deal with a wide range of types of goods, but in a narrowly bounded range of quality.[6] Quotas provide an incentive for consumers and producers to upgrade the quality of items bought and sold and tend to shift business from the importers that specialize in low-quality goods to those specializing in higher-quality lines. Moreover, as many of the higher-fashion goods are imported by retail stores directly, the quota will cause an absolute contraction in the role of the importer as a separate economic unit.

Hence, the impact of the bilateral quota on importers will be: an upward restructuring of the trade sector that was specializing in basic lines of clothing; a relative expansion of those firms that had been concentrating on the middle- and higher-quality ranges; an expansion of direct importing by retail stores, causing a relative decline in the overall import trade sector; and, in particular, a contraction in the trade carried out by importers of basic-quality items. These outcomes help explain why basic or traditional importers have tended to oppose the present bilateral export quota system more strongly than have the importers and retailers of newer, higher fashion.

How do the bilateral quotas affect domestic producers? Prior to the quotas, Canadian manufacturers had been concentrating their production on the top two-thirds of the quality range of clothing, leaving the lowest-quality segments of the market to be filled by imports. The import quotas have had two effects on domestic producers. First, the decrease in imports has allowed their prices to increase by more than they otherwise would have. Second, as noted, the quotas have encouraged foreign producers to move into the higher-quality ranges. As such, domestic producers have found increased, rather than decreased, competition from imports in the lines they have been producing. Moreover, because the quota has increased the relative cost of low-quality imports, there has been an incentive for domestic producers to restructure downward and to manufacture the low-quality goods previously imported. During 1978 and 1979, some importers even set up small manufacturing operations in Canada to supply their traditional basic lines, while importing some of their higher-quality lines.

Because of the wide flexibility in the manufacture of clothing, Canadian garment manufacturers have been able to respond quickly to opportunities for profits. The quotas have provided such an opportunity (though an artificial one), causing domestic producers to restructure into a segment of the market where, if economic forces were allowed to operate unrestricted, they would stand no chance of survival.

It is also ironic that the bilateral quotas imposed by Canada and other countries have probably strengthened the long-run true economic viability of the garment and textile industries in the traditional exporting countries. Hong Kong, South Korea, and Taiwan are all countries with relatively high rates of real economic growth, reflected in the high rates of growth of real wages. To prosper, the garment industry in those countries must move into areas where labor can become more productive. In the clothing industry, this tends to occur in the higher-quality clothing lines. Moreover, the governments of the exporting countries have been using the bilateral quotas to stimulate this restructuring. In doing so, however, the quotas have been helping the garment industry retain labor that should have been transferred to other industries, given that wage costs have been rising (e.g., in Singapore).

The Determination of Quota Values over Time

The economics literature contains extensive discussion of the impact of quotas and tariffs on imports, production and prices when either the exporter or domestic producer has a monopoly position in the market (Bhagwati, 1965, 1968; Shibata, 1968; Yadav, 1968; McCulloch and Johnson, 1973; McCulloch, 1973; Ophir, 1969). However, in the case of clothing, the industries in the supplying countries as well as the importers and domestic producers in Canada have been characterized by a high degree of competition. While the export quotas may have given a country a monopoly position, the firms within the country's clothing sector have been free to operate competitively within the constraints on national production. These conditions have certainly held for most of Canada's trading partners in clothing, with the possible exception of South Korea. Even there, given the ultimate competition from the high-cost producing countries, whose exports to Canada have not been subject to limits, it is unlikely that the concentrated position of Korea's producers will lead to a significant increase in prices over that generated by the restrictive quotas. Hence, in the following analysis, it was assumed that the supply of imported clothing to Canada has been provided by competitive industries in the exporting countries and that Canada's clothing importers have also operated competitively. (For some evidence of the large number of importing firms dealing in various clothing items, see Helleiner, 1978.)

In its simplest form, the quota will take on a value equal to the difference between the cost of imports, gross of the tariff, and the costs of domestic production. As illustrated in figure 9.1, if P_0 is the price of imported goods sold in the domestic market in the absence of a tariff, then the quantity demanded by consumers will be equal to Q_0^d, while the quantity supplied domestically will be Q_0^s, and the quantity imported (I_0) will be equal to the difference ($Q_0^d - Q_0^s$). When only a tariff of T is imposed, the domestic price will increase to P_1, or ($P_0 + T$), causing the total quantity demanded to fall to Q_1^d and the domestic supply to increase to Q_1^s. Imports (I_1) will now equal ($Q_1^d - Q_1^s$). If, in addition, a quota of K is imposed, then the domestic price of the good is no longer determined by the price of imports and the tariff, but is instead determined by the interaction of the domestic supply (augmented by imports of K), shown by the curve (SD + K), and the domestic demand for the good (DD). In this case, the domestic price with a quota of K units is equal to P^d or ($P_1 + V$).[7] It will in turn be equal to the world price P_0, plus the tariff of T plus a value of V for the quota.

This quota charge is determined as a residual, as are all other types of economic rents. If no tariff were imposed, then the quota

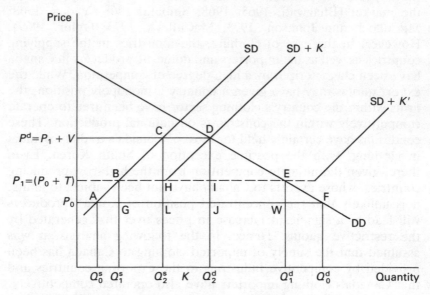

Figure 9.1　Determination of prices and quota values

value per unit would be equal to the distance CL, or $V + T$. When production costs in the producing countries increase relative to domestic production costs, then the quota value will fall and vice versa.

Suppose that instead of a quota of K, the quota is K'. In this case, the total supply curve is SD + K', creating an excess of quota. In theory, no value should be placed on the rights to use the quota. However, an examination of the administrative records of the Canadian bilateral quota system shows that, although not all the allocated quotas were utilized for many categories, positive and often very significant quota charges existed throughout the year. While at first this result may appear to be a contradiction, the nature of the market for garments is such that it is plausible, even when the markets in the exporting country are competitive. Alternatively, it may result from manipulation by the controlling authorities in the exporting countries in an effort to maximize total earnings.

Both these rationales arise because, although the quota for a category of garments is specified for one year, the bulk of the transactions that importers and producers enter into are carried out in the early part of the year. In addition, the organization of the market is such that the importers of basic items, which are not affected as much by fashion, generally place their orders first, followed by the importers and retail stores dealing in higher-quality lines, which must be more closely tuned to seasonal fashions.[8] The export licences used when a good is traded come from the quota of the year in which the good is shipped. However, the licence is purchased when the order is made, which may be months earlier.

As a general approximation, assume that the importers of basic items place their orders in November and December for the summer and fall seasons, while the importers of more fashionable items purchase in late January and early February. If the demand for an item is very strong (in the terminology of the textile trade, a 'hot' item), there might be repeat orders.

This brief description shows that at the time an importer of basic items completes the manufacturing agreements (in order to meet the delivery dates to retailers), there is very little information as to the likely scarcity value of the quota later in the year. If a manufacturer builds a quota charge of $2 a dozen into a sale made in January, but runs out of quota and thus cannot complete an opportunity for a transaction coming in July that pays $10 a dozen for the quota, it will have lost from the decision to sell early. At the same time, if it asks too high a price for the quota early in the year and turns away buyers, it will end up with a surplus of quota at the end of the year and also will have lost.

Most, if not all, items under the bilateral quotas have a positive probability of having their quota run out near the end of the year, despite a strong demand for the good. Where this is the case, the quota for an item is likely to have a positive expected value early in the year, when most of the orders are being placed. Thus, importers will be charged a positive amount for the right to import into Canada, even though at the end of the year a surplus quota may in some cases still be available. In Taiwan, where holders of unused quotas have future quotas taken from them, it is not uncommon for a positive quota charge to exist for an item throughout most of the year, only to take a negative value in the final months, as the holders try to utilize the quotas before the end of the period so that their present value in future years is positive.

The administration of the quota by the exporting countries may also lead to both high charges for export licences and surplus quota at the same time. Usually, the governments of the exporting countries hold back part of the total quota in the early months of the year when most of the buying is done. Hence, quota may be very scarce during this period when it is needed, becoming available later when there may be less demand. The exporting governments may carry out this action if they think they have some influence over the prices in the importer's domestic market and thus can extract some monopoly rents for their firms that own export quotas. As imported garments have dominated the lower-price levels of clothes in Canada for several years, this notion has some validity.

Because Canada has attempted to negotiate bilateral quota agreements with most actual and potential exporting countries or has threatened border actions, the quotas have effectively prevented importers from moving to new countries with lower-cost supplies. Therefore, if, over time, the traditional exporting countries are not able to maintain a rate of real productivity growth in the textile and clothing sectors equal to, or greater than, that experienced in other industries, their real supply costs for clothing will rise. If they rise faster than the increase in the costs of domestic producers in the importing country, then the quota charges should fall over time. In this case, however, a falling value does not mean that Canadians will pay less for their imports. Rather, it means that the costs of production in the exporting country are absorbing a larger portion of the quota's scarcity rent.

If new exporting countries such as China, Sri Lanka, and Indonesia are effectively restrained from taking over the role of producer of basic garments from the traditional exporters, then the quota charge as measured in the present exporting countries will seriously underestimate the loss to Canada from imposing this type of import constraint. This underestimate will increase the further Canada moves from the year on which the quotas were based, in this case 1975.

Estimating the Private and Economic Costs of Protection

To estimate the total cost to Canada of the protection provided to the garment industry, it is necessary to analyse not only the joint impact of the tariffs and quotas but also the costs inflicted on Canada because importers have not been allowed to purchase from the lowest-cost sources of supply. In practical terms, a comparison should be made between the FOB price paid for similar garments purchased by an importing country that does not have bilateral quotas, and the FOB price net of the quota charge faced by Canadian importers in the traditional exporting countries.

The following analysis of the costs of protection does not, however, take this latter source of economic loss into consideration. The principal reason is that, prior to 1979, Canadian importers were purchasing clothing from the lowest-cost sources. Although the base year for the bilateral quotas was 1975, the pattern of purchases in 1978 was not so different from the distribution in 1975 as to indicate major changes across countries in relative production costs. Given the present growth rates of real wages in Taiwan, Hong Kong, and South Korea as compared with China, Sri Lanka, and Indonesia, it is likely, nevertheless, that the economic costs arising as a result of being locked into a given set of suppliers will rapidly become a very significant factor.

An analysis of the costs of protection from the tariff and quotas was carried out in some detail for outerwear and shirts. These two products, which represent products in which manufacturers in Taiwan, South Korea, and Hong Kong could supply most of the product lines demanded by Canadian consumers, have been significantly constrained by the bilateral quotas. If all quotas and tariffs were eliminated entirely, it is likely that these sectors would be severely affected.

The same set of calculations was carried out in summary form for all the quota categories in the bilateral agreements with Hong Kong, Taiwan, and South Korea.

Figure 9.2 illustrates the market situation for a good that is subject to both tariffs and bilateral quotas. With a quota and tariff in place, the domestic price is P^d, resulting in a total demand for this item in the domestic market of Q_2^d. The quota is set at K units, which can also be shown as the difference between domestic demand (Q_2^d) and supply (Q_2^s), or $(Q_2^d - Q_2^s)$. If the CIF (import) price net of tariff and quota charges is denoted as P_0, then the difference between P^d and P_0 will be distributed between the quota charge and tariff. The higher the tariff, the lower the quota charge.

Figure 9.2 shows the value of the tariff collected as the area LHIJ, while the value of the quota and the charges is equal to HCMI. If the quotas did not exist and the amount of the tariff remained constant at T, then the market price would fall to P_1 and domestic demand would increase to Q_1^d, while domestic supply would decline to Q_1^s. Imports would then increase to $(Q_1^d - Q_1^s)$. However, because the quota charges are built into the base for calculating the amount of tariff due, if the quota is eliminated, the actual amount of tariff paid on a unit of imports falls from T to T', and the market price for the good becomes P_2. Therefore, final demand will settle at

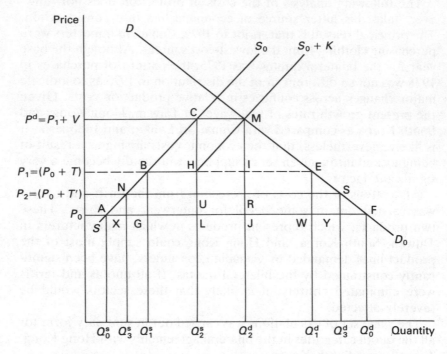

Figure 9.2 Market for goods subject to both tariff and quota

Q_3^d, with domestic suppliers cutting back further to Q_3^s, leading to imports of $(Q_3^d - Q_3^s)$.

If both the quotas and tariffs were eliminated, total domestic demand would increase to Q_0^d, while domestic supply would contract to Q_0^s because of the competition from imports. The quantity imported would then equal $(Q_0^d - Q_0^s)$.

The direct cash cost to Canadian consumers from the tariff and quota combined is shown as the area $P_0 P_d MJ$, which is the difference between the price (P^d) they are paying for clothing with this system, and the price (P_0) that would be charged if there were neither quotas nor tariffs, multiplied by their current level of consumption (Q_2^d). In addition, they suffer a loss in their standard of living because the prices of the goods are higher, causing them to decrease their purchases of the good from (Q_0^d) to (Q_2^d). The value they place on these goods is an amount equal to the area $Q_2^d MFQ_0^d$, or $\frac{1}{2}(P^d + P_0)(Q_0^d - Q_2^d)$. Under free trade, they would have had to pay only $P_0(Q_0^d - Q_2^d)$. Hence, they lose the difference between these two measures, shown as the area JMF and measured by $\frac{1}{2}(P^d-P_0)(Q_0^d-Q_2^d)$.

This total loss to the consumers is in turn distributed as gains to: the federal government, in the form of tariff revenues (area LHIJ, or $T(Q_2^d - Q_2^s)$); the producers, owners of export quotas and governments in exporting countries (area HCMI, or $V(Q_2^d - Q_2^s)$); and the domestic producers in the form of higher profits (area P_0PdCA, or $\frac{1}{2}(Q_2^s+Q_0^s)(P^d-P_0)$). It is also wasted through: the inefficient use of resources in the domestic garment industry (area ACL, or $\frac{1}{2}(P^d-P_0)(Q_2^s-Q_0^s)$); and depriving consumers of the opportunity to purchase clothing at international prices (area JMF, or $\frac{1}{2}(P^d-P_0)(Q_0^d-Q_2^d)$).[9]

Through interviews with exporters and quota brokers in Hong Kong, Taiwan, and South Korea, as well as with Canadian importers, it was possible to develop the information needed to estimate the various costs and transfers resulting from present Canadian policies. While the estimations described in the following sections were based on the levels of trade, production, and consumption in 1979, some of the quota charges could only be obtained for the early months of 1980. For several categories, it is believed that the quota charges in 1980 were lower than those in 1979, so the estimates have a slight downward bias when used as proxies for 1979 quota values.

Tables 9.1 and 9.2 present the FOB prices, quota charges and effective tariff rates for outerwear and shirts, respectively, imported from Taiwan, South Korea, and Hong Kong. The quotas have had the greatest effect on restraining imports in these two categories. Hence, the analysis for them was detailed. Table 9.3 presents the weighted averages across the three countries of the FOB prices, quotas charges, and effective duties for most of the garment categories subject to quotas.

As imports from these three areas have dominated the Canadian market, the error from extrapolating the information on them to the rest of the Canadian market for imports was probably small. However, the nature of the loss to Canada differs slightly according to whether the imports were obtained from low- or high-cost suppliers of garments. For the low-cost suppliers, the quota charge would be a pure rent to those holding the export licences. The existence of the quota charges in these economies would raise the CIF price and, therefore, induce Canadian importers to turn to the high-cost producers in countries such as the United States. When buying from these high-cost producers, the higher prices Canadian

Table 9.1 Determination of the import costs for outerwear from Taiwan, South Korea, and Hong Kong, 1979 (C$)

Taiwan	
FOB net of duty and quota $(5.98-1.57)$[a]	4.41
Quota charge[b]	1.57
Duty $= 0.25(1.25)(5.98)$[c]	1.86
Freight and insurance[d]	0.66
Foreign buying costs at 5% of FOB[e]	0.30
Landed cost each	8.80
Protection expressed as the ratio of net landed cost = 3.43/5.37	0.64

South Korea	
FOB net of duty and quota $(8.50-2.15)$	6.35
Quota charge	2.15
Duty $0.25(1.15)(8.50)$	2.44
Freight and insurance	0.66
Foreign buying costs at 5% of FOB	0.43
Landed cost each	12.03
Protection expressed as the ratio of net landed cost = 4.59/7.44	0.62

Hong Kong	
FOB net of duty and quota $(10.12-1.52)$	8.60
Quota charge	1.52
Duty $0.25(1.25)(10.12)$	3.16
Freight and insurance	0.66
Foreign buying costs at 5% of FOB	0.51
Landed cost each	14.45
Protection expressed as the ratio of net landed cost = 4.68/9.77	0.48

[a] The FOB values are the average unit import values obtained from official monthly import quantities and values by Import Commodity Classification (MCC) category. The reported values were reduced by 25% for Taiwan and 15% for South Korea to account for the administrative adjustment to the value for duty made by Canadian customs authorities.

[b] The quota charges were obtained from the exporters and quota brokers in the respective countries. They correspond to the values charged in February and March 1979 for Taiwan and South Korea and in March 1980 for Hong Kong.

[c] The rate of duty is 25% for outerwear and 22.5% for shirts with tailored collars. However, for 1979 they must be increased by 25% for Taiwan to reflect the increased value for duty imposed by Canada, and increased by 15% for South Korea. Since December 1979, the increased value for duty for Hong Kong has been 25%.

[d] The freight costs were estimated from an examination of the importers' costs.

[e] This is an estimate the importers gave of the costs for buying, banking, and brokerage charges.

Table 9.2 Determination of the import costs for shirts with tailored collars from Taiwan, South Korea, and Hong Kong, 1979 (C$)

Taiwan

FOB net of duty and quota $(2.59-0.78)^a$	1.81
Quota charge[b]	0.78
Duty $= 0.225(1.25)(2.59)^c$	0.73
Freight and insurance[d]	0.50
Foreign buying costs at 5% of FOB[e]	0.13
Landed cost each	3.95
Protection expressed as the ratio of net landed cost = 1.51/2.44	0.62

South Korea

FOB net of duty and quota $(2.87-1.10)$	1.77
Quota charge	1.10
Duty $0.225(1.15)(2.87)$	0.74
Freight and insurance	0.50
Foreign buying costs at 5% of FOB	0.14
Landed cost each	4.25
Protection expressed as the ratio of net landed cost = 1.84/2.41	0.76

Hong Kong

FOB net of duty and quota $(3.40-1.23)$	2.17
Quota charge	1.23
Duty $0.225(1.25)(3.40)$	0.96
Freight and insurance	0.50
Foreign buying costs at 5% of FOB	0.17
Landed cost each	5.03
Protection expressed as the ratio of net landed cost = 2.19/2.84	0.77

[a] The FOB values are the average unit import values obtained from official monthly import quantities and values by Import Commodity Classification (MCC) category. The reported values were reduced by 25% for Taiwan and 15% for South Korea to account for the administrative adjustment to the value for duty made by Canadian customs authorities.

[b] The quota charges were obtained from the exporters and quota brokers in the respective countries. They correspond to the values charged in February and March 1979 for Taiwan and South Korea and in March 1980 for Hong Kong.

[c] The rate of duty is 25% for outerwear and 22.5% for shirts with tailored collars. However, for 1979 they must be increased by 25% for Taiwan to reflect the increased value for duty imposed by Canada, and increased by 15% for South Korea. Since December 1979, the increased value for duty for Hong Kong has been 25%.

[d] The freight costs were estimated from an examination of the importers' costs.

[e] This is an estimate the importers gave of the costs for buying, banking, and brokerage charges.

Table 9.3 Weighted averages of the quota charges, duty payments and FOB prices for garments imported by Canada from Hong Kong, South Korea and Taiwan, China (C$)

Garment category	FOB net of duty and quota	Quota charge (per unit)	Duty	Total pro-tection	Freight insurance	Foreign buying cost	Landed cost	Pro-tection/ net landed cost
Outerwear	6.52	1.92	2.50	4.42	0.66	0.43	12.03	0.58
Structured suits, blazers	10.49	1.70	3.43	5.13	0.70	0.61	16.93	0.43
Shirts with tailored collars	1.89	1.07	0.80	1.87	0.50	0.15	4.41	0.74
Blouses and shirts	3.62	0.32	1.21	1.53	0.50	0.20	5.85	0.35
Sweaters, pullovers, cardigans	3.66	0.30	1.16	1.46	0.50	0.26	5.88	0.33
T-shirts and sweatshirts	1.39	0.34	0.48	0.82	0.50	0.11	2.82	0.41
Trousers, slacks (men's and boys')	3.15	0.33	1.22	1.55	0.60	0.25	5.55	0.39
Trousers, slacks (women's and girls')	3.34	0.40	1.02	1.42	0.60	0.22	5.58	0.34
Overalls and coveralls	1.24	0.28	0.45	0.73	0.50	0.10	2.57	0.40
Dresses and skirts	5.59	0.47	2.16	2.63	0.50	0.41	9.13	0.40
Underwear	0.40	0.14	0.10	0.24	0.15	0.03	0.82	0.41
Shorts	1.06	0.23	0.35	0.58	0.40	0.08	2.12	0.38
Pajamas and sleepwear	2.43	0.02	0.72	0.74	0.50	0.15	3.82	0.24
Foundation garments	4.72	0.31	1.41	1.72	0.50	0.32	7.26	0.31
Swimwear	1.09	0.19	0.36	0.55	0.40	0.08	2.12	0.35
Overcoats, topcoats and rainwear	13.66	1.57	4.23	5.80	0.66	0.94	21.06	0.38

importers would be willing to pay would be used largely to pay for the higher cost of the productive inputs in those countries and would only result in marginal increases in profits to the high-cost suppliers. As the CIF prices for garments of the same quality would be equalized across sources, the high-cost country production costs would place an upper limit on the low-cost country quota charges. The existence of the export quotas in the low-cost producing countries would result in the same economic losses to Canada regardless of whether it imported from low- or high-cost producers. However, the gain in profits from foreign producers would be determined by their relative production costs.

To measure the response in consumer demand and domestic production to a change in the level of protection, estimates of the elasticities of domestic supply and demand for these items were needed. Several were made for the demand elasticities for imports.[10] For overall imports, the demand elasticity estimates were in the range of −2 to −4. However, it would be expected that since only about one-third of the total clothing purchased was imported, the demand elasticity for imports might be somewhat higher. It would also be expected that the elasticity of demand for all garments would be less than the domestic supply elasticity. To be consistent with these observations, a value of −0.5 was used as the compensated own-price elasticity of demand for garments (imports plus those domestically produced), while a value of 1.0 was used for the elasticity of the supply of garments from domestic producers. These elasticities were evaluated at the current landed price and the retail price for supply and demand, respectively.[11]

Table 9.4 contains the data used to measure the various costs and transfers arising from the tariffs and bilateral quotas on outerwear and shirts. Table 9.5 presents the results of the estimations for these two sectors, along with aggregated effects for the remaining categories to which the bilateral quotas apply. The estimations in table 9.5 compare a completely free-trade situation and the present situation in which there are both tariffs and quotas.

As always, consumers ultimately paid the entire cost of the protectionist policies. In 1979, it amounted to approximately C$777.8 million for the garment categories under bilateral import quotas. Of this total cost, about 19 percent was associated with outerwear and shirts with tailored collars. This consumer cost included a gain to foreign suppliers of approximately $76.2 million, of which the foreign manufacturers of outerwear and shirts received about 37 percent. The Canadian federal government gained tariff revenues

Table 9.4 Information used in estimating the cost to consumers and the economic cost to Canada of the tariffs and quotas on outerwear and shirts, 1979 (C$)

	Outerwear	Shirts with tailored collars
Average landed cost per unit[a]	12.03	4.41
Average landed cost less duty and quota	7.61	2.54
Average tariff plus the quota charge	4.42	1.87
Quota charge	1.92	1.07
Tariff	2.50	0.80
Tariff plus the quota as a percentage of the net landed price	58%	74%
Tariff plus the quota as a percentage of the retail price	18.37%	21.20%
Elasticity of demand	− 0.5	− 0.5
Elasticity of supply	1.0	1.0
Total Canadian demand[b] (in thousands of units) (Q_2^d)	17,408	34,008
Imports[b] (thousand units) $(Q_2^d - Q_2^s)$	6 545	14,713
Canadian production[b] (thousand units) (Q_2^s)	10,863	19,295
Canadian consumption with no tariff or quota (thousand units (Q_0^d)[c]	19,128	37,882
Canadian production with no tariff or quota (thousand units) (Q_0^s)	6 872	11,114
Imports with no tariff or quota $(Q_0^d - Q_0^s)$	12,256	26,768

[a]   The values, prices, tariffs, and quota charges are taken from tables 9.1 and 9.2
[b]   The quantities for consumption, production, and imports were estimated using data for 1979 prepared by the Textile and Clothing Board unpublished report (1979).
[c]   The quantities of consumption, production, and imports were estimated according to the usual demand and supply elasticity relationships. Because of the differences in the producer and retail prices, the percentage changes in price for the latter were smaller when the tariff and quota were removed. From examination of the relationship between retail prices and landed prices, it was found that the former were approximately 200% of the latter. This broad average was used to estimate the changes in consumer prices as a result of the elimination of tariffs and quotas.

of approximately $183.3 million. Garment manufacturers in Canada gained approximately $418.2 million.

At the same time, there was a waste of economic resources (energy, capital, land and labor) through their use in this inefficient industry rather than in other sectors of the Canadian economy. The waste amounted to approximately C$71.3 million in 1979, with about 23 percent involving outerwear and shirts.

Table 9.5 Estimated costs of the tariffs and quotas combined, projects (C$ thousand)

Item	Outerwear	Shirts	All other garment categories	Total, all garments
1 Consumer cost	80,743	67,216	629,923	777,882
2 Additional payment to foreign suppliers	12,566	15,743	47,871	76,180
3 Tariff revenue	16,362	11,770	155,135	183,267
4 Gain to domestic producers	39,194	28,432	350,544	418,170
5 Economic waste of resources in production	8 820	7 649	54,791	71,260
6 Loss in standard of living from reduced consumption	3 801	3 622	21,582	29,005
Total (2+3+4+5+6)	80,743	67,216	629,923	777,882
7 Overall economic loss to Canada (2+5+6)	25,187	27,014	124,244	176,445

Because the estimation procedure assumed linear supply curves, the gain in profits to domestic producers may have been overestimated. However, to the degree that the gain in profits was *overestimated*, the loss in economic waste was *underestimated*, as there is a dollar-for-dollar trade-off between these two items in the estimations.

Last, part of the consumer cost arose because, at the artificially increased prices, consumers were discouraged from purchasing as many garments as they would have otherwise. This loss was equal to the difference between what they valued the items at and the price at which the goods would have been bought had there been no tariff or quota. In 1979, this consumer loss amounted to approximately C$29 million.

In table 9.5, row 7, all the transfers to the federal government through tariffs and to domestic producers through higher profits were subtracted from the consumer costs. The result was a net measure of the economic loss to Canada. For the garment sector, the tariff and quota policies in 1979 inflicted a loss of approximately C$176.4 million. About 43.2 percent was the result of the extra

Table 9.6 Weighted average duty payments, FOB prices and rates of protection with tariff but no quota

Garment category	FOB net of duty and quota (1)	Duty (no quotas) (2)	Freight and insurance (3)	Foreign buying costs (4)	Landed cost (5)	Protection/net landed cost (6)	Change in rate of protection due to quota (7)
Outerwear	6.52	1.93	0.66	0.43	9.54	0.25	0.33
Structured suits, blazers	10.49	2.94	0.70	0.61	14.74	0.25	0.18
Shirts with tailored collars	1.89	0.51	0.50	0.15	3.05	0.20	0.54
Blouses and shirts	3.62	1.02	0.50	0.20	5.34	0.24	0.11
Sweaters, pullovers, cardigans	3.66	1.03	0.50	0.26	5.45	0.23	0.10
T-shirts and sweatshirts	1.39	0.39	0.50	0.11	2.39	0.20	0.21
Trousers and slacks (men's and boys')	3.15	0.89	0.60	0.25	4.89	0.22	0.17
Slacks (women's, girls')	3.34	0.94	0.60	0.22	5.10	0.23	0.11
Overalls and coveralls	1.24	0.35	0.50	0.10	2.19	0.19	0.21
Dresses and skirts	5.59	1.57	0.50	0.41	8.07	0.24	0.16
Underwear	0.40	0.07	0.15	0.03	0.65	0.12	0.29
Shorts	1.06	0.30	0.40	0.08	1.84	0.19	0.19
Pajamas and sleepwear	2.43	0.68	0.50	0.15	3.76	0.22	0.02
Foundation garments	4.72	1.32	0.50	0.32	6.86	0.24	0.07
Swimwear	1.09	0.31	0.40	0.08	1.88	0.20	0.15
Overcoats, topcoats, and rainwear	13.66	3.84	0.66	0.94	19.10	0.25	0.13

payments Canadians must make to foreign suppliers because of the bilateral quota agreements, while 40.4 percent was attributable to the wasteful use of resources. The remaining 16.4 percent was the loss in the standard of living to consumers because they were induced to decrease their purchases of garments.

So far, the analysis has compared the present system (tariff plus a quota) with free trade in garments. It was also assumed that whatever distortions existed in the textile sector by way of tariffs or quotas remained in place. As textiles were an input into the garment sector, if protection was simultaneously removed from the domestic textile and garment industries, the latter would become more competitive by using imported textiles. Hence, the removal of both tariffs and quotas would require less adjustment by local garment producers than is indicated in table 9.5.

It may be unrealistic to assume that both the tariffs and quotas will be removed. Accordingly, the costs of protection were also evaluated for the case in which the present quota scheme was added to the prior system of tariffs. As the evaluation for duty has been based on the FOB price (including any quota charge), the import duties per unit would decrease if the quotas were removed. This aspect is illustrated in figure 9.2 by drawing T' (duty if there is no quota) less than T (duty if there is a quota).

Determining the impact of adding (or dropping) the existing bilateral quota system was a two-step procedure. First, the various costs and transfers were estimated for a situation in which there was only a tariff. Second, the values of the costs and transfers were subtracted from the corresponding items when both a tariff and quota were imposed to determine the incremental impact of adding the bilateral quotas.

Table 9.6 contains the basic data on the amount of duty that would be paid per unit if no system of import quotas were imposed (column 7). An estimation of the change in the nominal level of protection arising from the addition of the quota is presented in column 7.

Table 9.7 presents the results for three cases: tariff only (column 1), tariff plus quota (column 2) and the incremental effect of adding an import quota to the tariff system (column 3). In 1979, the bilateral import quotas on garments cost Canadian consumers approximately C$327.3 million. This was in addition to the consumer cost of the tariff alone of $450.6 million. The consumer cost of the quota system was made up of additional payments to foreign producers of $76.2 million, a loss in total tariff collections of $7.3 million, a gain to

Table 9.7   Estimated costs of protection from addition of bilateral quotas (C$ thousand)

Item	Tariff system alone (1)	Tariff plus quota (2)	Addition of bilateral quotas (2−1)
1. Consumer cost	450,575	777,882	327,307
2. Gain to foreign producers	0	76,180	76,180
3. Tariff revenue	190,548	183,267	−7,281
4. Additional profits to domestic producers	226,889	418,170	191,281
5. Economic waste of resources in production	23,458	71,260	47,802
6. Loss in standard of living from reduced consumption	9,680	29,005	19,325
Total (2+3+4+5+6)	450,575	777,882	327,307
7. Overall economic loss to Canada (2+5+6)	33,138	176,445	143,307

domestic producers of $191.3 million, economic losses from inefficient domestic production of $47.8 million, and a reduction in consumption of $19.3 million.

The incremental economic waste created by the quota was estimated to be C$143.3 million in 1979. This was made up of the additional transfers to foreign producers, inefficient domestic production, and a reduction in consumption resulting from the distortions. As compared with the economic waste created by the tariff alone, the *additional* loss created by the quota was 4.3 times as large. Hence, the bilateral quota was a relatively inefficient instrument to use to protect the domestic manufacturing of garments.

Employment and Protection Policy

Those who favor policies that increase protection for declining industries facing international competition principally argue that employment will suffer without those policies. There is no doubt that employment would have been reduced in the Canadian garment industry had it not been for the protection from imports provided by the tariffs and quotas. The critical questions are, however, how many person-years of employment the policies actually saved, and what was the cost to Canada?

From the model in figure 9.2, the number of units of each garment category that would have been produced under three cases can be estimated: free trade and no tariffs or quotas (Q_0^s); only a tariff (Q_3^s); and both tariffs and quotas (Q_2^s). The difference ($Q_3^s - Q_0^s$) is the additional number of units produced as a result of the introduction of a tariff into a free-trade situation, while ($Q_2^s - Q_3^s$) is the incremental quantity of units manufactured domestically resulting from the introduction of bilateral quotas into a market where tariff protection already existed. These values are presented in table 9.8, columns 1 and 2, for the tariff and quota respectively.

To move from the estimates of additional units produced to the person-years of additional employment, it was necessary to know the labor required to produce each garment class. Fortunately, the Department of Industry, Trade, and Commerce had obtained that information for a sample of Canadian manufacturers. The average labor input required per unit of output by garment category is presented in table 9.8, column 3. Assuming that a person-year of employment consists of approximately 2000 hours of work, the person-years of incremental employment were estimated and are presented in columns 4 and 5 for the tariff and quota, respectively.

The analysis indicates that the tariff was responsible for approximately 11,914 person-years of additional employment in garment manufacturing in Canada a year. At the same time, the quotas resulted in an increase in employment of 9231 person-years. However, these estimates overstate the total impact of the tariffs and quotas on employment because, by necessity, they also reduced the employment in the importing and retail parts of the sector. In the analysis that follows, these reductions were not netted out from the positive employment effects of the policies. Therefore, the measures of cost per person-year of employment are biased *downward*.

By combining the employment impact reported in table 9.8 with the costs imposed by the policies reported in table 9.7, the various costs and transfers can be expressed in terms of the incremental employment generated. The consumer cost of an additional person-year of employment in the garment industry produced by tariff protection was approximately C$37,800 in 1979. The consumer cost per person-year of employment created by the addition of the bilateral quota in this sector was approximately C$35,500. These consumer costs were measured over and above the normal cost of importing the goods produced by an additional person-year of

Table 9.8 Impact on employment in domestic garment production resulting from tariffs and import quotas

Sector	Increase in domestic prod. resulting from the tariff (1)	Increase in domestic prod. due to addition of quota (2)	Person-hours required per unit of production[a] (3)	Person-years of employment gained by tariff[b] (4)	Person-years of employment gained by quota (5)
	(thousand units)				
Outerwear	1743	2248	0.76	662	854
Structured suits, blazers	682	508	1.42	484	361
Shirts with tailored collars	2231	5950	0.50	558	1488
Blouses and shirts	5407	2703	0.50	1352	676
Sweaters, pullovers, and cardigans	3388	1414	0.50	847	354
T-shirts and sweatshirts	2908	3206	0.50	727	802
Trousers and slacks	8304	6158	0.53	2201	1632
Overalls and coveralls	492	534	0.53	130	142
Dresses and skirts	6039	4078	0.70	2114	1422
Underwear	9193	22,327	0.06	276	670
Shorts	270	252	0.40	54	50
Pajamas and sleepwear	5756	508	0.28	806	71
Foundation garments	3860	1170	0.45	869	263
Swimwear	564	436	0.20	56	44
Overcoats, topcoats, and rainwear	864	441	1.80	778	397
Total person-years increased employment in 1979				11,914	9231
Consumer cost per person-year of increased employment (annual)				$37,819	$35,457
Economic loss per person-year of increased employment (annual)				$2781	$15,525

[a] The values for labor input per unit of output in each garment category were obtained from a survey of garment manufacturers in Canada, carried out by the Department of Industry, Trade, and Commerce, from 1974 to 1978.

[b] To estimate the person-years of employment from person-hours, a conversion rate of 2000 person-hours per person-year was used. The values in column 4 = the values in column 1 × values in column 3 − 2000; the values in column 5 = the values in column 2 × those in column 3 − 2000.

employment. Clearly, these policies imposed a tremendous burden on the Canadian consumer relative to their impact on employment.

If the distinction of who gains and loses from these policies (producers versus consumers) is disregarded and the economy as a whole and, hence, the economic resource costs of these policies are considered instead, the results are very disquieting. The economic loss of Canada per additional person-year of garment worker employment generated by the tariff policy was approximately C$2781 per year, while the economic cost per person-year of employment created by the bilateral import quotas was approximately C$15,525 per year.

Given that garment workers have tended to be in one of the poorest-paid occupations in Canada,[12] the cost imposed on Canadians to preserve these jobs using either the tariff or the quota policies has been excessive.[13] However, the use of bilateral quotas has been clearly more inefficient than the tariff. It would have been better for Canada in economic terms had the people employed in the garment industry because of the quota been paid their garment industry salaries, but allowed to remain unemployed or free to engage in other non-market activities.

In summary, the argument that there are economic or social reasons for preserving employment in the Canadian garment manufacturing sector through the use of bilateral quotas is very difficult, if not impossible, to support. The magnitudes of the cost to the consumer and the economic waste from inducing employment in these sectors are so large that compensation of displaced workers for their private income losses would be preferable.

Such extreme alternatives are not realistic, or even necessary. Previous experience indicates that most, if not all, workers now employed in the garment industry would find employment elsewhere (Jenkins et al., 1978; Glenday et al., 1982). There is no evidence that artificial assistance to maintain an uncompetitive and declining sector improves the long-run employment conditions in the country. Such policies serve largely to continue to trap workers in areas of employment with no future.

The Distribution of the Costs of Protection by Income Group

Given these estimates of the costs and transfers and of the impact on employment induced by these protectionist policies, the next step was to assess the distribution of the costs across income groups.

Earlier in this study it was pointed out that imports have tended to dominate the lower-price and lower-quality ranges of each clothing category. Moreover, because the quota charge has been a fixed amount, it would have had a bigger percentage impact on the prices of the basic-quality items than on the higher-priced fashion goods. Both these factors have tended to make the cost of protection to consumers weigh more heavily on the poorest segments of the Canadian population, whose purchases of clothing have been contentrated in the lower, basic-quality imported types.

Average values of tariffs and quota charges were used to calculate the consumer cost of protection presented in tables 9.5 and 9.7, with no differentiation made between the high- and low-price grades. Still assuming that the tariff and quotas would increase the prices of all goods in each commodity class by the same percentage, it was possible to estimate the consumer cost to the various income classes. From the Survey of Family Expenditures in Canada (Canada, Statistics Canada, 1978), the proportion of total expenditures on clothing made by the various income levels was developed. The results are presented in table 9.9.

The analysis showed that the bilateral quotas on garments caused households earning less than C$12,000 in 1978 to lose at least $39.3

Table 9.9 Consumer costs of tariffs and quotas on garments by income class (C$ per year)

Income class by annual income distribution	Proportion of textile purchase (%)	Tariff alone (1)	Additional cost of quota (2)	Tariff plus quota (3)	Cost of quota per household (4)	Cost of tariff and quota per household (5)
Less than 12,000	12	54,069,000	39,276,840	93,345,840	17.70	42,06
12,000 to 19,999	24	108,138,000	78,553,680	186,691,680	36.49	86.72
20,000 to 29,999	33	148,689,750	108,011,310	256,701,060	54.60	129.75
30,000 and over	31	139,678,250	101,465,170	241,143,420	83.33	198.05
Total	100	450,575,000	327,307,000	777,882,000	43.25	102.78

million as consumers; those earning between $12,000 and $20,000, over $78.6 million; those earning from $20,000 to $30,000, $108.0 million; and households earning over $30,000, $101.5 million.

On a per household basis (column 4), families earning less than C$12,000 lost an average of $17.70 because of the bilateral quotas, while families earning from $12,000 to $20,000 lost approximately $36.49 each, those from $20,000 to $30,000, approximately $54.60, and those over $30,000, $83.33 each.

With respect to the combined consumer cost inflicted by both the tariff and quota on garments, the analysis indicated that households earning less than C$12,000 in 1978 paid at least $93.3 million for their clothes, or an average of $42.06 per family. For those earning between $12,000 and $20,000, the cost was more than $186.7 million, or $86.72 per family; from $20,000 to $30,000, at least $256.7 million, or $129.75 per family; and over $30,000, $241.1 million, or $198.05 per family.

A comparison of the average income of C$7172 for families earning less than $12,000 per year with the $40,479 of those earning over $30,000 per year shows that an average family in the low-income group earned only 17.7 percent as much as an average family in a high-income category. However, they bore over 21 percent of the burden of the consumer costs of protection as a high-income family. Hence, the tariff and quota policies on garments have hurt marginally the relative income position of poor families in Canadian society.

Policy Alternatives

The review of the impact of bilateral quotas on clothing imports does not provide any positive recommendations for that policy. It has wasted Canada's resources to an extent substantially in excess of the wages paid to the additional labor force it induced into this sector. It has transferred resources disproportionately from the poorer groups of Canadian consumers to the elites of the traditional exporting countries who have been privileged to get export licences. It has created an artificial incentive for the traditional exporting countries to shift their exports of garments to Canada into those higher-quality categories that compete more directly with Canadian manufacturers. The same mechanism has also provided an incentive for Canadian producers to shift their production downward into the lower-quality items that they had abandoned to low-cost suppliers years ago, as they stood no chance of attaining a comparable level of economic efficiency. In addition, the bilateral quotas have created an artificial disruption in the Canadian importing sector. The quotas have created artificial incentives that have caused traditional high-volume importers of basic-quality goods to be replaced by the higher-fashion wholesale and retail store importers.

The policy question is: what should Canada do now?

Given the magnitudes of the economic losses, the second-best policy is to eliminate the bilateral quotas and rely only on the present level of tariffs to provide some short- and medium-term protection to Canadian garment manufacturers, with the ultimate objective of reducing the level of tariff protection over time.

This approach will no doubt require some adjustment of the sector into the higher-quality ranges of production and some retrenchment. Accompanied by an enlightened adjustment assistance program for labor, the economic and private adjustment costs could be minimized. The adjustment assistance program could even be designed to yield positive income benefits for the vast majority of the displaced labor force. (See Glenday et al. (1982) for a detailed discussion of this question.)

If the government's policy objective is to maintain a healthy garment industry, then the logical first step is to reduce the level of protection provided to the domestic textile industry so that fabric can be imported at internationally competitive prices. In many fabric lines, the US textile industry is internationally competitive. With a North American (Canada and United States) rationalization of this sector, similar low costs of production could be enjoyed by Canadians.

An alternative to the bilateral garment quotas is a system of global import quotas administered in Canada. This policy would eliminate the approximately C$76.2 million annually that Canadian consumers of garments are transferring to foreign producers. Over time, as these import quotas became binding, they would also develop a scarcity value approximately equal to the quota charges now existing in the traditional exporting countries. For a short period of time, garment prices would likely be somewhat lower in Canada if the import licences were allocated to the traditional importers. This outcome is apt to arise because, in the low-quality ranges, the traditional importers have completely dominated the market, and thus the import quotas would be sufficient to provide a surplus of supply in these garment categories. At the same time, these importers would have some difficulty adjusting to serve the higher-fashion segments of the market. However, it would only be a question of time before the distribution of imports and the implicit value of the quotas would be similar to those in the present situation with the bilateral export quotas. The major (and very important) difference is, however, that the economic rent associated with the import licences would accrue either to Canadian importers (if the licences were distributed on the basis of historical performance) or to the Canadian government (if it sold the licences). In addition, global quotas would allow importers to go to the most efficient sources of supply, even if it meant importing from a different set of countries over time.

Usually, governments have avoided auctioning import or export licences for fear that the traditional producers or importers would be outbid and displaced. However, this happens no matter how the licences are allocated. In both Hong Kong and Taiwan, it has been very common for those who initially are issued the licences to sell them to others who can manufacture more competitively. Hence, the groups that initially received the quotas have earned large amounts of income as brokers of privilege instead of as manufacturers of garments. The important point, though, is that the reallocation of production has taken place in the same manner as if the quotas had been auctioned in the first place. The only difference is that instead of the government obtaining the revenue from the sale of the quotas, those privileged to receive the quotas obtained the income. There is no evidence that the Canadian import community would react any differently over time than the foreign export community would.

In the event that import quotas are sold, it should be done on both a permanent (two- or three-year) and a temporary (one-year) basis. This approach would allow importers to buy long-term quotas, thus enabling them to plan their business without the uncertainty of future import licences. Generous provisions should also be made for the carry-forward or carry-backward of quotas between years to help stabilize the prices of controlled items over time.

Nevertheless, it must be concluded that instituting one type of quota system for another will serve primarily to heighten the powers of ingenuity in the industry to circumvent the intent of the rules and to build up the stamina of the bureaucrats to regulate and control. In such situations, the interests of Canadian consumers and the long-term economic viability of the country tend to be overshadowed by the problems of the regulatory process. Given the relative competitive positions of the Canadian and foreign garment manufacturing industries and the costs inflicted on Canadians by the present protectionist policies, it would appear that the only viable alternative is for Canada to move to a more liberalized trade policy in garments.

Notes

1 Canada has followed the tariff structure prescribed by the multilateral trade negotiations under the General Agreement on Tariffs and Trade for a wide range of manufactured products.
2 For an estimate of the adjustment costs associated with the decline of firms, see Jenkins et al. (1978); see also Glenday et al. (1982).
3 Sri Lanka was such a case. The negotiated quota could not be based on the level of 1975 export sales to Canada because there had been no sales that year.
4 *Dantex Woolen Co., Inc. versus Ministry of Industry, Trade, and Commerce, C.D. Arthur, H. W. Wilson, Berys Budny and Millie Thompson*, Court files no. A–244–79, Ottawa, 6 June 1979.
5 This information on the quota systems of Taiwan, Hong Kong, and South Korea is based on interviews with the Taiwan Textile Federation and Taiwanese manufacturers, Hong Kong manufacturers, and Canadian importers who had had extensive dealings with all these countries.
6 Based on information obtained from interviews with Canadian importers, foreign producers, and Canadian retailers.
7 Figure 1 assumes that the commodity whose level of imports is controlled by the quota is homogeneous. Usually this is not so: instead, a single commodity class may contain several different qualities of the item. In this case, the market price of the different qualities of the commodity will have different market prices. However, the export or import licence will have the same market price no matter what the quality of the commodity traded with the permit. It is also assumed here that there are no wholesale or retail margins. As they exist in reality, the price received by the domestic producer would be lower than that paid by the final consumer.
8 Imports of clothing of basic quality are almost always shipped by sea. Hence, there is a two- to three-month shipping period between the time the clothing is made in the Far East and its arrival in Canada. By contrast, high-fashion items are transported by air, so the time interval between manufacturing and delivery in Canada is much shorter.
9 In this analysis of the tariff and quota on garments, a partial-equilibrium framework was used. As recent research has indicated (see, e.g., Baldwin et al., 1979), such a partial-equilibrium model is far from complete. It will tend to provide an upward bias to the employment impact of these policies.
10 The Micro-Economic Analysis Branch, Department of Industry, Trade,

and Commerce, recently completed a survey of empirical studies for clothing. At least three studies have been completed that have estimated the own-price elasticity of demand for Canadian imports on a partially disaggregated basis. Generally, the higher the level of disaggregation, the greater the absolute value of the own-price elasticities. Hence, the empirical estimates tend to give a downward bias to the value of the own-price elasticity of demand for clothing. For the aggregated sector, 'other manufacturers of other consumer goods,' which includes clothing, the following own-price elasticities of demand for imports into Canada were obtained:

estimated value −3.4   (Kreinen, 1967, table 4, p. 515)
estimated value −3.515 (Yadav, 1975, table 2, p. 416)
estimated value −3.176 (Yadav, 1977, table 2, p. 708).

11 The relationship between the compensated own-price elasticity of demand for imports of a good N_I^d, the compensated own-elasticity of total demand for the good N_T^d, and the elasticity of domestic supply E^s is

$$N_I^d = N_T^d (Q_T^d/Q_I^d)$$

where Q_T^d is the total quantity demanded, Q_I^d is the quantity imported, Q^s is the quantity of clothing domestically supplied in Canada, Q_T^d/Q_I^d is approximately three and Q^s/Q_I^d is two. If N_I^d is assumed to be −0.5 and $E^s = 1.0$, then the estimate of N_I^d is −3.5. This estimate is entirely consistent with the empirical estimates of this parameter (see note 10).

12 The average wage earned by a clothing worker in Canada in December 1979 was C$190.11 per week, or $9885.72 per equivalent person-year (Canada, Statistics Canada, 1980, table 2).

13 From Glenday et al. (1982, table 3, p. 48), it can be seen that the total present value over five years of the economic costs of adjustment for displaced textile workers in the Sherbrooke region (which is a worse labour market than the Montreal area, where the clothing workers are concentrated) is on the average not more than C$14,153. This is less than the *annual* cost of protection per worker through bilateral quotas of $15,525. Using a general equilibrium approach, which also includes the multiplier effect on the region, it was found (1982, p. 50) that the economic loss for displacing temporary workers was only 3.1 percent of their wage bill (annual cost $306 in 1979), although for workers employed throughout the year it could reach as high as 44.8 percent of their wages (annual cost $4428.80). However, in both cases, the annual cost of displacing the workers was small (not more than 31.3 percent) as compared with the welfare loss from the bilateral quotas.

References

Auer, L. and Mills, K. 1978: Confederation and some regional implications of the tariffs on manufacturers. In *Workshop on the Political Economy of Confederation*, proceedings of a conference held by the Institute of Intergovernmental Relations, Queen's University, and the Economic Council of Canada, Kingston, 8–10 November.

Baldwin, R. E., Stern, R. M. and Kierzkowski, H. 1979: *Evaluating the Effects of Trade Liberalization*. London: Trade Policy Research Centre.

Bhagwati, J. 1965: On the equivalence of tariffs and quotas. In R. E. Baldwin et al. (eds), *Trade Growth and the Balance of Payments – Essays in Honor of Gottfried Haberler*, Chicago: Rand McNally.

—— 1968: More on the equivalence of tariffs and quotas. *American Economic Review*, 58, 137–42.

Biggs, Margaret 1980: *The Challenge: Adjust or Protect?* Ottawa: North–South Institute.

Boadway, R. and Treddenick, J. 1978: A general equilibrium computation of the effects of the Canadian tariff structure. *Canadian Journal of Economics*, 11, 424–46.

Canada, Department of Industry, Trade, and Commerce, Policy Analysis Branch 1979: *Trade by Industrial Sector*. Ottawa.

Canada, Statistics Canada 1978: *Family Expenditures in Canada*, 3, Cat. no. 62–551. Ottawa: Queen's Printer.

—— 1980: *Employment, Earnings and Hours*, Cat. no. 72–002, Ottawa: January.

Canada, Textile and Clothing Board 1979: *Estimated Market for Clothing*. Ottawa: 13 November.

Dauphin, R. 1978: *The Impact of Free Trade in Canada*. Ottawa: Economic Council of Canada.

Falvey, R. E. 1979: The composition of trade within import-restricted product categories. *Journal of Political Economy*, 87, 1105–14.

Glenday, G., Jenkins, G. P. and Evans, J. C. 1982: *Worker Adjustment Policies: An Alternative to Protectionism*. Ottawa: North–South Institute.

Hazledine, T. 1978: The economic costs and benefits of the Canadian federal customs unions. In *Workshop on the Political Economy of Confederation*, proceedings of a conference held by the Institute of Intergovernmental Relations, Queen's University, and the Economic Council of Canada, Kingston, 8–10 November.

Helleiner, G. 1975: Manufactured exports from less developed countries and industrial adjustment in Canada. In *Adjustment for Trade: Studies on Industrial Adjustment Problems and Policies*. Paris: OECD Development Centre.

—— 1978: Market structure and buyer characteristics in Canadian imports of manufactures from low-wage countries. *Canadian Journal of Economics*, 11, 324–33.

Jenkins, G. P., Glenday, G., Evans, J. C. and Montmarquette, C. 1978: *Trade Adjustment Assistance: The Costs of Adjustment and Policy Proposals*, a report prepared for the Department of Industry, Trade, and Commerce, Ottawa.

Kreinen, M. E. 1967: Price elasticities in international trade. *Review of Economics and Statistics*, 49, 510–16.

McCulloch, R. 1973: When are a tariff and quota equivalent? *Canadian Journal of Economics*, 6, 503–11.

McCulloch, R. and Johnson, H. G. 1973: A note on proportionally distributed quotas. *American Economic Review*, 63, 726–32.

Ophir, T. 1969: The interaction of tariffs and quotas. *American Economic Review*, 59, 1002–5.

Pinchin, H. M. 1979: *The Regional Impact of the Canadian Tariff*. Ottawa: Economic Council of Canada.

Shibata, H. 1968: A note on the equivalence of tariffs and quotas. *American Economic Review*, 58, 137–42.

Szenberg, M., Lombardi, J. W. and Lee, E. Y. 1977: *Welfare Effects of Trade Restrictions: A Case Study of the U.S. Footwear Industry*. New York: Academic.

Wonnacott, R. J. and Wonnacott, P. 1967: *Free Trade Between the United States and Canada: The Potential Economic Effects*. Cambridge, Mass.: Harvard University.

—— 1972: Discriminatory aspects of Canada's imports of manufactured goods from the less developed countries. *Canadian Journal of Economics*, 5, 70–83.

—— 1980: *Free Trade Between the United States and Canada: Fifteen Years Later*, Working paper no. 8011, London/Ontario: Centre for the Study of International Economic Relations, Department of Economics, University of Western Ontario.

Yadav, G. 1968: A note on the equivalence of tariffs and quotas. *Canadian Journal of Economics*, 1, 105–13.

—— 1975: A quarterly model of the Canadian demand for imports, 1956–72. *Canadian Journal of Economics*, 8, 410–22.

—— 1977: Variable elasticities and non-price rationing in the import demand function of Canada, 1956:1–1973:4. *Canadian Journal of Economics*, 10, 702–12.

Index

Absolute-Wage Hypothesis
146–8, 152–3
accounting systems 22, 24,
34–5
for federal insurance budget
25–31
accrual accounting 25–7, 28–31
adjustment costs of investment 67,
69–75, 90
administration of bilateral quotas
in Canada 221–6
agricultural debt 15, 16, 19–21, 22
All Saver's Certificates 27, 29
Asset Price and Investment model
64–75
asset prices 62, 63, 64
effect of tax policy on 64–75,
81–5, 86–8, 89–91
variables 80–1

banking in Panama 172, 177
banks 16–20, 23, 29–31
benefits see social security
bilateral quotas 218, 219, 220
impact of 221–6, 230–47
books value accounting 30–1
borrowing rights (FDIC, FSLIC)
18
budget reporting 15, 22–4, 27,
31–2, 34–5
hypothetical 31–2

Canada
protection of clothing sector
217–53
Canadian Textile Policy 219
capital 4–6, 45–6
effect of tax on 84, 104
capital goods 52, 61–2, 64–7, 74–5
capital stock 3, 61–3, 69–75, 83
impact of indexation 85–6
capitalization effects 62
China 230, 231, 236
clothing industry
Canada 218, 219, 225–6
effects of policies on 230–42
commercial policies
Canada 217–26
alternatives to 247–50,
cost analysis of 230–46
Panama 167, 175
commodity taxes 40–1, 52–5
computational general equilibrium
analysis 110–7
see also general equilibrium
models
constant elasticity of substitution
(CES) and VAT 113
consumer sector
asset price model 78–81
effects of Canadian commercial
policy 237–41
effects of VAT 119, 120

corporate capital 62, 86
  accumulation 81
corporate stock 70–5
corporate taxes 62–3, 75, 82, 83–4
  effect of changing 83–4, 86,
    87–8, 90–1
  and VAT 113
cost benefit analysis
  of protection 230–42
  and wages 133–55
current cash flow accounting 27–8

debt
  and labour efficiency 135
default risk 15–24, 30, 32, 34
deposits, bank 17–18
  insurance of 15
  funds for 25, 28
depreciation allowances 63–4,
    71–5, 83
  effects of acceleration 86–7
discount rates in public
    expenditure 5–8, 45–6, 55–9
  Model 41–3
discretionary income see savings
disequilibrium versus equilibrium
    models 159–60
dividends, calculating 71
  effect of reducing 84

efficiency gains of VAT 119–20,
    122–7
efficiency–equity trade off of VAT
    109, 127–8
Efficiency–Wage Hypothesis 133–5
Efficiency–Wage Model 138–9
elasticity of external demand
    201–2, 206, 237
employment see labor
equilibrium models 61–3, 67–9,
    159–60
European VAT system and rates
    118
exchange rates 219
exports
  Canada 219

Panama 167–9
  statistics 168, 210–2
  subsidising effects 172, 177–8
  taxing effects 192–6

Farm Credit System (FCS) 16,
    19–21, 23, 24
Farm Home Administration
    (FmHA) 16, 21–2, 34
Federal Deposit Insurance
    Corporation (FDIC) 16–19, 23,
    28, 31
Federal insurance programs 16–35
Federal Land Bank Associates
    (FLBAs) 20
Federal Reserve System 16–19, 27
federal revenue see revenues
Federal Savings & Loan
    Insurance Corporation (FSLIC)
    16–18, 23, 31
  financial institutions
    and VAT 128
first period taxes control 47–8
foreign exchange earnings
    Panama 172
funds supply
  sensitivity of 90

garments in Canadian bilateral
    quotas 223, 236, 240
  see also clothing
General Agreement on Tariffs and
    Trade (GATT) 178
General Equilibrium Models 61–3,
    67–9, 159–60
Generalized Efficiency–Wage
    Condition 141
global import quota system
    Canada 219–20, 248–50
government insurance programs
    (US) 14–35
government policies
    commercial 167, 175, 217–26,
    230–46, 247–50
  insurance 14–39
  productivity 155–9
Gross Domestic Product (GDP)
  and trade ratios 167, 205, 206

Harris Todaro Model 143, 152
health care
  and labor efficiency 133–5
home goods
  price change effects 172–4, 175
Hong Kong 220, 221, 222, 226,
  231, 233–6, 249
horizontal equity 67–9
housing *see* residential capital

import demand models 180–90
import licences
  into Canada 219–21, 249
import substitution policies 167,
  169
imports
  Canada 219–22
  Panama 210–12
imports
  and duty 192–6, 203–6
  and prices 172–4
  and taxing 177–8, 179
incentives
  and bilateral quotas 221–6
  and productivity 136–7
Incidence of Protection Model
  185–8
incidence of taxes 61–2, 67, 173
  analysis 86–8
  effects of 86
income
  and labor efficiency 135
  personal use of 4–5, 8, 114, 117
  taxation of 27, 111, 118–19,
    120–5, 128, 177, 179
indexation of taxes 81–2, 85–8
Indonesia 230, 231
industry, Canada
  adjustment costs 218
  Panama 170–1, 175
inflation 30, 63, 75, 81–2, 88, 89
'inflation-taxation interaction'
  88–91
insurance programs
  government 14–35
interest income tax
  effect of eliminating 85

interest rates 28–9, 30, 82–3, 84,
  85
  corporate tax changes 87–8
  and indexation 86
  and inflation 89
international debt crisis 15, 18,
  29–30
investment
  and taxation 62–3, 64–91, 128
Investment and Asset Price model
  64–75

Japan 219

Korea, South 220, 221, 222, 223,
  226, 231, 233–6

labor
  in asset price model 72–3, 75
  and industrial adjustment 218
  and protection 242–5
  and tax 179–203
  and wages 110–6, 130–65
land *see* residential capital
less developed countries 15, 29–30,
  130–65
liberalization of trade
  in Panama 172, 175, 176
licences
  to export to Canada 222, 229
  to import into Canada 220–1,
    249
life cycle model for loan
  guarantees 32–4
life cycle theory 2–3
linear expenditure system (LES)
  115, 125–7
loan guarantees 15, 21–2, 23–4,
  32–5

market equilibrium
  Panama 172–3
  and wages 133, 138–50
market equilibrium model 144–5
  efficiency of 150–5
market failure
  and labor supply 154–5

Memoranda of Understanding
(Canada *et al.*, trade) 220
migration
and wages 143
monopoly position of Panama 176,
177–9, 190, 192–6, 198, 202–3
monopoly of supply through
quotas 223, 227, 230
morale
and labor efficiency 137
multiple shooting method 63

national output
maximization of and wages
150–5
Net Worth Certificate Act (US) 29
non-profit sector
effect of VAT on 128
nutrition
and labor efficiency 133–5

Office of Special Import Policy
(Canada) 221
oil prices 30
see also petroleum
Optimum Tariff for Panama 167,
201–2
overlapping generations model 2–5

Panama 166–216
Panama Model
Incidence of Protection 185–8
Optimum Tariff 190–6
Protection and the Volume of
Trade 188–90
Pareto–Efficiency
and labor supply 154
pensions 1–12
petroleum products 167, 168, 169,
204
policies, commercial 167, 175,
217–26, 230–46. 247–50
insurance 14–39
productivity 155–9
policy implications of tariffs 202–3
portfolio equilibrium 69
equation for land 76–7

premiums for import licences
220–1, 222
premium incomes (FCIC, FSLIC)
17–18, 28, 32
prices, 172–4
and protection 169–74, 239–41
private intra-generational discount
rate 5–8
private production control 49–52
probability of payouts for
insurance 28, 30–1, 35
Producer Credit Associations
(PCAs) 20
production 224–5, 226, 228–30,
231
in Canada 225–6, 233–42,
control of 47–55
and export quotas (Taiwan) 223
productivity and wages 130–65
prohibition of imports 221
property tax 62, 68, 88, 113, 128
protection and trade
Canada 217–53
other countries 183
Panama 166, 167–79, 188, 190
variables 183
public expenditure analysis 40–59
public production control 49–52
public workmen's compensation
taxes 113

quality of labor
and efficiency 137
quit rates
and labor turnover 135–6, 140
quota protection
Panama 169, 176
quotas
analysis of economic costs
231–42
quotas
allocation 222–3
Canada 217, 219–20, 221
determination of values over
time (model) 226–30
sale of 222–3
usage 228–9

recruitment techniques
  and labor efficiency 137
Relative Wage Hypothesis 148–50,
  153
residential capital
  asset price model 76–8
  and indexation 85–6, 88
  and inflation 88
  investment in 82, 83
  and tax policies 62, 68, 88, 113,
    128
resource cost of policies 218,
  221–6, 230–47
resource taxation 95–108
revenue
  income tax 27
  and protection 205–6, 239–41,
    241–2
  and tariffs 205–6
  and VAT 120
risk
  deposit insurance 15, 17, 18, 23,
    28–30
risk aversion
  labor supply 152
risk premium 88, 91
  on assets 75
  on consumption 78
  on land 76, 77

Samuelson, Paul
  life cycle theory 2–3
savings 1–11, 88, 90, 104, 111, 117
  general equilibrium model 114
  and VAT 122
scarcity rent
  tax on 96–100, 102
service trade
  Panama 172, 175, 176, 177–9
  tax on (models) 191–2, 192–6,
    198
shadow prices 46, 56
  capital 69, 72–3
  and wages/productivity 157–9
Singapore 226
Small Business Administration
  (SBA) 16, 21, 34

smuggling
  and tariffs 201, 202–3
social inter-generational discount
  rate 5–8
social security 1–11
  and VAT 113
South Korea 220–3, 226, 233–6
Sri Lanka 220, 230, 231
steady state effects of tax reforms
  81–5, 87
stock market values 63, 88, 90–1
subsidies
  on capital investments 66–7
  on exports 177–8
  and wages/productivity 155–6

Taiwan 220–3, 226, 229, 231,
  233–6, 249
Taiwan Textile Federation 222–3
tariffs
  Canada 217, 219, 221
    analysis of economic costs
      230–42
  Panama
    exonerations 169, 176, 204
    and internal prices 172–4
    and quotas 176
    revenue from 168–9
tax
  of capital stock 61–91
  of resources 95–108
  of service exports 177
  from social security 3–9
  and wages/productivity 133,
    155–7
  value added 109–129
tax reform 62–3
  and asset prices 64–91
tax system
  indexation 81–2, 85–8
  non-indexation 68
  tax weighted averages models
    46–54
textile industry
  Canada 219–26
  US 248
thrift institutions 15–18, 27, 28–9

tourism
  Panama 172
trade
  barriers 166–216
  equation 198–201
  and GDP ratios 167, 205, 206
  statistics
    Panama 210–2
Trade and Relative Prices Model
  166–7, 179–90
training and labor turnover 136
Treasury funds 18, 21, 23, 27

United States textile industry 248
urban wages 131

Value Added Tax (VAT) 109–29
voluntary export restraints
  Canada 219

wage differentials 131–3
Wage–Productivity Model 139–41

wages
  and productivity relationships
    130–65
  and protection 243–5
  and tax/subsidy 177–8, 202
  and trade liberalization 175
  and trade restrictions 176
Weighted Average Discount Rates
  Model 41–6
weighted average matrices 48–59
welfare 1–2, 6, 9, 10
  analysis 91
  and resource taxation 97–105
  and tariffs 218, 230–42
  and VAT 117, 119–25
welfare cost triangle 100–1, 102–3
windfall effects of indexation 85–8,
  90
windfall income from quotas 221
windfall profits tax 95

Zona Libre de Colon 166, 172,
  177

*Index compiled by
Pamela Le Gassick*